THE COMELY FRONTISPIECE

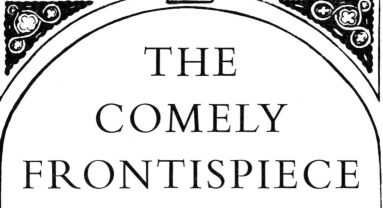

THE
COMELY
FRONTISPIECE

THE EMBLEMATIC TITLE-PAGE
IN ENGLAND
1550–1660

Margery Corbett

and

Ronald Lightbown

Routledge & Kegan Paul
London, Henley and Boston

First published in 1979
by Routledge & Kegan Paul Ltd
39 Store Street,
London WC1E 7DD,
Broadway House,
Newtown Road,
Henley-on-Thames,
Oxon RG9 1EN and
9 Park Street,
Boston, Mass. 02108, USA
Set in 12 point Bembo
and printed in Great Britain by
Ebenezer Baylis & Son Ltd
The Trinity Press, Worcester, and London

British Library Cataloguing in Publication Data

Corbett, Margery
The comely frontispiece.
1. Title-page—History 2. Emblems—History
I. Title II. Lightbown, Ronald William
769'.5   Z242.T6   78–40618

ISBN 0 7100 8554 0

CONTENTS

CONTENTS

ACKNOWLEDGMENTS

First we must record our gratitude to the British Academy for its generous grant towards the cost of publication of this book.

We thank Dame Frances Yates for her encouragement at the inception of our work and during the whole period of its execution.

We gratefully acknowledge the help given us by Mr John Gere, Mr Paul Hulton, Mr John Rowlands and the staff of the Print Room of the British Museum; by Mr Hugh Tait of the Department of British and Mediaeval Antiquities, the British Museum; by Dr Dennis Rhodes and Miss Anna Simoni of the Department of Printed Books, the British Library; by Mrs S. Tyacke and Mr E. J. Huddy of the Department of Maps, the British Library; by Mr J. P. Hudson and Mr T. Pattie of the Department of Manuscripts, the British Library; by Mrs J. E. Tucker of the Department of Pictures, the National Maritime Museum, Greenwich; by Mr B. W. Bathe, ISO and Commander A. G. Thoday formerly of the Science Museum, London; by Professor J. B. Trapp, Miss Jennifer Montagu and Miss Elizabeth McGrath of the Warburg Institute, London; by Sir Oliver Millar, Keeper of the Queen's Pictures; by Dr Roy Strong, Director of the Victoria and Albert Museum; by Professor H. M. Colvin, St John's College, Oxford; by the Reverend C. W. Dugmore, Emeritus Professor of Ecclesiastical History in the University of London; by Mr J. Nevinson; by Mr Jeremy Potter, formerly Deputy Keeper of College Collections, Eton College; by Mr R. J. Loewe, MC of the Department of Hebrew and Jewish Studies, University College, London; by Mr K. G. Boon, former Director of the Ryksprentenkabinet, and Mrs D. de Hoop Scheffer, Curator of Prints, at the Ryksprentenkabinet, Amsterdam; by Dr M. L. Wurfbain, Director of the Stedelijk Museum de Lakenhal, Leiden; by Professor Vittore Branca of the Fondazione Giorgio Cini, Venice; by Mr Walter Oakeshott; and lastly by our ever-patient consorts.

We thank the British Library for permission to reproduce Plates 1, 2, 4, 5, 7, 8, 10, 11, 12, 13, 15, 16, 17, 18, 19, 20; Plate 6 is reproduced by kind permission of the University of London Library; Plate 9 is reproduced by kind permission of the Provost and Fellows of Eton; Plates 3 and 14 and Figure II were taken by Mr Noel Wright.

ABBREVIATIONS

Bartsch:	A. Bartsch, *Le Peintre Graveur*, 1803–21.
BL:	British Library.
Hind, I, II:	A. M. Hind, *Engraving in England in the 16th and 17th centuries. A Descriptive Catalogue*. Part I, *The Tudor Period*, 1952. Part II, *The Reign of James I*, 1955.
Hind, III:	Margery Corbett and Michael Norton, *Engraving in England. . . .* Part III, *The Reign of Charles I*, 1964.
Hollstein:	F. W. H. Hollstein, *Dutch and Flemish Engravings and Woodcuts ca. 1450–1700*, 1949ff.
Johnson:	A. F. Johnson. *A Catalogue of Engraved and Etched English Title-pages . . .* , 1934
JWCI:	*Journal of the Warburg and Courtauld Institutes*.
McK. and F.	R. B. McKerrow and F. S. Ferguson, *Title-page Borders used in England and Scotland. 1485–1640*, 1932.
STC:	A. W. Pollard and G. R. Redgrave, *A Short-title Catalogue of Books printed in England, Scotland and Ireland . . . 1475–1640*, 1926.

INTRODUCTION

From Death, and darke Obliuion, (neere the same)
The Mistresse of Mans Life, graue Historie,
Raising the World to good, or Evill fame,
Doth vindicate it to Æternitie.

These are the opening lines of the verses written by Ben Jonson to explain the engraved title-page of Raleigh's *History of the World*, published in 1614. The design shows the monumental figure of History holding up the globe, which is flanked by two other figures representing good and evil fame. It is a title-page of a special kind, known as emblematic. This was the contemporary description: George Wither speaks of his desire to have a title-page 'That's Emblematicall' to his book of *Emblemes* of 1635. The term may be rendered as iconographical, that is, made up of a number of complex images which require a literary interpretation to be understood. The execution of such title-pages is usually humdrum, nor, with the exception of one or two artists, are the engravers at all well known. The contrast which exists between the learned invention and the dull craftsmanship offers the clearest proof of what contemporaries well knew, though we have forgotten it, namely that in these designs we are confronted with conceits of the author, represented at the front of his book in visual symbols that he himself had chosen and designed as its most fitting emblems. In other words, they are images in which some of the greatest of sixteenth- and early seventeenth-century poets, dramatists, travellers, scholars, philosophers, statesmen and divines express themselves in a second language. To interpret that language, to explore its sources, to draw out the meanings, some plain, some deliberately obscure, that it was intended to hold for contemporaries, is the task we have set

A*

ourselves in this book. Some two hundred emblematic title-pages were published between 1570 and 1660 and it would obviously be impractical to elucidate them all in a single volume. A choice was therefore imposed and we have taken as our illustrations title-pages which represent English culture of the sixteenth and the first half of the seventeenth century in its multiple aspects.

Over the years the significance of these title-pages dropped into obscurity. Since the engraver very generally signed his plate, title-pages came to be considered as part of the œuvre of the engraver. Evelyn in his *Sculptura* mentions the name of various engravers who made frontispieces to books but does not give any further details. Pepys collected them separately from their books and mounted them as examples of the art of engraving. In modern times the significance of the engraved title-page in the presentation of the late Elizabethan and Jacobean book has been neglected, for all our increased awareness of the interdependence of the visual emblem and verbal expression in Renaissance and Baroque culture. Even now the importance of the title-pages which adorn so many of the literary works of the age has not been properly understood,[1] perhaps because bibliographical studies have to a certain extent concentrated on textual matters. Then again, English engraving hardly exists at this period outside of books, with the exception of portraits, and possibly it is for this reason that the engraved title-pages have not been studied as a subject in themselves by specialists in Elizabethan and Jacobean art.

THE DECORATION OF THE TITLE-PAGE

The origins of the title-pages we study are international and go back to the late fifteenth century. In this first part we shall give an indication of the various kinds of Renaissance title-page and of the evolution of their iconography. Certain types of design were used constantly for title-pages throughout our period and became traditional patterns, and it is as well to be familiar with these so that we do not confuse what is original invention in individual title-pages with what is convention.

The various forms that the decorated title-page was given as its use

[1] Certain individual title-pages have been studied in connection with the books to which they belong, notably by the historian Sir Charles Firth (see 10) and by Sir Peter Medawar (see 16). Dr Roy Strong describes the title-page to Dr Dee's *General and Rare Memorials* in *Portraits of Queen Elizabeth*, 1963, and Jean Robertson that to the *Arcadia* in her edition of *The Countesse of Pembroke's Arcadia (The Old Arcadia)*, 1974.

became general in the early sixteenth century spread quickly from their places of origin and were used throughout Renaissance Europe, together with the ornamental motifs that they incorporated. This rapid diffusion was partly due to the flourishing trade in books and partly to the migrations of artists and engravers. Engravers were an international community and there were always foreign engravers, generally from Germany and the Netherlands, in England. Indeed most of our title-pages are typical expressions of international Northern Mannerism.

The four types of design which occur in this book are the title-page divided into geometrical compartments, the title-page which is a single overall design, the title-page whose dominant motif is a cartouche and, most important and interesting of all, the architectural title-page. The title-page divided into compartments appears to be German in origin and it is significant that it first appears in England on Coverdale's Bible of 1535, which is now thought to have been printed in Cologne or Marburg. The overall design usually takes the form of a scene and is also a German invention. The first English example is the title-page of the Great Bible of 1539 which is generally attributed to the School of Holbein. Both the compartmental and the overall types of design had a long and vigorous life well into the seventeenth century and examples of them figure among those we study. It was the Lutherans of Germany who in the 1520s had seized on these types of title-page as a means of pictorial propaganda for their religious beliefs, and it is in their tracts and in Reformation Bibles that we find the first title-pages whose iconography bears more than an illustrative relation to the text, in that their images are deliberately chosen for doctrinal and controversial significance.

The strapwork cartouche was originally the invention of the School of Fontainebleau. It was immediately adopted by decorators and engravers and remained popular both north and south of the Alps well into the seventeenth century. It first appears on title-pages in the 1530s. The design may consist of one big cartouche simulating three-dimensional scrollwork or it may be made up of a number of such cartouches whose splaying curling scrolls are ingeniously interlocked. In addition there may be isolated architectural forms, masks, swags and garlands. This complicated formula, together with a general irrationality which allows, for instance, a solid obelisk to be poised on a shell-like volute, delighted the eye of the Mannerist. The three examples included here are all of this kind. One, in all probability by Richard Haydocke, was done for his translation of Lomazzo's treatise on the arts (3);* the other two, on the title-pages to *The Covntesse of Pembrokes Arcadia* (2) and Van Linschoten's *Discours* (4), are by William Rogers, an artist in his own right and the most accomplished English engraver of the period.

When used decoratively this form of cartouche design was animated by beings from the classical world, gods, goddesses, nymphs and satyrs, monsters and grotesque figures. The representations within the cartouches and those embodied in the overall design of the title-page are closely associated with or may even be the subject of the book to which it belongs.

The cartouche appears on many title-pages in other forms. Particularly favoured by the Mannerist designer was the oval cartouche enclosing in its vertical or horizontal frame titles, coats of arms and portraits. There are certain other frame motifs that warrant special mention. The tablet and the tabernacle were both more monumental than the cartouche. From the first, designers of ornamental borders in the Renaissance borrowed the forms devised by other artists for frames of sculptured reliefs or paintings, notably tabernacles and altarpieces, and also (we may surmise) those devised for goldsmith's work. Enclosed within such frames the title simulates a carved inscription, a conceit that appealed to the Renaissance cult of antiquity. An illusionist variation of this practice was to transform the tablet into a cloth or scroll of paper. In England an early use of this device occurs in William Burton's *Description of Leicestershire* of 1619 where the title is on a cloth, probably a cloth of honour. Another cloth of honour is shown on the title-page to the *Leviathan*, 1651 (20).

The Renaissance took an even livelier interest in architecture than in any of the other arts. From the 1490s a number of antique architectural forms were used as frames for title-pages, especially in Italy. But from the first the most popular of all was the classical recess flanked by wings, standing on a base and surmounted by a pediment. This form was developed into a variety of structures by the addition or subtraction of various members. Its adaptability for many purposes was explained by Sebastiano Serlio in his *Architectura*, 1537, f. xxiv (quoted here in the English version of 1611, book IV, folio 24):

> This figure following [i.e. the recess] may be used by the learned workeman for divers things, and may bee altered according to the accidents that shall happen: it will also serue for a Painter to

* The numbers in brackets refer to the numbers of the entries.

beautify an Altar withall, as men at this day doe in Italy: it may also serue for an Arch tryumphant, if you take away the Basement in the middle. Likewise, you may beautifie a Gate withal, leauing out the wings on the sides: sometimes for setting forth a Window, a Niche, a Tabernacle, or such like things: . . .

The title, enclosed in a cartouche or frame, generally hung from the overall architectural frame or was affixed to it, at the top or across the recess of the plinth. We are probably justified in regarding the underlying principle of all these variations as that of creating a front or façade to the book.

It is important not to class the architectural forms developed for the title-page too rigidly. They are not architectural drawings: rather they are fanciful, even fantastic, essays on architectural themes. In style they reflect in turn the exuberant caprice of late fifteenth-century and early sixteenth-century ornamental forms, the complex inventions of Mannerism and the stately pomp of the Baroque. The earlier Renaissance designs need not be considered here, but those of the 1540s and the two following decades, which saw the advent and triumph of Mannerism, are all-important to our subject. One of the most significant innovations of the new Mannerist style from our point of view was the introduction of allegorical figures as simulated sculptures into the architectural design. Just as the designer never felt it necessary to create an exact imitation of real architectural forms, so these allegorical figures are not represented as true statues but as illusory beings. In other words, the title-page always maintains its character as graphic art.

Unlike its predecessors, the architectural title-page of Mannerism was generally executed in a full three-dimensional style in which monumentality, solemnity and congruity are deliberately sought. This new illusionism also gave greater freedom of display to the engraver; his architectural structure rose beneath the sky; he was able to represent God and his angels in the heavens where they reside; to show on the title-page to Drayton's *Poly-olbion* (13) the sea as the proper background for the maiden Britannia, or the hills and streams of Berkshire where Eton lay and where Savile's Chrysostom (9) was made and printed.

THE INTRODUCTION OF THE ENGRAVED TITLE-PAGE

We must note an important change in technique which eventually was to affect the very nature of the title-page. This was the introduction of the engraved title-page. Engraved title-pages only become common from the middle of the century: the earliest English example, early even in a continental context, is that to Thomas Geminus' book, *Compendiosa totius anatomie delineatio* of 1545. English scholars and literati must have been familiar from the 1550s onwards with many of the majestic engraved title-pages produced in Italy and the Netherlands. Those engraved for Plantin's press at Antwerp and those of Hubert Goltzius of Bruges were certainly in their libraries. Only three of the title-pages studied in this book are woodcuts. Where the title of a woodcut title-page was set in movable type as for the *Arcadia*, the border could be used for other books and Rogers' design also appeared on the title of the 1595 edition of Machiavelli's *Florentine historie*. Copper-cut title-pages, on the other hand, because of the different technique in printing, were made for a particular book, with the letters of the title and the imprint also engraved. By their nature, therefore, they were tied to the book for which they were first intended. Details might be changed in later editions but only occasionally were they altered sufficiently for them to appear in a totally different book.

Line engraving on copper is a technique that allows of greater pictorial illusionism, of much more richness and precision of detail than the woodcut. Probably it was these qualities that helped to produce the transformation of the engraved title-page into an independent work. This emancipation reached its fullest form in the seventeenth century when a second printed title-page followed the engraved title-page. This practice, first developed on the continent, also became general in England. Obviously it encouraged the tendency to make of the woodcut or engraved title-page an elaborate allegorical and emblematic visual introduction to the book.

THE SIGNIFICANCE OF THE ARCHITECTURAL SETTING

In sixteenth- and seventeenth-century England the architectural inventions of title-pages employ the fantastic, highly ornamental forms of Flemish Mannerism with their rich decoration of sculptures and relief, their crowns of lanterns, obelisks, pediments, cartouches and tablets. Inventions of this kind are often loosely termed portals or triumphal arches. There can be no doubt that the arch proper of these imposing structures was often regarded as a triumphal arch, which itself was an adaptation of the gateway into the walled cities of Roman times. Such an arch on the title-page of *Poly-olbion* is described by Drayton as a

'Triumphant Arch' (13). So too Guillim in 1610, writing an explanation of the title-page to his *Displaye of Heraldrie*, describes the arch on which he places the shields of the Heptarchy as a 'Triumphal Arch'. Set on the title-page it may symbolise the formal entrance to the work within. However it is a mistake to assume that such forms are always or only triumphal arches, since a constant feature on the title-page is the continuous high plinth which runs across the opening. In fact, these designs often closely resemble a type of Renaissance architectural structure made for triumphal entries in the Netherlands and in Italy in the sixteenth century. This was the stage on which an allegorical tableau was presented in honour of the hero of the day. It was set in a free-standing architectural framework with the central area usually flanked by columns which supported the cornice and the pediment; the whole was raised on a substantial base so that the spectacle could be seen and was placed in a prominent position beside the route of the procession. The term used to describe it by Corneille de Schryver in his account[1] of the entry of Philip of Spain into Antwerp in 1549 is *pegma*; in the French and Dutch editions of his work it is also called a scaffolding. Sir Thomas Elyot renders this classical word in his *Dictionary* of 1538 as 'a stage whereon pageantes be set, or whereon plate and jewels do stand to be looked on'. De Schryver's book was issued in three languages; it had many illustrations and must have had an influence on engravers. But the design based on the *pegma* was used in England actually before de Schryver's book appeared, on the title-page to Thomas Geminus' book on anatomy referred to above. It shows a tableau in glorification of Henry VIII. Geminus was a Fleming and his *pegma* is a characteristic example of Flemish Mannerism. The central feature is a stylised scalloped niche, probably intended to suggest a throne. Before the niche two winged putti hold the imperial crown of England over the royal arms which are upheld by their supporters, the lion and the dragon. Above in a domed open lantern sits Victory. Two youthful angels, one holding the Tudor portcullis, the other the Tudor rose, are poised to either side of her. With her left hand she extends Victory's laurel wreath to the angel holding the rose. On the left arm of the central recession of the plinth sits a river nymph, pointing upwards with her right hand to a figure of Justice standing on a pot of flowers in a niche in the left side of the arch. A river god, almost certainly Father Thames, reclines on the right arm, looking upwards at the confronting figure of

[1] Cornelius Scribonius Grapheus, *Spectaculorvm in svsceptione Philippi Hisp. Prin. . . . Antverpiae aeditorvm, mirificvs apparatvs,* Antwerp, 1550.

Prudence. The decorative motifs include swags, satyrs, fruiting branches, lion-masks, herms (and the inscribed cartouche) that will reappear constantly in various forms in later title-pages.

Geminus chose to make his tableau a vehicle for honouring the Sovereign; Remigius Hogenberg, another Fleming, had the same intention in his title-page to Saxton's *Atlas of England and Wales*, published at London in 1579. Here Queen Elizabeth is seen in a tableau enthroned between two figures representing Geography and Astronomy. As the idea of the emblematic title-page developed, the allegorical tableau comes to be entirely concerned with the subject of the book while the design of the *pegma* integrates into a single coherent whole the meaning and allusions enacted by the symbolic figures and emblematical motifs. Sometimes the figures occupy all the available space and the title is inscribed on the cornice (10, 13); more generally, the central area is reserved for the title with the figures on the flanking members, on the pediment or superstructure.

Finally these architectural inventions in many ways recall the free-standing monument of architectural reality, whose purpose was to celebrate the living or commemorate the dead. Graven monuments, they celebrate the fame of the living author and his work. From the time of their invention woodcut and engraving were classed under the category of sculpture—partly because the block or plate from which they were made were of the same durable materials, wood or metal, as sculpted work; partly because they were cut with knife or burin. So there was something not entirely strange about an engraving as a monument. The enormous woodcut representing a triumphal arch made to celebrate the achievements of the Emperor Maximilian was erected before him 'as in olden times the *arcus triumphales* before the Roman Emperors in the city of Rome'.[1] A similar conceit occurred to the publisher Hieronymus Cock. At the end of his book of funerary monuments addressed to 'Pictores statuarii . . .' (1563), is the engraving of a large monument (plate 27) with verses underneath which tell us that it has been made by Cock himself, since lacking heirs he fears that there will be no one to remember him fittingly after his death. Along the entablature runs the inscription, 'Hout den Cock in Eeren' (Let Cock be honoured); in the vault below lies his tomb with the figure of Fame above it. This is the monument to his life and work.

---

[1] The opening words of the legend composed by Johann Stabius which runs below the woodcut. Stabius, royal historiographer, was author of the programme for the triumphal arch which was carried out by Dürer.

The single members and adjuncts may have a laudatory intent, as well as the architectural whole. The arch recalls the triumphal arch to honour the author or the subject of his work; the obelisks celebrate his renown. The intricate decoration of the stonework on the title-page to the *Workes* of James I (11), is in compliment to the king; the name of Ben Jonson is glorified by the bay leaves and garlands which adorn the title-page to his *Workes* (12); the swags of cockleshells and marine creatures on the *Poly-olbion* (13) are a tribute to the sea nature of its heroine, Britannia.

It would seem then that the architectural title-pages of Mannerism had both the connotations of a stage and a monument. A still further meaning may be attached to them. As we have indicated there had probably always been the desire to give the book a decorative front. This sentiment is consciously expressed in '*An Epigram explaining the* Frontispiece *of this Worke*' which occurs in John Guillim's *A Displaye of Heraldrie*, 1610:

> The noble Pindare doth compare somewhere,
> Writing with Building, and instructs vs there,
> *That euery great and goodly Edifice,
> Doth aske to haue a comely Frontispice.
>
> (*Olymp. Ode 6)

The architectural design admirably met this demand. It formed a stately and imposing front to the book.

THE EMBLEMATIC BACKGROUND

The emblematic title-page, an invention of the late Renaissance, is an expression of the same profound and far-reaching imaginative current that gave so powerful an impulse to the emblematic fashion from the 1550s. In this section, therefore, we have given some account of emblem literature, of the motives which inspired it, of the qualities and character of its authors, of the nature and sources of the pictorial images which they devised.

Very few books of emblems and devices and only two or three treatises on allegorical personification or the imagery of ancient myth and religion were produced in England during our period. We are in fact studying an iconography whose sources were continental and which was known here principally from books. Accordingly we have taken particular note of works that circulated in England, usually in the original but sometimes in translation as well. We have tried to characterise the different sorts of symbolism embodied in each variety of book and to illustrate the various levels of interpretation they received. We have also laid particular stress on a neglected aspect of all this literature, the relationship between author and illustrator, between inventor and artist. In this way we hope to paint a general background to our special study, and at the same time demonstrate certain conclusions that are highly pertinent to its theme.

Devices and Emblems

By the last decade of the sixteenth century there was already a rich literature of devices and emblems. The older of the two forms was the device (French, *devise*; Italian, *impresa*; in Latin usually rendered as *symbolum*). In origin the device was a characteristic invention of northern fourteenth-century chivalric culture, and spread from France into Italy during the fifteenth century. The French invasions of Charles VIII and Louis XII increased its vogue, throughout north Italy especially, and in its Renaissance guise it was imported north of the Alps where it was believed by many in the late sixteenth century to be an Italian invention. Essentially the device was a heraldry of the mind, a symbol chosen to blazon a personal preoccupation in war or love, an aspiration, an ambition, a vow, a declaration of courageous purpose, of amorous hope, constancy or despair. An individual might change his device as his circumstances changed and different devices might be used simultaneously by the same person to express different meanings. But they remained constant in their use of a visual language which disguised their meaning from vulgar eyes and left it to be divined by the sharp-witted or divulged to a small circle of intimates. Their application or meaning was often pointed by the addition of a motto: in the sixteenth century it was even ruled that their explanation ought not to be wholly contained either in the image or the motto, but should emerge from the combination of the two.

The choice of a device involved an allusiveness that required both visual and verbal ingenuity and a certain amount of learning. Those who wanted a clever device often turned therefore to poets or learned men for a witty invention. But the invention of a device was always considered a proper employment for persons of royal, noble or knightly degree and carried with it no debasing associations. The imagery of devices was usually drawn from a common stock. Its source might be the real or legendary lore of the natural and animal world—the constancy of the turtle-dove, the chastity of the ermine, the eternal infrangibility of the diamond. Or it might be drawn from the metaphors of the Petrarchan love-convention—the flames of love were especially popular. Or common objects of daily life, a candlestick, a yoke, a rudder, might be given a personal significance.

By the first decades of the sixteenth century devices had already assumed two forms, that of a simple symbol and that of a symbolic scene in which symbols interact. Far from declining under the influence of the Renaissance the device flourished even more and it was not to expire as an expression of ceremonial and courtly life until the end of the Baroque age. Learned authors endeavoured to show that its ancestry derived from classical antiquity—had not classical warriors worn crests of real animals or fabled monsters and did not the coins and medals of the ancients bear devices just like those of modern times? Classical motifs and mottoes were borrowed in abundance and incorporated into devices—gods and their attributes, nymphs and other figures from antique myth, altars, sarcophagi and temples. Yet motifs from the old repertory of imagery inherited from the Middle Ages still continued to be just as popular—the unicorn, the wild man, the pelican in her piety—and there was always a consciousness that devices, like heraldry, were an inheritance from the chivalric past. Nor is this surprising, for the aristocratic society of the sixteenth century was as entranced by the paladins of romance as its mediaeval forefathers.

Since those who used devices were often personages of high rank and importance, contemporaries were greatly interested in them and we have many descriptions of how and why they were assumed, what form they took and how they were worn. Those displayed on shields, banners, surcoats and housings in war or tournament necessarily vanished with or shortly after the occasion for which they were composed. But devices were also used in less evanescent forms, on buildings, on furniture, in books, on jewellery, especially hat-badges and pendants, on medals. Some became famous from the famous personages with whom they had been associated, others from some particular grace of ingenuity or appropriateness.

The literature of devices dates from the publication in 1555 of the famous *Dialogo dell' Imprese*, written at Florence in 1551 or 1552 by the aged Monsignor Paolo Giovio (1483–1552).[1] This little work won an

[1] For the literature of the device in Italy see especially Abd-el-Kader Salza, *Luca Contile: uomo di lettere e di negozi*, Florence, 1903, pp. 205–52.

immediate success, and was reprinted at Venice in 1556 and 1557, at Milan in 1559 and again at Venice in 1560. All these unillustrated editions were surpassed in richness and elegance of presentation by the edition published at Lyons in 1559 by Guillaume Rouillé. In this the book was adorned with woodcuts taken from an illustrated manuscript sent to Rouillé by Ludovico Domenichi, Giovio's friend and translator and one of the two interlocutors in the actual dialogue. Giovio gives a vivid picture of the use of devices in Renaissance Italy, France and Spain. He explains that the right to bear them belongs to those of royal, noble and knightly rank, and to those of equivalent degree in the Church—popes, cardinals and prelates. Among literary men only 'those of the first class' can be allowed to bear them without incurring the charge of presumption. Giovio tells us that some of the devices he describes were invented by those who bore them, but that others were invented by poets and learned men for their patrons or friends. Thus he himself had invented many devices, and he tells us of those devised by such famous *literati* as Castiglione, Molza and Sannazaro. We should not imagine that men such as these actually drew the devices they invented. It was their task to invent the image and a suitable motto, after which their conception would be realised in visual form by a craftsman—goldsmith, embroiderer or painter. Thus a device Giovio invented for the Genoese nobleman Girolamo Adorno was designed in colours by Titian and then embroidered by a celebrated Venetian embroiderer named Agnolo di Madonna.

For Giovio indeed the collaboration of a literary or learned man was essential to the contriving of a perfect device, since to make one it was necessary to have a knowledge 'of the things written by the ancients'. Devices had to be of brave appearance so as to make 'a beautifull shewe, which makes it become more gallant to the vew, interserting it with Starres, Sunnes, Moones, Fire, Water, greene trees, Mechanicall instruments, fantasticall birds'. Their images and mottoes had to be well-matched, and no human figure should appear in them. Above all, a device must not be so obscure 'that it neede a *Sibilla* to interprete it, nor so apparant that euery rusticke may vnderstand it'.

The success of Giovio's *Dialogo* was widespread and long-lived. A Spanish version was issued at Venice in 1558 and was reprinted in 1561. In 1585 the poet Samuel Daniel published an English translation entitled *The Worthy tract of Paulus Iouius, contayning a Discourse of rare inuentions,*

both Militarie and Amorous called Imprese, with many other notable devises.
A plain little volume, it has no illustrations. Daniel and N.W., an
Oxford friend of Daniel's who wrote a preliminary letter of commendation for the book, show themselves well acquainted with the other
great codifier of the laws of the device, Girolamo Ruscelli. As early as
1556 Ruscelli had added a *Discorso intorno all'inuentioni delle imprese* to
the Venice edition of Giovio, and he prefaced his great collection of
devices *Le Imprese illustri*, published at Venice in 1566, with an abbre-
viated version of this dissertation. Ruscelli took issue with Giovio on a
number of matters, but his most important objection was to Giovio's
rule that human figures should not be used in devices. He pointed out,
quite rightly, that in this Giovio's practice had not been consistent with
his precept, and that no later book of *imprese* had followed him. *Le
Imprese illustri* set the pattern for future collections of the kind. Each
device is engraved under the name of its illustrious bearer, and is
followed by a long and learned exposition of its meaning and purpose,
occasionally illustrated by other devices. A feature of the illustrations
in this and later Italian books of devices are the extremely elaborate
cartouche frames enclosing the devices. Sometimes indeed Ruscelli had
device and frame engraved as full-page plates, usually when the device
was that of a royal or princely personage, and in these instances the
designs closely resemble those of the title-pages which are the theme of
this book.

In Italy the books of Giovio and Ruscelli were only the first wave of
a flood of books of *imprese*, illustrated and unillustrated. Already in the
1530s and 1540s the invention of devices had become a favourite
amusement of the literary academies that flourished in Italy and something of their popularity can be attributed to this. The *Ragionamento
sopra la proprietà delle imprese con le particolari de gli Academici Affidati et
con le Interpretationi et Croniche* of Luca Contile, published at Pavia in
1574, is a typical expression of this academic vogue. It opens with a
treatise on the history and rules of devices, followed by an illustration
of those of the members of *Accademia degli Affidati* at Pavia. The book
was known in England, and is cited together with Giovio and Ruscelli
as an authority both by Daniel's friend N.W. and by Abraham
Fraunce in his *Insignivm, Armorvm, Emblematvm, Hieroglyphicorvm, et
Symbolorvm, quae ab Italis Imprese nominantur, explicatio*, published in
1588. Fraunce also cites the treatises of Alessandro Farra (*Settenario*
1571) and Scipione Bargagli (*La prima parte delle imprese*, Siena, 1578;
fuller editions from 1589).

13

Meanwhile two other books, also well known in Elizabethan England, had appeared in France. They seem wholly or partly independent of Giovio. First and most important was the *Devises héroiques* of Claude Paradin, Canon of Beaujeu, originally published without text in 1551, and then published with text at Lyons in 1557. In this, the earliest of all illustrated treatises on devices, we find the form which became characteristic of such books. Each device is illustrated separately together with its motto and accompanied by an explanatory text. Paradin's little book is a mixture of personal devices, of heraldic emblems, such as the insignia of the Golden Fleece, and of moral devices or emblems of general application, such as the ostrich for hypocrisy or the chariot of Elijah for the elevation of the spirit to the contemplation of celestial beauty. The moral devices are usually illustrations in visual form of some anecdote or saying from a classical author, but some are from the Bible and some are of Paradin's own invention or borrowed from the great emblematist Alciati, whose work we shall discuss below.

In his 'moral devices' Paradin was imitated by the Italian polygraph Gabriello Symeoni, whose *Imprese heroiche et morali* was issued at Lyons in 1559, in the same year and by the same publisher as Giovio. Symeoni's 'heroic' devices consist partly of devices invented to flatter great personages of the court of France, partly of devices he had invented for his friends. The 'moral' devices link his book, as they link Paradin's, with the literature of emblems. They are devised to symbolise various qualities or types of character—feigned friendship, true nobility, gratitude, a quarrelsome man, an overweening man. Symeoni makes it clear that the invention of these emblems is his own, but that they were drawn out for him by others using his instructions as a guide.

Both Paradin and Symeoni gained immediate popularity, and were reissued in a joint edition by Christopher Plantin at Antwerp, first in Latin (1562) and then in French (1563). From the Latin they were translated into English by an anonymous P.S. and published in 1591 as *The Heroicall Devises of M. Claudius Paradin, Canon of Beauieu, whereunto are added the Lord Gabriel Symeons and others.*

The Emblem

From its first appearance the emblem was closely linked with the device and the two genres were often confused even in the sixteenth and seventeenth centuries.[1] There was indeed one obvious social distinction between the two. The device was primarily a courtly genre, framed by or for persons of royal, noble or gentle birth, and it long retained associations of one kind or another with heraldry. Printers indeed early adopted it to their use as a nobler form of merchant's mark. The example of Aldus who took his famous device of a dolphin and anchor from a medal of Titus was soon imitated by others. N.W. writes in his commendatory letter to Daniel's translation of Giovio:

> Haue not our Printers also of late honored this profession? Haue they not been at emulation for ingenious *Deuises. Stephen* [Estienne] glorieth in his tree, and moderateth those (that love to mount by loftie witts) with this Posie: *Noli altum sapere. Plautin* [Plantin] beareth a compasse in a hande stretched out of the cloudes which measureth all, *Constantia* & *labore.* I will omit *Griphius Episcopus:* I will forget all artificers, who commonly buy such inuentions at second hand.

The emblem by contrast was essentially a language of the learned and literary, who were of lower degree, if only by their profession, than the gentry and nobility. Yet it was a great nobleman, Ambrogio Visconti of Milan, who in the early 1520s first hit on the idea of the genre. But apparently the only use he made of his invention was to suggest it to the celebrated jurist Andrea Alciati (1492–1550) and to another Milanese jurist Aurelio Albrezi, who both realised it in poems. The author of its popularity was in fact Alciati, a typical international scholar of the Renaissance. The first, apparently unauthorised edition of his *Emblemata* was published at Augsburg in 1531 by Heinrich Steyner. In this edition each emblem consisted of a small allegorical picture, a motto, and an explanatory verse epigram. The part of author and publisher in the book must be carefully distinguished. For Alciati the *emblema* was primarily the poem, whose verses, on the model of so many ancient Greek and Latin epigrams, contained a description of a pictorial invention. The pictures were added to the text of the *Emblemata* by the

[1] For the emblem in general see A. Henkel and A. Schöne, *Emblemata: Hardbuch zur Sinnbildkunst des XVI. und XVII. Jahrhunderts,* Stuttgart, 1967 and M. Praz, *Studies in Seventeenth-century Imagery,* Rome, 1964. There is an excellent bibliography of the subject in *The New Cambridge Bibliography of English Literature,* ed. G. Watson, i, 1974, pp. 1327–34. Special studies and bibliographies are R. Freeman, *English Emblem Books,* 1948; J. Landwehr, *Emblem Books in the Low Countries,* Utrecht, 1970; idem, *German Emblem Books 1531–1888,* Utrecht, 1972. For the circulation of foreign emblem-books in England the only study is still H. Green, *Shakespeare and the Emblem Writers,* 1870.

publisher, Steyner, in order to make their meaning plainer 'to the less learned', for in his opinion the learned would gather it for themselves 'without such assistance'.[1]

The term *emblem* long preserved its original meaning. The Elizabethans Abraham Fraunce and Geoffrey Whitney define the emblem primarily as a poem. In this they were influenced by Sambucus, whose *Emblemata*, published at Antwerp in 1564, were much read in England. Writing in 1588, Abraham Fraunce gives the etymology of emblem after Sambucus and explains its modern meaning.[2]

> An emblem is anything inserted for the sake of ornament. Emblems are so called because it was the custom to insert sententious images in inlaid work on walls and vessels. . . . Thus the ancients adorned the houses of the great with small square stones, cut and worked, in which pictures were to be seen interwoven. Accordingly by metaphor those poems are called emblemetical by which images, pictures and *pegmata* and other ingenious inventions of the kind are learnedly explained.

Nevertheless in practice emblems were generally regarded from the first as the combination of picture, *sententia* and explanatory verse which is usually understood by the term. Thus in the dedication to his *Theatre des bons engins, auquel sont contenuz cent Emblemes*, published at Paris in 1539, Guillaume de la Perrière excuses himself for not having been able to get the pictures ready in time for the arrival of his patroness Marguerite of Navarre. He can only offer her the verses by themselves. And he explains that emblems were used in the form of hieroglyphics by the ancient Egyptians before the invention of letters and that in modern times 'lautheur Polyphile en la description de son songe, Celien Rhodigien en ses commentaires des elections anticques, Alciat a semblablement de nostre temps redigez certains Emblemes & illustrez de vers latins'. La Perrière's book was translated into English by Thomas Combe and published at some date between 1593 and 1614 as *The Theatre of Fine Devices*.

In a letter of 9 September 1522 Alciati declared that his intention in writing his emblems was not to produce a series of arcane symbols, but

[1] On this point see H. Miedema, 'The term *emblema* in Alciati', in *JWCI*, xxxi, 1968, pp. 234–50, where Alciati's own references to the emblem are collected. For Alciati see also H. Green, *Andrea Alciati and his Books of Emblems*, 1872. An up-to-date biographical sketch and bibliography in the article by R. Abbondanza in *Dizionario biografico degli italiani*, ii, 1960, pp. 69–77.

[2] Fraunce, op. cit., Sig. N1v–N2r.

'something choice taken from history or natural things from which painters, goldsmiths, founders can make the sort of piece which we call badges and fix in our hats, or else use as devices, like the anchor of Aldus, Froben's dove or the elephant of Calvo'. It will be obvious that emblems, being intended to suggest subjects for craftsmen, were bound to differ from devices, whose application was purely personal, even when their significance might have a wider interest or appeal. Accordingly Alciati's subjects all have an amorous, moral, philosophical or political theme of general import.[1] For Ruscelli this was one of the great distinctions between the emblem and the device: and Daniel's friend N.W. explains the difference neatly: '*Impreses* manifest the special purpose of Gentlemen in warlike combats or chamber tornaments. *Emblems* are generall conceiptes rather of moral matters then perticulare deliberations, rather to give credit to the wit, then to reueale the secrets of the minde.' Similarly Whitney writes in 1586 that emblem[2]

is as muche as to saye in Englishe as *To set in, or to put in*: properlie ment by suche figures, or workes, as are wrought in plate, or in stones in the pauementes, or on the waules, or suche like, for the adorning of the place: hauinge some wittie devise expressed with cunning woorkemanship, somethinge obscure to be perceiued at the first, whereby, when with further consideration it is vnderstood, it maie the greater delighte the behoulder. And althoughe the worde dothe comprehende manie thinges, and diuers matters maie be therein contained; yet all Emblemes for the most parte, maie be reduced into these three kindes, which is *Historicall, Naturall, & Morall. Historicall,* as representing the actes of some noble persons, being matter of historie. *Naturall,* as in expressing the natures of creatures, for example, the loue of the yonge Storkes, to the oulde, or of suche like. *Morall,* pertaining to vertue and instruction of life, which is the chiefe of the three, and the other two maye bee in some sorte drawen into this head. For, all doe tende vnto discipline, and morall preceptes of liuing.

The other great distinction between the *impresa* and the emblem was that in the *impresa* part of the meaning is conveyed by the image and

[1] For the themes of emblematic literature see R. J. Clements, *Picta Poesis: Literary and Humanistic Theory in Renaissance Emblem Books*, Rome, 1960.

[2] Geoffrey Whitney, 'To the Reader', in *A Choice of Emblemes*, Leyden, 1586.

part by the motto, whereas in the emblem the verse is a full exposition of the image. Accordingly the emblem, unlike the *impresa*, needs no explanation beyond what its attendant epigram supplies. Alciati's emblems are in fact far from recondite in their imagery: they make plentiful use of the traditional lore of beasts and of familiar stories from classical mythology, and as their first publisher claimed, their meaning must have been quite plain to the learned.

If there was nothing abstruse in Alciati's conception of the genre—the enormous number of editions of his *Emblemata*, both in the original and in translation, testifies to the ready appeal of its precepts and their emblematic clothing—there were at the same time obvious possibilities of haughty abstruseness in the invention of emblems. Alciati himself conceived the emblem as a means of signifying one thing by means of another. In 1530 he wrote 'Words signify, things are signified. However things by themselves may sometimes signify, for instance the hieroglyphics in Horus and Chaeremon. On this argument we ourselves have written in verse a little book whose title is *Emblemata*.' Hieroglyphs are more fully considered below, but we should note that under their influence some of Alciati's many imitators were inclined to make their emblems abstruse and difficult. Thus in the introductory verses to his *Symbolicae Quaestiones* (Bologna, 1555), Achille Bocchi declares:

> Symbols were long used in the arcane mysteries of the ancients:
> as, to take an example, the poppy signified a fertile year. Of this
> kind are the Pythagorean symbols, allegories and enigmas:
> similarly the emblems of Alciati are called silent pictures, full of
> mysteries, which contain most useful and beautiful lessons in
> life and morals, open to the sound part of mankind, but unknown
> to the ignorant.

The general view of emblems, however, was that expressed by Sambucus in 1564. In his opinion it was better to devise them so that there would be no need 'for hesitation or questioning'. But their images, if commonplace, should 'indicate some hidden meaning', and if obscure 'should teach more openly'.

Like the device then, the emblem was intended to be not so complete a puzzle as the enigma, yet at the same time not so plain that it deprived the ingenious reader of the pleasure of working out its meaning. Like the device too its meaning was to be closed to the vulgar and open to the learned. Hadrianus Junius, who like Bocchi and

Sambucus was much read in England, explains in his *Emblemata* (Antwerp, 1565) that

> in writing of this kind we know there is the greater addition of beauty and grace the more they sharpen the wit: that is to say, the longer they keep the reader's mind in suspense and surmise. Accordingly, after they are understood, they draw him to admiration with an increase of his delight, especially when they conceal in a pleasant obscurity, as if beneath a veil, something of solid excellence under apt and subtle inventions.

Accordingly, he printed the prose explanations of his emblems all together at the end of his collection, rather in the fashion of a modern key to a book of crossword puzzles.[1]

We know from Abraham Fraunce, Henry Peacham and other sources that of the many emblem books produced in the sixteenth century certain were regarded in England as 'best approved'. These included the *Picta Poesis* of Barthélemy Aneau (Anulus), published at Lyons in 1564, the *Icones* of Théodore de Bèze (Geneva, 1580), the *Emblemata* of Nicolaus Reusner (Frankfurt, 1581), the *Symbola* of Camerarius (1593, 1595, 1596, 1604) as well as the emblems of Alciati, Bocchi, Sambucus and Junius. Those of the first English emblematist, Geoffrey Whitney, are borrowed from continental emblem-literature, partly from Plantin's editions of Alciati, Junius, Sambucus and Paradin—indeed, 202 of his book's 248 woodcuts were taken from the same blocks. This is hardly surprising, for his *Choice of Emblemes* was '*Imprinted* at Leyden, In the house of Christopher Plantyn'.

Most emblem books in the sixteenth century were written by learned humanists who are most unlikely to have been able to draw. In spite of Castiglione's pleas in his *Cortegiano* the social prejudice against the practice of art as base and mechanical was still powerful and drawing rarely formed part of public, private or even self-education. The general method of working was for the author to write the poems containing the inventions of the subjects. Then he, or more often his publisher, would commission artists to draw the pictorial subjects and engravers to execute them.[2] Thus the privilege granted in 1554 to Matthieu

---

[1] Sambucus, 'De emblemate', in *Emblemata*, Antwerp, 1564, pp. 3–4; H. Junius, *Emblemata . . . : eivsdem Aenigmatvm Libellvs*, Antwerp, 1565, p. 65.

[2] For the intervention of Alciati in the illustration of his book, a subject which has received virtually no attention, see an inconclusive article by E. F. Bosanquet, 'The first Paris edition of the Emblems of Alciat, 1534', in the *Library*, 4th series, iv, 1924, pp. 326–331.

Bonhomme, publisher of Pierre Cousteau's *Pegma cum narrationibus philosophicis* (Lyons, 1555) granted him six years' copyright for his 'frais & depence pour faire tailler figures & histoires respondantes à la variété des epigrammes y compris'. The illustrations were executed according to verbal or written instructions, more or less detailed, from the author. Many inventions in later emblem books were so learned that such instructions must have been quite indispensable. Traces of them survive in the prose explanations appended by Hadrianus Junius to his emblems, which seem in fact to be elaborated versions of what he actually wrote to his *pictor* or designer. He tells us in his preface that the appearance of his book had been delayed partly by the need 'to explain the composition of the illustrations, lest the artist [*pictor*] should be at a loss because we were not in the same place'. Similarly, Sambucus tells Junius that his own book of emblems is held up 'because of the delays of the engraver and artists [*pictores*]'. It is true that Barthélemy Aneau plumes himself in the preface to his *Picta Poesis* on having fitted his verses to a set of small engraved plates he found lying in his publisher's *Musaeum*. But he explains that this was a reversal of the usual course 'for I have not adapted the picture to the poem, as was fitting, but the poem to the picture which had already been executed, as was necessary'.

We have here then the same relation as obtained between the author and the engraver of his title-page. In actual fact, however much they subscribed in the abstract to the Renaissance theory of *picta poesis*, most of the emblematists borrowed from each other. Partly, no doubt, they felt the imagery of emblems belonged to a common stock. In one or two instances, where the author was also an artist, he might both write the poems and draw the emblems that accompanied them. We have two opposite examples of this in the case of Vaenius and Peacham. Otto Vaenius (1558–1629) or Otto van Veen, to give him his Flemish name, was not an ordinary artist-craftsman, but a humanist-artist of the type who sought to realise the ambitions of Renaissance theorists by uniting humanistic learning with the practice of art. The son of a burgomaster of Leyden, he claimed to be of noble descent, and his image of himself as a gracefully learned gentleman-artist was no doubt confirmed by his training at Liège in the studio of Lampsonius, an artist who was more of a humanist and poet than a painter. Later, Vaenius became court-painter to Alessandro Farnese at Brussels, and after Alexander's death, settled at Antwerp in 1593. He is of interest to England because one of the several emblem-books he published from 1607 to 1618 was partly intended for the English market. This is the

Amorvm Emblemata: Emblemes of Loue with verses in Latin, English, and Italian which he published in 1608 from his own studio in Antwerp, with a dedication to William Herbert, Earl of Pembroke and his brother Philip, Earl of Montgomery. For this Vaenius drew all the designs and may have engraved them, though at least one of the engravings is signed by Cornelis Boel. It is a question whether he also wrote the Latin verses that accompany the emblems: their English and Italian versions must surely have been composed by his friends, perhaps the Englishman R.V. and the Italian Pietro Benedetti who sign commendatory verses in their own languages at the opening of the book. Vaenius' *Emblemata Horatiana*, first published in 1607, in which *sententiae* and images from Horace are given visual form, was also popular in England, as might be expected from the author emblematised.

Conversely Henry Peacham was a courtier and tutor who made himself an advocate of the Renaissance doctrine that gentlemen and noblemen should know how to draw. Peacham was a deviser of *imprese* and emblems in the old tradition. To Prince Henry he presented c. 1610 an illustrated manuscript of emblems based on the 'Divine Instructions' contained in the *Basilicon Doron* of the Prince's father King James I, 'done by me', he says, 'into Latine verse, with their pictures drawn and limned by mine owne hand in their liuely colours'. To these he then added more 'newly inuented, with some others collected' and issued the whole in 1612 as *Minerva Britanna or a Garden of Heroical Deuices, furnished, and adorned with Emblemes and Impresa's of sundry natures. Newly devised, moralized, and published.*

SOURCES OF EMBLEMATIC, ALLEGORICAL AND OTHER IMAGERY

The lore of animals, plants and other branches of natural history and the Petrarchan imagery used in devices and emblems derived, as we have seen, from classical antiquity and mediaeval traditions. We have now to consider more fully certain other sources of imagery in the Renaissance that are especially relevant to our theme. Our concern will be with hieroglyphs, medals and other classical antiquities, with figures of the ancient gods and from ancient myth, with allegorical personifications, and with representations of historical figures. Much of this imagery was taken directly from the antique, but some was derived from mediaeval tradition, developed, altered or corrected according to later interpretation or historical knowledge.

Hieroglyphs

Renaissance writers on emblems and devices were fond of tracing their origin to the hieroglyphs of the ancient Egyptians.[1] In 1539 La Perrière claimed that at the very beginning of the world, before the invention of letters, men wrote in figures and images which were emblems of their meaning. Paradin illustrates and discusses a Tau cross as an Egyptian hieroglyph signifying a divine mystery. This fanciful origin was current in Elizabethan England. Samuel Daniel's friend N.W. observed in 1585:

> concerning the arte of *Imprese*, I neede not draw the petigree of it, sith it is knowne that it descended from the auncient *Aegiptians*, and *Chaldaeans*, in the Schoole of *Memphis:* who deuised meanes before Charecters were founde out, to vtter their conceiptes by formes of Beastes, Starres, Hearbes. . . . But to what end serued this? to shadow surely their purposes and intents by figures. As by the picture of a Stork they signified [family devotion]. By a serpent pollicie. By an Olive peace. By a Gote lust: drawing these Charecters from the world, as from a volume wherein was written the wonders of nature. Thus was the first foundations layd of *Imprese*. From hence were deriued by succession of pregnant wittes *Stemmata* Coates of Armes, Insignia *Ensignes*, and the old Images which the Romaines vsed as witnesses of their Auncestors, *Emblemes* and *Deuises*.

Yet it was a more powerful motive than antiquarian fancy that invested hieroglyphs with mystical prestige among Renaissance scholars. The ancient Greeks had never attained to any true understanding of hieroglyphs as a system of writing: instead they gradually evolved the notion that the connection between each sign and the word it signified was allegorical. Thus the hawk was interpreted as a symbol for swiftness, the crocodile as a symbol for evil. In his treatise on Isis and Osiris, Plutarch extended this notion to claim that the hieroglyphs embodied occult wisdom and sacred knowledge, picturing ideas that ought not to be disclosed to the vulgar and profane. The Neo-platonic

---

[1] For the tradition of the hieroglyph see E. Iversen, *The Myth of Egypt and its Hieroglyphs in European Tradition*, Copenhagen, 1961. Alciati's own declaration of the purpose of his emblems (see p. 15) indicates that they were a kind of generalised device. Their origin is therefore to be sought in the device rather than in the hieroglyph, as has been claimed.

philosopher Plotinus gave the final consummation to this hermetic interpretation of the hieroglyphs. He declared that to the initiate hieroglyphs revealed the essence of things, in other words, a knowledge of their transcendental origin in the ideal world of Platonic philosophy. In this way he conferred philosophical respectability on the belief that the priests of ancient Egypt had concealed within their hieroglyphs the mysterious truths of their religion and philosophy.

The prime source from which the Renaissance derived its knowledge of hieroglyphs was not one to weaken such a belief. This was the *Hieroglyphica* of Horapollo, now thought to have been written in or about the fourth century A D, and to have been translated not long afterwards from Egyptian into the Greek version which alone survives.[1] Horapollo himself was said to have been born at Nilopolis. Whoever he was, he did not have a full and accurate knowledge of Egyptian hieroglyphs and interpreted their meaning according to the old allegorical system which gave a philosophical or scientific explanation of why a given sign expresses certain ideas. Thus for Horapollo the year is symbolised by Isis because her star predicts by its waxing and waning, its brightness or dimness, the happenings of the year. Similarly a frog represents an unformed man because frogs are born of the mud of rivers.

Horapollo's book was rediscovered in 1419 and brought to Florence. In fifteenth-century Italy it was eagerly copied and studied and was printed in the original Greek in 1505 and in a Latin translation in 1515. During the sixteenth century some twenty-nine more editions and translations of the original appeared, a number of them illustrated in a fashion imitated from emblem books. Meanwhile Marsilio Ficino's translation of Plotinus had given fresh currency to the notion of hieroglyphs as a symbolic language enfolding divine truths. This was the view that was embodied in the most influential Renaissance treatise on hieroglyphs, the *Hieroglyphica* of Pierio Valeriano (1477–c. 1558). First published at Basle in 1556, the *Hieroglyphica* obtained European fame, circulation and authority.

> If it is the case [says Valeriano] that no little nobility is conferred
> on things by their antiquity, the opinion of authors is that the
> letters used by the Egyptians were first thought out when those
> early men before the Deluge who are said to have been the first

[1] For Horapollo see especially G. Boas, ed. and trans., *The Hieroglyphics of Horapollo*. New York, 1950.

mortals ever to investigate the causes of celestial things raised up two columns of different materials. One was of brick, the other of stone, and on them they wrote the entire secret of the consummation of the world. There are indeed some who claim that they couched this description in figures of animals and other things, yet in these philosophers, poets and historians have also seen hidden the precepts of divine teaching. For there was a most constant report that those old priests of Egypt declared all the obscurities of nature to be so plainly known to them that they possessed this learning as an inheritance handed down from one to another (Epistle Dedicatory).

Pierio Valeriano justifies the study of hieroglyphics by claiming that Moses, David and the prophets wrote 'with mystic sense', and that when Christ spoke in parables, he spoke hieroglyphically and allegoric-ally. In fact he interprets the term hieroglyphics in the widest possible sense. In addition to Egyptian symbols, he made a collection of symbols from classical antiquity, from coins and medals, from stone monuments, from literary texts. He also draws on the Bible and the Bible commen-taries of the Fathers. His work is divided into fifty-eight books, each of which takes one or more symbols and discusses the various qualities it can symbolise and the various images that have been made of it. The books range over animals, birds, fishes, parts of the human body, plants, trees, precious stones, metals—in fact, all the constituent elements of nature. Caelius Augustinus Curio, editor of the edition published in 1567 at Basle, added two more books, one of which treats of the Greek and Roman gods and the figures of mythology.

The importance of Valeriano for our theme springs not only from his text but from its woodcut illustrations. These are sometimes drawn from ancient sources that are specified, but sometimes, like emblems, they seem to have been drawn in obedience to the indications of his text. Their resemblance to emblems is in fact often very close, and is increased by Valeriano's practice of inscribing the thing they illustrate—quality, principle, personage—as a brief caption above them. This often takes a form resembling the motto of a device or the *sententia* of an emblem. Hence, the user of the book had at his disposal a rich visual vocabulary of emblems, personifications, allegorical and mythological personages in visual form, together with texts giving them a literary or historical explanation.

Valeriano's *Hieroglyphica* was well known in England. Writing in

1588 on how to use hieroglyphics in composing symbolic images, Abraham Fraunce remarks

> that many, indeed most of the hieroglyphics explained by Pierio are brought up from the innermost vitals of nature herself and are celebrated in the letters and tongues of all nations. Let us keep to these, let us make up the bodies and figures of our symbols from these, and let us leave on one side the others, which are more abstruse, and contain I know not what mysteries of the Egyptians, but have no commerce with the works of nature.

And he adds, with sturdy common sense, but contrary to the general trend of Late Renaissance and Baroque learning:[1]

> To speak what I feel without hesitation, the hieroglyphics which were collected by Horapollo and have come down to us do not appear to be so deep and recondite that they cannot be understood by any ordinary man who has saluted the Muses, if only from the threshold. And I so firmly hold this opinion, that I esteem all those excellent mysteries of the Egyptians to have perished from the injuries of time, and that only some remains of them have come down to us, like fallen and scattered ruins of buildings. Accordingly we need have no fear of deriving our symbols from them, since they are ready to all and are as widely plain as may be. Pierio certainly performed a great work in collecting them: and almost all the examples we shall set before you are taken from him. Not that we would wish by making this epitome of them to lead the eyes or minds of our readers away from those great commentaries of Pierio, but rather to point a finger towards his founts.

Coins and Medals

Classical coins and medals began to be collected in the late fourteenth century and they were to remain the chief pride of royal, noble and learned collectors until the beginning of the nineteenth century. These small antiquities had of course survived in considerable quantities. They were valued as providing true portraits of Roman emperors and other great personages of antiquity, as commemorations of great events in

[1] Fraunce, op. cit., Sig. P1v–P2r.

B

ancient history, and as authentic representations of classical antiquities. 'Finally,' says Peacham, in the *Compleat Gentleman* of 1634,

> there is also much learned pleasure and delight in the
> contemplation of the severall figures stamped on each side of
> these Antique Coynes . . . bookes and histories and the like are
> but copyes of Antiquity bee they never so truely descended unto
> us: but coynes are the very Antiquities themselves. But would you
> see a patterne of the *Rogus* or funerall pile burnt at the canonization
> of the Roman Emperors? would you see how the *Augurs* Hat, and
> *Lituus* were made? Would you see the true and undoubted modells
> of their Temples, Alters, Deities, Columnes, Gates, Arches,
> Aquaeducts, Bridges, Sacrifices, Vessels, *Sellae Curules*, Ensignes
> and Standards, Navall and murall Crownes, Amphytheaters, Circi,
> Bathes, Chariots, Trophies, Ancilia, and a thousand things more;
> Repare to the old coynes. . . .

The reverses of coins and medals were also of great interest because of the allegorical motifs figured on them. Here too writers on devices and emblems were pleased to trace the pedigree of their favourite fancies back to ancient Rome, and in practice medals were used even earlier as sources for *imprese*. As we have seen Aldus' famous device of a dolphin and anchor was taken from a medal of Titus. In England, Abraham Fraunce had some doubts about their usefulness to the contriver of devices.

> Coins [he says] are histories and witnesses to things done rather
> than indications of things to come. Accordingly they are not
> devices, though it is allowable to represent devices or emblems or
> hieroglyphs in metals or other substances, according to choice. But
> the ancients appear not to have used coins in this way or to such
> an end, though some coins are found which contain certain
> emblems and hieroglyphs, but not devices, saving only imperfect
> ones, and such as signify the past rather than predict the future.

But in general medals were highly esteemed as a source for allegorical figures and representations of the ancient gods.[1]

Knowledge of them was, however, derived much more from books than from the originals. A number were illustrated in antiquarian treatises: the most important and most used of these was the *Discours de*

---

[1] Peacham, op. cit., Oxford, 1906, p. 123; Fraunce, op. cit., Sig. N3v–N4r.

la religion des anciens Romains (Lyons, 1556 and many later editions) of Guillaume du Choul, an antiquary of Lyons. Special illustrated treatises on medals appeared in increasing number from the 1550s. The famous *Promptuaire des Médailles*, first published at Lyons by Guillaume Rouillé in 1553, is a collection of portraits, and contains no reverses. Enea Vico's important *Discorsi sopra le medaglie de gli antichi* (Venice, 1558) appeared unillustrated, but Gabriello Symeoni's *Illvstratione de gli epitaffi et medaglie antiche* (Lyons, 1558) was adorned with handsome woodcuts. And in 1559 there appeared in Venice the first book specially devoted to illustrating the reverses of medals, Sebastiano Erizzo's *Discorso sopra le medaglie antiche*, edited, significantly, by Girolamo Ruscelli, whom we have already encountered as a deviser and theorist of the *impresa*.

Ancient Myth and the Images of the Gods

By 1634 Peacham could write that it was fitting for every 'ingenuous Gentleman' to be familiar with ancient statues, and that it was not enough

> to behold these with a vulgar eye: but he must be able to distinguish them, and tell who and what they be. To doe this, there be foure parts: First, by generall learning in History and Poetry. Whereby we are taught to know *Iupiter* by his thunderbolt, *Mars* by his armour, *Neptune* by his Trident, *Apollo* by his harpe, *Mercury* by his winges on his cap and feet, or by his Caduceus; *Ceres* by a handfull of corne, *Flora* by her flowers, *Bacchus* by his Vine-leaves, *Pomona* by her Apples, *Hercules* by his club or Lyons skin, *Hercules* infans by his grasping of Snakes. *Comedy* by a vizard in her hand, *Diana* by a crescent, *Pallas* by her helmet and speare, and so generally of most of the Deities. Some mortals also are knowne by their cognisances, as *Laocoon* by his Snakes stinging him to death, *Cleopatra* by a viper, *Cicero* by his wert, and a great many more.

The second way to discern them, he continues, is by the study of antique coins and medals, and the third is by studying the *Icones statuarum quae hodie visuntur Romae*, a collection of engravings of ancient statues which could be seen in Rome. Lastly, the best way of all is to visit them in company 'of such as are learned in them'.[1]

[1] Peacham, op. cit., p. 109.

Peacham's assumption that men would familiarise themselves with the ancient gods and their attributes principally from literary sources was characteristic of the Renaissance, even in Italy.[1] The work of compiling systematic encyclopaedic accounts of ancient gods and ancient myth had been begun in the fourteenth century by Boccaccio, in his *Genealogia Deorum*. Boccaccio and his successors relied heavily on the mythological treatises from antiquity and the early Middle Ages— those of Hyginus, Fulgentius and Albricus, for instance. More read than any other mythological author, either in the original or translation, was Ovid, editions of whose *Metamorphoses*, complete or abridged, illustrated or unillustrated, poured from Renaissance presses. It was probably Ovid who whetted the appetite for a complete knowledge of classical mythology.

Among the earlier Renaissance treatises on the ancient gods one at least is known to have been used in England. This is the *Theologia mythologica* of the German scholar Pictorius (Georg Pictor). First published in 1532, this book gives an account of a number of classical gods and goddesses, mostly Roman, and of Osiris and Isis. The account of each deity is divided into three sections, the first giving an etymology of its name, the second a description of its image, and the third a historical and allegorical explanation of its attributes. The form of the book and many of its descriptions were copied by England's only sixteenth-century mythographer, Stephen Batman (Bateman), in his little work of 1577, *The Golden Booke of the Leaden Goddes. Wherein is described the vayne imaginations of Heathen Pagans and counterfaicte Christians: wyth a description of their seueral Tables, what ech of their Pictures signified*. Batman omits Pictor's etymologies, however, and the *Signification* in which he explains each of the images, is usually very different from Pictor's *allegoria*. Among the ancient authors he claims to have used are Lactantius, Martianus Capella, Ovid, Fulgentius and Hermes Trismegistus, among the moderns Caelius Rhodiginus (Ludovico Riccheri) whose *Lectiones antiquae*, first published at Venice in 1516, were a typical erudite miscellany of information on antiquity of the sort first popularised by the *Miscellanea* of Politian (1489).

In the middle of the sixteenth century three important mythographic

[1] The standard work on this subject is J. Seznec, *The Survival of the Pagan Gods*, New York, 1953. On the myth and mythographers see also D. C. Allen, *Mysteriously Meant: the Rediscovery of Pagan Symbolism and Allegorical Interpretation in the Renaissance*, Baltimore and London, 1970. For a study of the first illustrations to Cartari see R. L. McGrath, 'The "old" and "new" illustrations for Cartari's *Imagini*', in *Gazette des Beaux-Arts*, 6th series, lix, 1962, pp. 213–26.

treatises appeared. The *De deis gentium varia et multiplex historia in qua simul de eorum imaginibus et cognominibus agitur* of the Italian humanist Lelio Gregorio Giraldi was published at Basle in 1548. In 1556 Vincenzo Cartari issued the first edition of his *Le Imagini colla spositione de i dei de gli antichi* at Venice. Finally, the *Mythologiae, sive explicationvm fabularvm libri decem* of Natale Conti appeared in the same city in 1568.[1] These books, though professedly works of literary and antiquarian research, are closely linked to other kinds of Renaissance symbolic imagery because they attempt to explain the allegorical meanings of the attributes given to gods in antiquity. Conti, it is true, did not make this his principal study: following a tradition of philosophical antiquity he was concerned instead to discover the moral or philosophical teachings of which the myths are allegories. But all three authors proceed by the same method, the accumulation of literary references from the authors of antiquity, which they interpret and expound. Since references to the gods and myths are scattered throughout ancient authors, many of them obscure and in the sixteenth century often very difficult to obtain, it is not surprising that these three books came to be much used by the learned as well as by the less learned in preference to the original sources.

None of them was originally issued with illustrations, and the much-read and much reprinted Conti did not acquire any until as late as 1616. Even Cartari, whose equally popular treatise was concerned exclusively with representations and who was much used by artists, did not appear in an illustrated edition until 1571. And when his book was at last given illustrations, these mostly represented the gods not after surviving antique images, but in accordance with literary descriptions of their aspects. Indeed Cartari goes out of his way to praise the engraver of his illustrations for the faithful execution of figures that were well adapted to his text.

There could be no clearer evidence of the primacy of literary over visual authority so characteristic of all this literature, and exactly the same relation was to obtain between the inventors of our title-pages and their engravers. It has already brought itself to our attention in

---

[1] Owing to an error in the article by A. Guillon in the *Biographie Universelle Michaud*, ix, pp. 121–2, a general belief still prevails that the first edition of Conti's *Mythologiae* was printed in 1551. Since Guillon also claims that it was printed by Aldus, it can be shown that he has confused the *Mythologiae* with Conti's poem *De Venatione*, which was printed by the Aldine press in 1551 (Renouard, *Annales de l'Imprimerie des Alde*, Paris, 1834, p. 152). The terms of Conti's dedication (dated 1567) of the edition of Venice, 1568, to King Charles IX of France make it perfectly clear that this edition was the first edition.

connection with the device and emblem, where we saw that the invention precedes and dictates the pictorial shape they assume. Indeed for some six decades the only considerable corpus of pictures of the ancient gods with some pretence to authenticity remained Du Choul's *Discours de la religion des anciens Romains*, with its illustrations taken from medals. Those added by Curio to Valeriano's *Hieroglyphica* are much more fantastic.

In 1599 Cartari's book appeared in an English version by the poet Richard Lynche as *The Fovntaine of Ancient Fiction. Wherein is liuely depictured the Images and Statues of the gods of the Ancients, with their proper and particular expositions.* Beyond a brief, affected preface Lynch added nothing to the text, which had no illustrations. Robert Burton, author of the *Anatomy of Melancholy*, knew Cartari not from this edition, but from an illustrated edition of the Latin translation of Du Verdier, first published in 1581. Boccaccio, Giraldi and Conti were also well known in England. Spenser and Marlowe both used Boccaccio, while Chapman made careful study of Giraldi. Perhaps the most generally read of all the mythographers was Conti: the number of his editions, their close print and duodecimo format all indicate his popularity as a general manual for ready reference. He was used by Chapman even more than Giraldi: he and Cartari are mentioned in the same breath by John Marston in 1598, and his moral and philosophical interpretations of the ancient myths influenced Bacon.[1]

Allegorical Personifications

The Renaissance inherited a number of allegorical personifications from the Middle Ages—we may cite the Virtues, cardinal and theological, and the Arts. Others it derived from the deified abstractions and symbolic figures of imperial Rome as represented on medals. We have already seen that the *Hieroglyphica* of Pierio Valeriano added to the vocabulary of representations of allegorical figures. Other personifications were devised during the sixteenth century as a result of collaboration between learned men and artists—yet another instance of the division in such creations between the invention, which was the task of poets and scholars, and its realisation in visual form which was executed by artists under their guidance. The splendid princely pageants and ceremonies of the Renaissance—weddings, triumphal entries, funerals—provided typical occasions for the devising of such

[1] See B. C. Garner, 'Bacon and Comes', in *JWCI*, xxxiii, 1970, pp. 264–91.

personifications, and when described in commemorative publications provided yet another literary source for compilers of symbolic images.

The consummation of the fashion for ingenious allegorical figures that prevailed from c. 1540 was the *Iconologia* of Cesare Ripa, first published in an unillustrated edition at Rome in 1593.[1] This book was to enjoy an extraordinary vogue for two centuries and to become a Bible of allegory for the learned, for men of letters and above all for artists. Ripa held much the same view about the images of the pagan gods as other Renaissance scholars held concerning Egyptian hieroglyphs and classical myths. He believed that they had been composed by the ancients as veils to conceal philosophical secrets about nature and astrological secrets about the heavens. They had been invented 'so as to advance the instruction of the vulgar and at the same time to prevent the ignorant from understanding these mysteries equally clearly with the learned, which they would have done had their meaning been more openly declared'. Moreover, they had been partly invented for the sake of later generations, which would certainly be wiser than their predecessors. As we have already seen, this Janus-faced approach, half-favouring the arcane, half-advocating the illumination of the understanding, is typical of Renaissance symbolism.

Although images of the heavenly bodies, of the gods, of the elements, of the arts and sciences, of the times and seasons all figure in the *Iconologia*, Ripa's true concern is with images of another kind, with those that signify the properties of man or of things closely connected with him, above all his conceits and the various comportments that proceed from them. Conceits Ripa defines as all that can be signified in words. They can be divided into two sorts; those that affirm or deny something about someone and those that do not do so. The former provide the subject-matter of devices and emblems; it is the latter which are the subject-matter of Ripa's images, since they concern only virtues and vices and things connected with virtues and vices. The difference could perhaps be defined in our terms as the difference between a prescriptive image, such as was devised for *imprese* and emblems, and a descriptive image, which characterises a quality, property or attribute. Accordingly Ripa's images are properly expressed by human figures, since to use his Aristotelian terminology, the accidental form of man's qualities can be expressed by the accidental form of his exterior. It follows that his images, however abstract the concept they

[1] For Ripa see E. Mandowsky, 'Ricerche intorno all'Iconologia di Cesare Ripa', in *La Bibliofilia*, xli, 1939, pp. 7, 111, 204, 279.

represent, had to be anthropomorphic, and such indeed they are.

It also follows that they must be varied both in their aspect and attributes so as to express the conceit they represent. Among the means of achieving this are the disposition of the limbs in conformity with our humours and passions, and differences of complexion, size and age. All these are things, explains Ripa, that allow of great diversity because they fall under the four Aristotelian heads of matter, efficient, form and purpose. It is from this diversity that there has sprung a diversity of images intended to express one single thing. Ripa has tried to use all four categories in his images, but he points out that it is perfectly meritorious to use only one since the image-maker's 'principal regard must be to teach an occult matter in a fashion that is not ordinary, so as to delight by ingenious invention'. As regards attributes, he must search out his similitudes either by choosing two different things which have a relation in common, or by choosing two which share a quality. Thus a column can signify fortitude because it sustains a building as fortitude sustains a man: this is an instance of a shared relation. A lion signifies magnanimity because it is very magnanimous: this is an instance of a shared quality.

In its final form Ripa's *Iconologia* is a remarkably full repertory of allegorical images of man's emotional, moral, intellectual and physical nature and of the external adjuncts of his existence, wealth, poverty, dominion, glory, the political forms of his societies. It represents his qualities and properties, virtues and vices, not merely under broad categories, as had formerly been usual, but with considerable particularity of analysis. He himself declares that some of his images he had collected from antiquity, some from modern times and some he had invented himself or got his literary friends to invent for him, 'dressed out in mystic symbols'. The sources from which he borrowed were mostly not very recondite—Pierio Valeriano, Cartari, descriptions of pageants such as Vasari's *Descrizione dell'Apparato per le nozze del Principe Francesco de' Medici* (Florence, 1565).

Again it is significant that although the *Iconologia* is a compilation of images, it appeared in its first and second editions without illustrations. In fact, though it so swiftly became a handbook for painters, it was originally also intended as a handbook for authors and for the contrivers of ceremonies and pageants, in other words for the literary and learned. Indeed Donato Pasquardi, printer of the Paduan edition of 1630, describes it as 'a work pertaining to the representation of dramatic poems, comic and tragic, and to the devising of every sort of ceremony, nuptial, funeral, triumphal or spiritual'. The book's alphabetical arrangement by concepts, as well as its underlying scheme, implies an audience of this kind. And its learned text, with its many allusions to classical literature and its many Latin quotations, its citations of authors like St Thomas Aquinas, can never have been intended primarily for painters. The history of its illustrations demonstrates once again the ascendancy of the author and his text over the artist who drew the figures. Many of the figures of the first illustrated edition, that of 1603, were drawn by Cesare d'Arpino, to whom Ripa no doubt showed or lent the books from which he wanted him to copy certain figures. For the newly invented images he and the engraver were instructed to follow the text, as we know from an advertisement Ripa added to the book on publication. This complains 'that the engraver of these our figures has in some places not been an observer of the text; therefore, whenever the figure does not match with the text, you shall conform it in accordance with our words on every occasion it shall please you to represent it for your own service.' And for the editions of 1625 and 1630, edited by Giovanni Zaratino Castellini, a friend of Ripa, some new images were devised by Castellini himself and as such are expressly attributed to him.

Ripa also insisted that names should be added to identify symbolic images, just as the ancients had done on their medals.

> It seems to me a thing to be observed that a name should be added, except when images are to take the form of an enigma, for without knowing the name we cannot penetrate to a knowledge of the thing signified, except in the case of trivial images which are ordinarily recognised by all at first sight from familiar use.

It is perhaps because of this precept given in a very influential book that seventeenth-century allegorical personifications are more frequently identified on title-pages than their sixteenth-century predecessors.

Ripa was soon known in England, though because of the weak native artistic tradition his book was not translated into English until 1709. Its influence was therefore confined to the literary and learned. But by 1610 Peacham was already familiar with the illustrated edition of 1603.

Conclusions

Certain conclusions emerge from our survey of this literature of device, emblem, hieroglyph and allegory which flourished so vigorously from the 1550s onwards. In the first place it is not a literature addressed to artists, but to the courtly, to the literary and to the learned. Its authors came from these three classes: Alciati was a jurist, Giovio a bishop, Symeoni a typical polygraph of his day. As might be expected, it is the literary text that predominates in their works, even if it is a literary text that expounds, like Giovio's *Dialogo*, a collection of earlier devices. And even in the case of these earlier devices we are given to understand that their invention was the work of great personages or of poets, courtiers or humanists in their employ. Consequently the role of the artist is that of a more or less literal illustrator of a given text: he does not suggest inventions, he merely gives them pictorial form. Moreover all this literature is book-nurtured and book-bound. Even when the authors use visual rather than literary sources—antique medals and the like—more often than not their source was an illustration in a book. Only one or two authors—Giovio and Valeriano are perhaps the most important—draw directly on visual sources.

Two other conclusions define the nature of the visual figures contrived by these collectors and inventors of devices, emblems and allegories. We have already seen that in scope and application they include the personal preoccupations of the device, the moral preoccupations of the emblem, the transcendent symbolism of hieroglyphs, the philosophical and moral symbolism of myth and the descriptive symbolism of allegory. A common feature none the less is the anxiety of the authors to be not so obscure as to be enigmatic nor so commonplace as to exclude all ingenuity of invention in the contriver or all ingenuity of solution in the reader. If the courtiers, poets and humanists of the Renaissance shared with antiquity the opinion that learning was not for the vulgar, and should be hidden under veils so as to make it inaccessible to them, those veils were not to be so thick and dark that the truths they concealed were totally obscured. All these authors recommend a middle path between the occult impenetrability of the enigma and the tedious obviousness of the familiar.

THE IMAGERY OF THE TITLE-PAGE

It was towards the end of the sixteenth century that emblematic title-pages began to appear in England. Like the emblem, their intention was to communicate complex ideas by means of visual images. They were addressed to the same learned readers who enjoyed the books of emblems; who would in like fashion be edified or interested by their message and ready to savour the erudition with which it was conveyed; who would be entertained by the allusions and fascinated by the manipulation of the sources and by the neat and ingenious presentation. As we shall show in the analysis of one title-page after another, the designer was certainly the author (or in some instances, the editor). Again there is a parallel with the emblem which was the brain-child of a scholar or poet, a literary concept which with the help of an engraver was translated into a pictorial figure. However, in important respects the two forms differ; the title-page is not a general statement of a moral or philosophical aphorism. It does not exist in its own right but, on the contrary, is always closely related to the contents of the book for which it was made, be it the Bible, a history, a political tract, the collected works of a famous dramatist or a treatise on the alleviation of deafness.

To express their ideas the designers of title-pages used the rich collection of motifs inherited from Egyptian and classical antiquity, from the Middle Ages and from the more recent contrivers of symbolic figures. But since the title-pages were essentially modern, even topical in character, further invention was necessary and their devisers drew on a great variety of traditional and contemporary sources which might be literary or pictorial. Generally the design was not confined to the expression of one idea or one theme. It was the vehicle for the thoughts of the author on his work, but might also seek to give an indication of its scope, and include pictorial representations which could be understood only by perusing the book, thus stimulating the reader's curiosity. All the themes were carefully interwoven into the set patterns for the design of title-pages, according to an inner logic, to make up the meaning of the whole. The twenty examples chosen for this study exemplify the main characteristics of the emblematic title-page in England, both in their decoration, which we have already considered, and in their content.

A decade or so before they became fashionable in England, John Dee devised an emblematic title-page to his *General and Rare Memorials* (1), published in 1577 (dated 1576). He did so self-consciously, as we can see from the motto 'Plura latent quam patent' (More things are hidden than are revealed) at the top. This alludes to the symbolic representation below, whose Greek inscription in the border reads in translation 'The symbolic picture of Britain'. The book is a plea to the Queen and her counsellors to establish a strong naval force of small ships to police the narrow seas and so put an end to the current plague of piracy;

among the duties of its soldiers on land would be the abolition of hoarding of necessary commodities. In the picture the cause of Britain's plight is shown by the presence of the pirate ships in the darkness, the cover for evil-doing; the hoarding and the dearth are symbolised in the upturned ear of corn and the skull. The allegorical figure of Britain, a woman, kneels in supplication to the Queen who must seize her opportunity. Opportunity is personified in traditional allegorical form. The policy in action is demonstrated by the ship of the new force riding at anchor near to the soldiers on guard on the shore. Her Majesty aided by the heavenly powers will reap a splendid reward by becoming the mistress of Europe; she is, therefore, shown enthroned on the allegorical ship of Europe with the lesson repeated below in the figure of Europa carried to her glorious destiny by the bull. Dee urges as a model the successes of the fifteenth-century Greek rulers of the Peloponnese who strengthened and held their country by building fortresses; hence, centrally placed, the 'Fortress of Security' with Byzantine details. To bring the Greek theme home he has written most of the inscriptions in Greek. Or was this a deliberate mystification intended to act as a challenge to the reader to open the book and digest the contents? Although over-burdened, this title-page, with its several themes, its ready use of symbol and allegory and its contemporary features foreshadows the developed examples of the next generation.

It was usual for the designer to select individual motifs from the repertory of emblematic imagery for inclusion in his title-page; the obelisk signifying the monument to fame, the cut diamond, symbol of enduring worth, the wreath of bay, the reward of glory, appear again and again. The title-page to the *Discours of Voyages* (4) made by Van Linschoten displays the branches of the pepper and the vine; the vine is an emblematic symbol of spiritual wealth taken from the Bible, the pepper, which was of course a real source of riches, when placed in confrontation with the vine becomes a symbol of material wealth. By this means the editor has suggested the fruits to be gathered by follow-ing in the steps of Van Linschoten; while the coats of arms, one of the City of London, the other of a private gentleman, the secretary to the Archbishop of Canterbury, point to the great parties whose interest lay in eastern ventures.

Yet a visual emblem, complete in itself, may form the central theme of a design. The title border to the *Covntesse of Pembrokes Arcadia* (2) shows the representation of a pig backing away from a bush of mar-joram. Among the branches is a scroll bearing the appropriate motto,

'Spiro non tibi' (I breathe out [sweet scents] but not for thee); the whole is encased in an oval frame. This emblem may well have been invented by the editor of the *Arcadia*, Hugh Sanford. It also appears in Camerarius' contemporary book of emblems where it is accompanied by verses which tell us that wholesome teaching is poison to corrupt minds, just as the filthy pig flies from the sweet smell of marjoram. On the title-page it declares that Sidney's work is not for the mean and vulgar-minded, but only for the virtuous and generous-hearted. The rest of the space is taken up with the portrayal of the novel's two leading characters, and in the centre, Sir Philip Sidney's crest.

The image of a pig 'to represent a pernicious man' occurs in the first printed edition of Horapollo; it was elaborated by Pierio Valeriano whose work must have been consulted by Sanford and Camerarius. Interest in hieroglyphics continues throughout our period. Burton placed a hare in his illustration of Solitudo on his title-page (17) because the Egyptians 'in their Hieroglyphicks' used this solitude-loving animal to express a 'melancholy man'. A rhetorical gesture which Bulwer shows on the title-page to the *Chirologia* (18) of 1644, well known to have come down from classical antiquity, was none the less given an Egyptian provenance by him as evidence of its universal adoption. Raleigh's adaptation of the Divine Eye is described below.

Tired or worn-out inventions would not have been acceptable to the lively spirit which informs these title-pages. A traditional allegorical figure may, of course, be adapted in accordance with the new meanings it is required to convey, a process which can be observed in the evolution of the figure of Britannia. It is possible that Dee in showing Britannia as a woman in classical dress had the Britannia of Roman coins in mind. William Camden was already in London in 1576 and preparing his material for his great antiquarian work. In the first edition of *Britannia*, 1586, he discusses how Britannia herself should be portrayed and in the edition of 1600 she appears on the title-page holding standard and spear, seated on a rock within a rocky bay; in 1607 she has the spear reversed, perhaps to show that her wars are over. This is the model which Drayton had in mind for the representation of Britannia on the title-page of *Poly-olbion* (13), which the scholar John Selden, who wrote the notes and commentaries on his poem, helped him to devise. Much is changed; the spear has gone and the sceptre which she holds instead associates her with the kings and queens of England. Poised on her island amidst the seas, she is prosperous and serene. Two features suggest that nostalgic enchantment with the memory of Queen Elizabeth which was prevalent towards the end of James I's reign: her dress reveals one breast, traditionally an indication of chastity, and her robe is decorated with a map of her kingdom which recalls a well-known painting of the Queen in which she is shown standing on the map of Britain.

The characters of classical mythology likewise undergo a change as fresh ideas may occur to the author. In the title-page to Chapman's *Homer . . . twelve Bookes of his Iliads*, 1610, the hero Achilles appears as a mature warrior, not unlike Hector who stands opposite him. For the complete translation published in 1611 (8), he is shown as elegant and youthful and newly equipped with the armour forged for him by Vulcan, ready to re-enter the fray. Gods and goddesses are made to fit the roles assigned to them. Juno, Queen of Heaven, is transformed by Haydocke (3) into patroness of painting. The title-page of Bulwer's *Chirologia* asserts that Nature requires the assistance of art in supplementing and perfecting speech; accordingly, Nature is portrayed as a wild unkempt woman, a form never envisaged in antiquity. In Bulwer's later work, *Philocophus* (19), she takes part in a masque and dances with the personifications of the Senses in order to illustrate the author's theory of the senses.

A personification may be chosen from a recently published collection of engravings or from other contemporary sources. Some figures become popular and appear more than once, though with a different meaning. The figure of Religion in the title-page to the *Workes* of James I (11), was first shown in Théodore de Bèze's *Icones* of 1580 accompanied by a set of verses describing her attributes. Martin de Vos, the Flemish artist, adapted her for a broadsheet and translated the verses into Dutch, German, Flemish and French. She then appears in Ripa's *Iconologia*. De Bèze was the great Calvinist whose pupil Peter Young had been tutor to James I; Martin de Vos had the Protestants of the north in mind; Ripa labels her *Religione vera christiana*. In James's *Workes* she represents *Ecclesia Anglicana* as conceived by the King. In this latest manifestation, coloured by the different shades of opinion with which she had been imbued, she makes her appeal to the various streams of religious thought current in England. The companion figure of Peace holds a cornucopia symbolising riches. For this emblematical note there exists a model in Hadrianus Junius' book of emblems of 1565. James, like Solomon, to whom he is compared in the Preface to the *Workes*, was granted wisdom: 'Wisdom brought him Peace; Peace brought him Riches.' In her role as peacemaker, the figure treads the arms of war underfoot. Ripa expatiates on the qualities of the peace-maker who is of those who know 'how peace may be restored through suffering . . . both by their own means and with the help of others, not only by bodily force against external enemies, but . . . in the spirit against the powers of Hell'. But she is best understood in reference to the portrait of James I which was intended to face the title-page; there on the backcloth hanging behind the enthroned king is the inscription BEATI PACIFICI, for James, after years of effort in the cause of peace, felt justified in associating himself with the Seventh Beatitude.

Many of our title-pages display religious symbols which are quite different from those commonly found in the pictorial art of the Middle Ages. They were brought into being to meet the demands created by the religious developments of the sixteenth century. In common with the emblem the religious symbol always has the sanction of tradition, Egyptian, biblical, early Christian or mediaeval. Calvinist doctrine was the predominating influence on Protestant thought during the reign of Elizabeth and it proscribed the 'graven image' and most emphatically forbade any anthropomorphic representation of God the Father. Biblical figures either alone or in scenes might not suggest the act of adoration to the beholder; they were to be portrayed as historical personages carrying out the functions proper to them or taking part in historical events. The artistic formula might be traditional or it might be a version modified by a sixteenth-century master.

It was the work of translating the Old Testament into the vernacular and the study of the original Hebrew necessitated by the undertaking which led to the discovery of a fitting substitute for the figurative representation of the Almighty. In the Hebrew Bible the four letters of the name of God, JHWH (Jehovah) were written but were considered too sacred to be uttered. They were given therefore the vowel points belonging to the Hebrew for Lord, ADONAI, by which the reader was reminded each time to use the permitted word. This was the Tetra-grammaton. In the Middle Ages it appears in a few isolated cases in churches and because of its arcane quality it acquired magical properties and is to be found on amulets. It was also sometimes inscribed on church bells which ring in the name of God. Now it assumes a new life. Protestants were imbued with the writings of the Old Testament. They believed God to be unknowable; the Tetragrammaton was non-representational and at the same time a symbol enshrouded with reverence; the letters of a strange alphabet incomprehensible to all but the few who were Hebrew scholars, enhanced the effect of awe which it was meant to convey. Holbein placed it at the top of his design for the title-page to Coverdale's Bible of 1535 surrounded by a radiant light; after the Great Bible of 1539 the figure of God the Father never appears again as a human figure at the top of an English title-page. By contrast, many early vernacular Bibles, in German, Dutch and French do show God the Father as the bearded patriarch. The Tetragrammaton was also very popular in Protestant countries on the continent; after Leyden became Protestant c. 1572 the figure of God the Father in Lucas van Leyden's *Last Judgment* was painted out and the Tetragrammaton put in its place.[1]

A few tomb inscriptions have been found of the fourth and fifth centuries showing a triangle framing the monogram of Christ.[2] But throughout the Middle Ages it is an extremely rare motif and there is only one known example which may be associated with a text which explains its meaning. On the first illuminated leaf of the Uta Gospels,[3] produced in Regensburg in the eleventh century, the design includes a triangle with an open hand superimposed, surrounded by concentric circles. On the outer circle are hexameters which read in translation 'God encompassing all eternity with his will, which he established by his eternal word'.[4] These lines should refer to the triangle, the central figure of the whole diagram, which thus represents the Godhead. This interpretation is reinforced by a definition given by Johannes Belethus, one time Rector of the Theological School in Paris, in a work of 1165:[5] 'The divine nature is symbolized by delta [Greek letter Δ] which closed by a round represents the divine nature which has neither beginning nor end.'[6] It occurs more frequently in the fifteenth and early sixteenth centuries, but again it was religious controversy which led to its widespread adoption in the latter part of the century. At this period the anti-Trinitarian movement was well organised and constituted a threat to all the established churches; as a manifesto of the true faith, the triangle, symbol of the Trinity, was placed on title-pages to Bibles and other religious literature and broadsheets in both Catholic and Protestant countries.

[1] Information kindly given us by Dr Wurfbain of the Stedelijk Museum 'De Lakenhal', Leyden. The Tetragrammaton has now been removed.

[2] See G. Stuhlfauth, *Das Dreieck. Die Geschichte eines religiösen Symbols*, 1937.

[3] See G. Swarzenski, *Der Regensburger Buchmalerei*, I, 1901, no. 28, plate XII.

[4] 'perpetuo totum nutu cingens deus aevum sanxit ab aeterno quae condidit omnia verbo'.

[5] J. P. Migne, *Patrologiae Cursus Completus*, 1855, vol. 202. 'Rationale divinorum officiorum', c. 44.

[6] 'Per delta enim circulariter clausum, divina figuratur natura, quae nec principium nec finem habuit'.

Often the triangle is represented enclosing the Tetragrammaton. Quite apart from its polemical value this invention was one solution to the problem of representing God the Creator and Law-giver as He appears in the Old Testament and the Godhead of Christian doctrine.

The Trinity may be represented by three entities and on title-pages to Catholic Bibles God the Son may be shown as Christ crucified; on Protestant Bibles He is symbolised by the Paschal Lamb. This image can be traced to the sixth century. It appears beside the cross on Erhard Altdorfer's title-page to the Lübeck Bible of 1533–4 which was used for the English Bible of 1537. Signifying the Crucifixion prefigured by the first Passover it was pre-eminently suited to Protestant thinking.

With the accession of James I there is a change in the religious climate and the imagery of high Anglicanism, reflecting the views of the King himself, as well as of some of the bishops, begins to make a tentative appearance. Thus on Gaultier's title-page to the *Workes* of Chrysostom the Greek doctors are shown with haloes and there is certainly a transcendental quality about the figures on the title-page to the Authorised Version. At the bottom of this title-page there is a representation of the pelican in her piety. This symbol of Christ's sacrificial death and resurrection appears in the Middle Ages on crosses, on pictures of the Crucifixion above the figure of Christ, on the doors of tabernacles for the Host and on monstrances. It was therefore connected with the Eucharist. It had never previously been shown on an English title-page and its presence suggests a high Anglican feeling towards the Eucharist.

Our period sees the invention of a new religious symbol. This is the Eye of God. There are many references to it in the Bible but no representations occur before the sixteenth century. In the early editions of the *Hieroglyphica* of Horapollo an eye together with a sceptre is said to signify the Egyptian god Osiris. However, the form of an eye was an authentic Egyptian hieroglyph which scholars could observe on Egyptian monuments in Rome, and in the augmented editions of Horapollo published by J. Kerver in Paris,[1] the eye has been added as a separate image and given a meaning. Accompanying the woodcut of the Eye is an explanation:

> Pour signifier Dieu ils paignoient un oeil,
> pource qu' ainsi que l'oeil veoit & regarde ce qui est
> audeuant de luy, ne plus ne moins Dieu
> veoit, considere & cognoit toutes choses.

[1] See p. 135 note 2.

It thus becomes a hieroglyph in the Renaissance sense symbolising the all-seeing and all-knowing eternal God.

This work was republished many times and may well have been the source used by Raleigh who placed it on his title-page of 1614, where it is labelled Providentia. The Eye of Providence appears in prints of the Gunpowder Plot[1]—it foresees politico-religious terror. In a broadsheet of 1621 its beam spies out Guy Faux; thus God intervenes actively in human affairs. The author of this design was Samuel Ward, the well-known Puritan who was also an emblematist.

The juxtaposition of spiritual symbols, of allegory and myth with the factual world was a commonplace of visual art; it was characteristic of the tableau mounted on its *pegma* and of the contemporary masque. Similarly on our title-pages there is an interplay of symbol and reality; indeed they derive much of their impact from the interaction of the different spheres of imagery. Reality may be represented by historical characters, living people, the stuff of geography and astronomy, architectural views. All these features were delineated with the greatest care since they were to be scrutinised by the reader for novel and interesting detail just as the allegorical matter was searched for recondite allusion.

Renaissance biblical studies, though mainly philological, influence the appearance and attributes of the figures which appear on the title-page of the Authorised Version (7). The horns of Moses have gone, to be replaced by a radiant light playing about his hair; the figure of Aaron standing opposite was taken from an engraving made under the instructions of the great Hebrew scholar Arias Montanus which was included in the last volume of the Royal Polyglot Bible of 1573. Certain Hebrew commentaries, available in print in the sixteenth century, contain passages on the emblems of the twelve Sons of Israel; these were interpreted as descriptions of their insignia and on the title-page to the Bishop's Bible of 1602 (5) are shown emblazoned on their shields.

In the portrayal of historical and semi-historical figures there is evidence of the antiquarian research which found expression in the formation of the first Society of Antiquaries. Brutus on the title-page to the *Poly-olbion* (13) is wearing a leather surcoat which may well be adapted from the coat worn by one of the 'more civille Britaines' in the illustration in Speed's *History of Great Britain*, 1611. Recourse may have been made to a manuscript in Robert Cotton's collection to find

[1] Hind, II, pp. 342 and 394.

the proper contemporary attire for Hengist the Dane. Jonson recon-
structed the original seat of drama shown on his title-page from literary
sources—and got it wrong. He took the theatre from one of the several
books on the antiquities of Rome. Richard Lyne's plan of Cambridge
was used by Savile for the view of King's College, Cambridge, but he
must have had a sketch made of Eton, for what is the first known
representation of the College (9).

The continuing intellectual excitement of the geographic discoveries
and advances in astronomy is reflected in the many representations of
the globe and the celestial sphere, of maps and projections—the globe
terrestrial and celestial globes as God's creation for Du Bartas' *Deuine
Weekes* (6); the terrestrial globe as the subject of Raleigh's *History* and
the stage for some of the exploits of which he had personal knowledge;
as the world revealed by man's intelligence, for Bacon's *Natural History*
(16).

The Portrait

In some instances portraits appear on title-pages without any reference
to the iconographical scheme. An old tradition led to their inclusion.
During the Middle Ages living authors often had themselves portrayed
on presentation copies of their manuscripts. In the case of the printed
book such portraits were long placed on the verso of the title-page and
in the seventeenth century we frequently find an engraved portrait
following the engraved title-page. But from the first decade of the
sixteenth century we also find the portrait of the living author trans-
ferred to the title-page itself. One of the earliest if not the earliest
example of this practice is the title-page of Sir John Harington's translation of the *Orlando Furioso*, 1591, where an oval miniature or
medallion of Harington leans against the protruding wings of the
plinth on either side of the central recess. Where a book was the work
of two authors, notably in the case of translations, it became the
custom to place the portrait of the original author at the top and that of
the translator at the bottom. We find this arrangement on the title-
page of Haydocke's translation of Lomazzo, 1598 (3), on Philemon
Holland's translation of Xenophon's *Cyropaedia*, 1632, and on Richard
Tomlinson's translation of Jean de Renou's *Dispensatory*, 1637. The
only other portraits that are found on English title-pages of our period
are those of royal personages: these are placed according to the dictates
of the design. In one instance (3) it is possible that the author's portrait
was engraved from a miniature by Hilliard; indeed, portraits in the

form of a miniature or medallion are a feature of these title-pages. They are not exclusive to England. Other portraits were taken from paintings and engravings and perhaps, as in the case of the portrait of Hobbes for the *Leviathan*, from a drawing done from the life specially for the occasion.

The invention of engraving had, in fact, greatly altered the approach to portraiture. Likenesses were taken several times in a man's life; in the case of royal persons, many times. It was essential, therefore, that when a portrait was shown, it should be as recent a likeness as possible. Burton who presents himself as teacher to the reader of the *Anatomy* and so plays a living role in the work, took pains to have his portrait changed in the later editions to that of the ageing man. Then again, when the contents were, even in part, propaganda nothing would have been more fatal to the sense of immediacy than an out-of-date portrait. In the drawing for Dee's title-page the Queen is depicted, possibly without too much thought, as a smiling girl, but in the wood-cut her features are those of the stern and regal woman as befitted her seventeen years of rule. The portrait of James on the title-page to the *Historie of Virginia* (15) is from the late engraving done for his *Workes* in 1616, while that of the Prince of Wales must have been taken from a likeness made within a few months of publication.

Changes in the Design of the Title-page

As an answer to the needs of Elizabethan and Jacobean iconography the architectural front was satisfactory. Symbolic in itself, it might house any number of allegorical symbols. But in the 1620s and 1630s other kinds of design begin to appear in response to different needs. A new conception may be embodied in a new symbol which will not fit into the old scheme; Bacon envisaged the mind of man as a ship sailing out to discover fresh worlds of knowledge; to Hobbes the state was a crowned giant, Leviathan towering over his kingdom. Or propagandist aims may demand a more direct form of imagery; Captain John Smith, who was pressing for the extension of royal power in the colonies, simply imposed the effigies of the monarchy on the map of North America. The author who wished to show the categories under which he had considered his work might turn to the compartmental design; Hobbes placed the emblems of secular and ecclesiastical power in confronting compartments and a similar scheme was adopted by Burton for his almost clinical illustrations of the various kinds of melancholy with which he had dealt.

The Making of the Title-page

Enough has been said to confirm the assumption that the authors them-selves were responsible for the complex ideas expressed in these title-pages. To this the signatures of the engravers are a tacit witness for they nearly all read *fecit* or *sculpsit*. William Rogers is an exception. Although he would have discussed the title-page to the *Discours* with the editor, John Wolfe, since he signs it *Inuentor* he must have made the design himself. He had as a model the famous title-page to the first volume of *America*, 1590, made by Théodor de Bry, who shows some of the figures drawn by John White while he was in Virginia. The title-page to Philemon Holland's translation of the *Cyropaedia* is signed H H *invent*. This might be the monogram of Henry Holland who wrote the dedica-tion to James I and presented the book to the king on behalf of his aged father. If indeed he invented the design, this is the only work among the great number which he published with which he proclaims any artistic connection. Again John Jackson signed the frontispiece to his *Pedigree and Peregrination of Israel*, *J.J. ye Author invēt*.[1]

Unfortunately, however, lack of such evidence often makes it diffi-cult to assess the nature of the co-operation between the author and engraver. In the Renaissance when a programme was devised for a work of art, it would be proposed to the artist or his patron either verbally or in written instructions. We have seen that this was almost invariably the case with books of devices and emblems. In the case of an engraving, the patron might then commission an artist to make a design which would then be handed over to the engraver for execution. This was the procedure followed by Plantin for the first title-page of volume I of the Royal Polyglot Bible. Alternatively, the engraver might use his own invention working on the basis of the literary pro-gramme. With the possible exception of Dr Dee and the certain exception of Haydocke and Peacham, both of whom were amateur artists, it is most unlikely that any of the authors whose title-pages we discuss were able to provide engravers with working sketches. Both Robert Burton (17) and George Wither in his *Emblemes* complain that the engravers of their title-pages have failed to carry out their instruc-tions correctly, and we are surely justified in deducing that such mistakes arose because the engravers had to devise images partly on the basis of purely verbal guidance.

There were perhaps conferences to which the engraver brought

[1] Hind, III, p. 169.

pattern books. We know that a man might design his own sepulchral monument—the French historian Thevet wrote in 1584, 'La coutume est . . . que chascun . . . fait dresser son tombeau'; James I would have had to approve the monuments which he raised to Elizabeth and Mary in Westminster Abbey; so that an author might well be sufficiently familiar with architectural forms to select what he thought would be effective on his title-page. Books of emblems, allegorical personifications would also have to be provided; these might be owned by the author. We know that Raleigh had a copy of Cartari's *Le imagini . . . de i dei de gli antichi* and that James I owned Alciati's *Emblemata*. Many books or series of allegorical representations were produced especially for the use of craftsmen who held them as part of their stock-in-trade.

Sketches must have been made for submission to the author or editor and for use in the actual engraving of the plate but hardly any are known from our period. The sketch for Dee's *General and Rare Memorials* survives though it is not the final version. There is a preliminary drawing in existence by John Webb for the title-page engraved by Hollar for the Polyglot Bible of 1657; in the engraving more figures have been added and part of the design has been altered.

The Explanation of the Frontispiece

We have already seen that from the middle of the sixteenth century the purpose of the ambitiously designed title-page was more than simply to decorate the book; rather its purpose was to epitomise the book and glorify its author and his work. Such title-pages do more than illustrate the contents of the book; they can have an independent message of their own. But if some title-pages are clear enough in the delivery of their meaning, others were obscure even to the learned in their own day because their invention interwove images whose association was not obvious. The message of the title-pages of the Coverdale Bible of 1535 and the Great Bible of 1539 must always have been patent to anyone familiar with the great controversies of the day, but a more esoteric knowledge of allegorical language was required to interpret the complex title-pages of Mannerism. The figures, strangely dressed and with singular attributes, were often difficult to identify even for contemporaries and in order to give some clue to the witty devising of their allegorical conceit, it was customary to name them in inscriptions. But sometimes this was not done, and sometimes the association of thought that linked them was difficult to perceive. Accordingly, there soon arose a demand for a text to explain the meaning both of single features and the whole. This was generally couched in the favourite form of a poem which took a place among the preliminaries of the book. The earliest example we have been able to trace is the 'Frontispicii Explanatio' appended by Hubert Goltzius to his *Fasti Magistratvvm et Triumphorvm Romanorvm* published at Bruges in 1561. A dialogue in Latin hexameters between Goltzius and a spectator, it explains that the title-page represents Rome seated on the two hills enclosed within her first walls. To either side of her Fortune and Virtue join hands to signify the long and happy union of these two powers that made Rome great. On the left is the Tiber, on the right the wolf that gave suck to Romulus and Remus. These figures are all set on top of a rusticated structure whose upper part bears a tablet inscribed with the title. In a dungeon underneath, flanked by trophies, are the nations Rome has taken captive: conspicuous in the front, right, is the mourning figure of Carthage. In England such explanatory verses are first found appended to Jacobean title-pages; to some, that is, by no means all. The 'Epigram' already quoted from Guillim's *Displaye of Heraldrie* of 1610 appears to be an early example. Entitled 'The Minde of the Front', 'The Explanation of the Embleme', or 'The Argument of the Frontispiece', they gracefully indicate to us the principal meanings of the designs they illustrate, but without elucidating their every detail or association. Nevertheless they are a great assistance to the reader's understanding and in this book they are reproduced in every instance where they occur.

Conclusion

Some of these title-pages are pleasing to the eye, others less so. It would be wrong to judge them solely for their aesthetic qualities since they were not primarily intended as harmonious compositions and now and then the urgency of communicating concepts may have outweighed artistic requirements. Their value and importance lies in the content, the author's contribution. Through them we perceive great authors in a new light, translating their intellectual and literary concepts into the forms of pictorial art, exercising their imagination in another sphere. Perhaps something is added to a knowledge of their minds; on a different level the idiosyncracies of character which are revealed from time to time afford us an unexpected glimpse of their personalities.

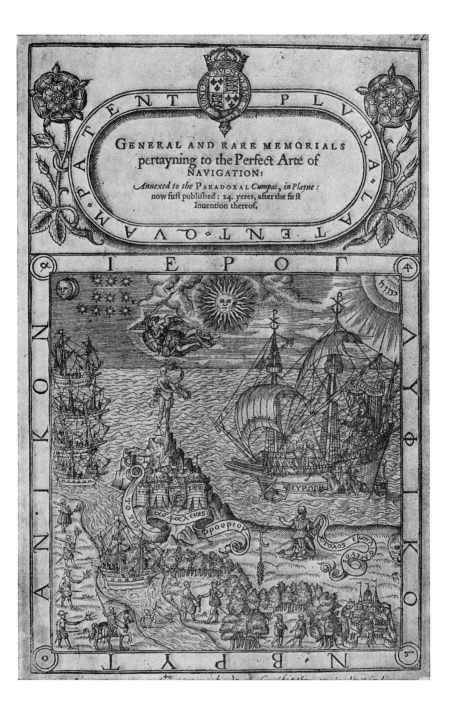

PLVRA · LATENT · QVAM · PATENT

ΙΕΡΟΓΛ ... ΑΝΙΚΟΝ ... ΛΥΦΙΚΟ ... ΝΒΡΥΤ

GENERAL AND RARE MEMORIALS
pertayning to the Perfect Arte of
NAVIGATION:

Annexed to the PARADOXAL *Cumpas, in Playne :*
now first published : 24. yeres, after the first
Inuention thereof.

I

JOHN DEE

General and Rare Memorials pertayning to the Perfect Arte of Navigation...

1577

(McK. and F., no. 157)

The woodcut title-page is divided into two compartments; the upper one contains an oval frame enclosing the title which continues: *Annexed to the* PARADOXAL *Cumpas, in Playne:*/now first published: 24.yeres, after the first/Inuention thereof. Round the border of the frame, the motto, PLVRA : LATENT : QVAM : PATENT (More things are concealed than are revealed). At the top, the royal arms encircled by the Garter and surmounted by the crown. Secured by loops on either side of the outer frame, the Tudor rose. The border of the lower compartment is lettered ΙΕΡΟΓΛΥΦΙΚΟΝ . ΒΡΥΤΑΝΙΚΟΝ (the Hieroglyph of Britain). In the corners are circles each containing a Greek letter, top l., α with lower prime (the stroke), top r., φ, bottom l., ο, and bottom r. ϛ. the Greek symbol for 6; Greek letters have a numerical value and the three together with the symbol add up to the date when the book was completed, 1576. This was first pointed out by William Herbert, the eighteenth-century bibliographer.[1]

The coastal scene which fills the lower compartment is lit by the Tetragrammaton whose rays extend across a cloudy sky in the centre of which shines the sun with human face. To the left, below the sun, is the descending figure of the Archangel Michael, whose name in Hebrew characters is inscribed on a fold of his robe. In his right hand

---

[1] William Herbert, *Typographical Antiquities* . . . , begun by Joseph Ames, 1785, pp. 66of.

he clenches a raised wavy sword, in his left, a shield blazoned with the cross. He has a fillet round his forehead. On the extreme left on the nightward side is the moon, also with a human face, showing one quarter, and ten stars. In the waters on the right is a great ship with the anchor drawn up. On the hull is the inscription ΕΥΡΩΠΗ (Europe) with the mythological figure of Europa on the bull swimming alongside. The χρ sign, the monogram of Christ, surmounts the two masts. Sitting on a high-backed and canopied throne on the poop deck is the Queen with ELIZABETH lettered on a scroll above. She is crowned and wears a richly patterned dress. She extends her right hand and holds a sceptre in her left. Three gentlemen, her counsellors, all cloaked and dressed alike, stand bareheaded on the deck amidships. Marked on the rudder is the royal coat of arms. A woman in classical dress kneels on the shore facing the ship, her arms outstretched in supplication to Her Majesty; she holds a long scroll lettered, Στολος εξωπλισμενος (a fully-equipped expeditionary force). On her left is a stalk of corn turned head down in the ground; on her right is a skull half cut off by the border. The estuary of a river divides the land on which she kneels. A walled town rises on the rocky headland in the centre. Two round castellated towers flank its great gate; within the ramparts is a church with a central tower and steeple; a scroll twists about the town with the legend, ΤΟ ΤΗΣ ασφαλειας φρουριομ (sic) (the fortress of safety). Balanced on the pinnacle, one foot on a rock and the other on a pyramid, is the figure of Opportunity pointing up to her lock of hair with one hand, while with the other she extends a laurel wreath in the direction of the Queen. Near the mouth of the river a ship rides at anchor with three masts, six gunports visible and a flag with four bands flying from a flagpole at the poop. Further upstream is a dinghy tied to the bank with an oarsman sitting in it; in a clearing on the wooded right bank is a soldier, seemingly just landed from the dinghy, grasping a bag of money and conversing with a gentleman who holds out his hand in a gracious gesture; in a second clearing a similar pair, differently attired, walk towards the walled town which fills the bottom right-hand corner; they appear again within its walls. The buildings inside the town include a heavy round tower, two churches with spires, a cupola raised on columns and various other buildings; the wall facing the spectator is pierced by an arched gateway with moat, drawbridge and portcullis. On the left bank are four soldiers holding torches. All four wear morions, two shoulder arquebusses, two hold unsheathed swords. Another helmeted soldier on horseback in the foreground carries a lance. Beyond these soldiers, out to sea, is a line of four ships riding at anchor; all three-masted, the first with six gunports in view, the furthest away with eight or nine; there is much activity on board. Men are on the look-out in the forecastles and others are carrying what appear to be lances on the decks.

A preliminary drawing ascribed to Dee exists among the papers of Elias Ashmole.[1] It precedes a copy of the manuscript which had been sent by the author to his cousin William Aubrey[2] and was returned to him at the end of July 1577. This was in time for a final drawing to be made from it for inclusion in the book which was published in September. It measures 19·3 × 18·2 cm. There are various discrepancies between the drawing and the cut; in the drawing there is no margin enclosing the roses and the oval at the top. The sky on the left is very dark and half obscures the stars; there is no one on the ships; the name 'Michael' is written on the sky alongside him and he has a straight sword; the gentleman engaged in a money transaction has his left hand extended; the Queen is shown as very much younger and so are her counsellors who are wearing ruffs, jerkins and doublets while one of them has a hat decorated with feathers; the figure of Opportunity is definitely looking at the Queen; the town, bottom right, has two gates. There are flagpoles instead of *flèches* on the twin towers.

General and Rare Memorials was written in four parts;[3] the second part deals with navigation proper. The woodcut title-page is to the first part, the only one to be printed. Its running title is 'The Brytish Monarchie'. After the introductory matter, it consists of a plea by the author to Queen Elizabeth for the creation of a 'PETY-NAVY-ROYALL' distinct from the 'Grand-Nauy-Royall', numbering 'Three score Tall Ships, (or more)'[4] and smaller ones, whose duty would be to police the narrow seas, sweep away pirates both British and foreign, and stop foreigners from fishing in England's waters. A great deal of information is given about both the pirates and the foreign fishermen who came from Flanders, France, Portugal and Spain.

[1] Bodley, Ashmole MS. 1789. See Peter French, *John Dee*, 1972, plate 14.
[2] Bodley, Ashmole MS. 1789, ff.116–17v.
[3] See E. G. R. Taylor, *Tudor Geography 1485–1583*, 1930, p. 181.
[4] John Dee, *General and Rare Memorials . . .* , p. 53.

The subject was extremely topical. At her accession the Queen had thirty-five, or according to another source thirty-two, ships in good and bad condition. She was determined on an active policy of naval armament and henceforward the shipyards were fully occupied with new ships or repair work. Nevertheless things went slowly. In 1563 there were still four hundred known pirates in the seas round Britain; during a vigorous campaign in 1573 hundreds were captured but owing to the complicity of shore authorities only three were hanged.[1] It was against this background that Dee put forward his own far-reaching and ambitious plan, which he suggests should be financed by 'A perpetuall Beneuolence'[2] levied on goods and rents, not only of the citizens of coastal towns, but throughout the kingdom; a tax of this nature would burden neither the Crown nor the Commons.

At the end of the book are two Addresses by Gemistus Pletho, the famous late Byzantine philosopher, one to the Emperor Manuel II, the other to his second son Theodore, Despot of the Peloponnese. These works written probably about 1400, were first printed in 1575[3] when they were issued both in the original Greek and a Latin translation. Dee says, 'I need not Dowbt, but they, to whom, the chief Care of such causes is committed haue Diligently selected the Hony of those Flowres'[4]—he includes them therefore for a wider audience. The Byzantine Empire, despite the disaster of 1453, still held an important place in contemporary minds; it had endured for so many centuries and was the direct heir and transmitter of Greek thought and learning. During the fourteenth century most of the Peloponnese had been reconquered for Byzantium from the Franks and a provincial government was then set up at Mistra under the son of the Emperor. Mistra became a brilliant centre of learning and it was here that Gemistus held a school of philosophy. In his first Address Gemistus advises the Emperor to continue the well-proved policy of building strings of fortresses up and down the country. These defences were to be financed by a tax on the non-fighting population.

Dee felt that what he had written bore strongly on the state of affairs of Britain; though not directly, 'much thereof, might be a good

---

[1] See M. Oppenheim, *A History of the Administration of the Royal Navy* . . ., 1896, pp. 119, 177.

[2] Dee, op. cit., p. 13.

[3] John Stobaeus, *Eclogarum libri duo:* . . . *Una G. Gemisti Plethonis de rebus Peloponnes. Orationes duae, eodem G. Cantero interprete* . . ., Antwerp, 1575.

[4] Dee, op. cit., p. 65.

Aduise for the framing of an Analogical Ciuile Consideration'.[1] 'But, here and there, the Idea generall, is to be answered with due application, particularly, for our Cuntry, and these our Dayes.'[2] Because of his earnest desire to bring the Greek example to the notice of his readers, he wrote all the captions on the title-page in Greek, excepting only the name of the Queen and the Archangel. And as we shall see, it plays a central role in his pictorial theme, which is part fact and part allegory.

Towards the end of the book there occurs the description of the 'Hieroglyph of Britain'[3] which partly explains the title-page.

Why should not we *HOPE*, that, *RES-PVBL . BRYTANICA*,   I
on her knees, very Humbly, and ernestly Soliciting the most   E
Excellent Royall Maiesty, of our *ELIZABETH*, (Sitting at the   P
HELM of this Imperiall Monarchy: or, rather, at the Helm of   O
the *IMPERIALL SHIP*, of the most parte of Christendome: Γ
if so, it be her Graces Pleasure) shall obteyn, (or Perfect Policie,   Λ
may perswade her Highnes,) that, which is the Pyth, or Intent   Υ
of *RES-PVBL . BRYTANICA*, Her Supplication? Which is,   Φ
That, ΣΤΟΛΟΣ ΕΞΩΠΛΙΣΜΕΝΟΣ, may helpe vs, not onley,   I
to ΦΡΟΥΡΙΟΝ ΤΗΣ ΑΣΦΑΛΕΙΑΣ: But make vs, also,   K
Partakers of Publik Commodities Innumerable, and (as yet)   O
Incredible. Vnto which, the *HEAVENLY KING*, for these   N
many yeres last past, hath, by *MANIFEST OCCASION*,   B
most Graciously, not only inuited vs: but also, hath made,   P
EVEN NOW, the Way and Means, most euident, easie, and   Υ
Compendious: In-asmuch as, (besides all our own sufficient   T
Furniture, Hability, Industry, Skill, and Courage) our Freends   A
are become strong: and our Enemies, sufficiently weake, and   N
nothing Royally furnished, or of Hability, for Open Violence   I
Vsing: Though their accustomed Confidence, in Treason,   K
Trechery, and Disloyall Dealings, be very great. Wherein, we   O
beseche our *HEAVENLY PROTECTOR*, with his *GOOD*   N
ANGELL to Garde vs, with *SHIELD AND SWORD*, now,
and euer. Amen.

First, divine assistance; the 'Heavenly Protector' is represented by the Tetragrammaton—the four Hebrew letters for the Name of God. This non-representational form was chosen by the Protestants to replace 'the

---

[1] Ibid., in the margin.
[2] Ibid., p. 73, in the margin.
[3] Ibid., p. 53.

graven image' of God the Father. Here it lights the sky whose radiance is increased by the rays of the sun. 'The *Good Angell* to Garde us' with shield and sword is Michael, agent of God's command—he carries forward the divine influence, pushing back the darkness. He is 'the great prince which standeth for the children of thy people'.[1] Thus Britain is identified with Israel. Michael is often represented with the cross of Christ on his shield in works of the Renaissance and earlier.

'Res-publ[ica] Brytanica' is personified by the woman on her knees pleading with the Queen for 'a strong expeditionary force' which 'may helpe us' to be 'a fortress of security'. In the estuary is one of the 'Tall ships' of the new force for which she asks. The flag at the poop is the British ensign which at this date might show four, five or more bands[2] as distinct from the Dutch which had three bands only. She carries twelve guns; there would also have been mobile cannon so she is well armed and warlike, though at this period there was no difference between warship and merchant ship, except perhaps that the former were more strongly constructed. With her high poop she resembles a warship of 1570, perhaps the *Bull* or *Tiger*.[3] The four ships off the coast are of the same build as the one in the estuary, therefore not fishermen. St Michael has raised his sword against them—they are the Queen's enemies—'the Pety forrein Offender'[4] or 'Pyrats, our own Cuntrymen (and they to no small number) [who] wold be called, or constrayned to come home'[5] by the 'Pety-Navy-Royall'. It is not possible to say whether they are preparing a raid under cover of darkness, which shields the evil-doer, or whether they have been captured and the armed men on the decks are members of boarding parties. As pointed out above, the darkness is more firmly indicated in the drawing.

There is more night activity on the left bank where soldiers are using their torches to keep watch on the shore. They too are members of the naval force whose scope was to extend to various duties on land, 'For, skilfull Sea Soldiers are, also, on land, far more traynable to all Martiall exployts executing'.[6] One of the great troubles of the time was shortage of corn and other victuals brought about by hoarders, 'diuelish Greedy

---

[1] Daniel 12.1.

[2] See BL, Add. MS. 22047, The second Rolle declaring the Nombre of the Kynges Maiestys own Galliases [1546], and Bodley, Rawlinson MS. A1 92, 20; both reproduced in Oppenheim, op. cit., frontispiece and plate at p. 130.

[3] Oppenheim, op. cit., plate at p. 130.

[4] Dee, op. cit., p. 5.

[5] Ibid., p. 6.

[6] Ibid.

guts, ouer long keping back their Corn from the Common Market';[1] they 'Counterfet a Dearth: And all, for Priuate Lucre onely.'[2] In the picture hoarded corn is symbolised by the full grain of wheat turned downwards, and dearth or near dearth by the skull. Another of the tasks assigned to the soldiers of the Pety Navy was to commandeer corn and store it in the 'Publik . . . Store-Houses' located in the twenty Pety-Navy-Royall towns on which the force was to be based, whence it would be distributed in times of need.

The couple furthest away from us on the other bank may be an officer from the ship and a counsellor who has handed over the monies necessary for the ship's maintenance; alternatively, it is perhaps the officer who is about to hand over some of these 'liberall Presents and forrein Contributions' made by a foreign captain in gratitude for the succour and 'good and ready Pilotage'[3] afforded him by the Pety-Navy-Royall.

Another counsellor accompanies the messenger who must render weekly, 'the Certificat, of the Affaires, and State, of the PETY-NAVY-ROYALL, . . . to our Gracious Soueraign, and her most Vigilant Priuy Cownsailors' and 'Attend and Receiue . . . their will and pleasure'[4]— they go into one of the appointed towns.

The mountainous headland which dominates the landscape is most unEnglish in character and is only summarily connected with the gentle valley below. It is surely intended as an allusion to the Peloponnese. On its steep slopes is set one of the walled places referred to by Gemistus, both a real fortress and to the latterday Englishman a symbol of the security he so urgently needed. In all contemporary maps of the Peloponnese the rocky ranges are shown dotted about with fortified towns and castles so that Dee's impressionistic sketch would have been easily understood; if the city is meant to be Mistra, the great portal with flanking towers would be the Nauplion Gate, of which Dee, who knew many geographers, might have had a description. If it is imaginary the individual features might have been taken from woodcuts such as those in Münster's *Cosmographia*.[5] The flat domes with *flèches* give the towers a Byzantine flavour.

The pyramid perched on the highest rock of the headland, on

[1] Ibid., p. 41.
[2] Ibid., p. 39.
[3] Ibid., p. 9.
[4] Ibid., p. 61.
[5] Sebastian Münster, *Cosmographia*, 1550, see woodcut at p. 1018.

which Opportunity stands, may according to a later source[1] signify prudence, 'post collectum robur' (after strength has been gathered); so the 'Little Lock of LADY OCCASION, Flickring in the Ayre, by our hands, to catch hold on':[2] must be seized now, when our 'Freends are become strong' and 'our Enemies, sufficiently weake'.[3] The Queen shown severe and dignified in the engraving, is advised by her sober counsellors; she will respond to the gaze of Opportunity, set up the strong expeditionary force and so reap the laurel wreath of victory for which indeed she is holding out her right hand.

Elizabeth enthroned on the ship of Europe represents the sum of Dee's prophetic hopes. The Pety Navy Royall will 'waft and garde our own Marchants Fletes, as they shall pas, and repas betwene this Realm'; [also] 'forrein rich Laden Ships, passing within, or by any the Sea Limits, of her Maiesties Royallty'[4] so that they would be, 'now, in most Security'; from which it would follow that she like King Edgar, will be 'the True and Souerayn Monarch, of all the Brytish Ocean, enuironing any way, his Impire of Albion, and Ireland'[5] and as such, with the royally marked rudder under her hand, assume her place as the helmsman of Europe and therefore 'of the most part of Christendome'.

The motto 'Plura latent . . .' alludes to the complicated imagery of the frontispiece, only to be made plain by reading the book and particularly the passage containing the Hieroglyph. Dee thus anticipates the later form of iconographical title-page which was often followed by the Explanation.

---

[1] F. Picinelli, *Il mondo simbolico*, 1669, p. 661.
[2] Dee, op. cit., p. 54.
[3] See above, p. 53, on the hieroglyph.
[4] Dee, op. cit., p. 9.
[5] Ibid., p. 160.

THE
COVNTESSE
OF PEMBROKES
ARCADIA.

WRITTEN BY SIR
Philip Sidney Knight.

NOW SINCE THE FIRST EDI-
tion augmented and ended.

LONDON.
Printed for William Ponsonbie.
Anno Domini. 1 5 9 3.

2

SIR PHILIP SIDNEY

The Covntesse of Pembrokes Arcadia

Written by Sir Philip Sidney Knight.
Now since the first edition
augmented and ended

1593

(McK. and F., no. 212)

A woodcut border of strapwork and grotesque motifs encloses the title and the imprint, LONDON./Printed for William Ponsonbie./*Anno Domini.* 1593. In the top centre a vertical cartouche framing the crest of Sir Philip Sidney, 'a porcupine passant . . . quilled collared and chained'. Behind the cartouche depends a canopy to hang over the title; at the top an acanthus bud; outer l. and r., a winged naked putto each with a trumpet proclaiming the fame of the author. Flanking the crest are animals in the guise of heraldic supporters, l., a bear, r., a lion. A shepherd with a crook, l., and an Amazon, r., stand on plinths decorated with grotesque male masks, and grasp the scrollwork above. The shepherd's surcoat, buttoned on the slash and right shoulder, is worn over a jacket with high neck and turned-back cuffs and full breeches to mid-thigh; his hat is banded with ribbon. His feet and legs are shod in classical boots. The Amazon has long curly hair and a feathery headgear with a flowing tassel; she wears a doublet with plated shoulder piece, a robe and cloak. A curved sword with a pommel in form of a bird's head and a decorated chape hangs at her waist, from a chain attached to the breast-plate. At the bottom, within a horizontal oval frame studded with pearls and diamond lozenges is an emblem, the representation of a boar backing away from a bush of marjoram. On a scroll entwined in the branches is the motto, SPIRO NON TIBI (I breathe out [sweet scents] but not for thee); in the background, hills, and a river on whose banks rises a tree-embowered church with a tower in the middle of the nave. Elaborate strapwork surrounds the frame, interlaced with tasselled swags; in the centre above and below, is a grotesque male mask. On the outer edge of the border on either side, are perched two confronting birds. Upward branches of the scrolls are linked to the consoles which support the plinths.

The design of the title-border is typical of the latter half of the six-teenth century; light scrollwork incorporating figures, groteschi, swags and so on derive primarily from the engravings of the Fontaine-bleau school which had a continuous popularity for over fifty years. That there is a resemblance between this woodcut border and one designed for *Willobie his Avisa*, 1594,[1] which is signed *W R*—William Rogers, has long since been pointed out.[2] In the disposition of the figures, in the delicacy and ingenuity of the scrollwork, it is also quite close to engraved title-pages by Rogers, that for Gerard's *Herball*, and Linschoten's *Discours of Voyages*.

The porcupine of the crest has the tusks of a boar though in other respects it resembles the heraldic animal shown in one of the plates depicting the *Funeral Procession of Sir Philip Sidney*[3] engraved by Théodor de Bry and published in 1587. Possibly the artist has made an attempt to give it the features which might be expected in a *Porcus spinosus*, but he cannot have referred to the representation in the most famous of contemporary zoological works, Conrad Gesner's *Icones animalium*.[4]

The two human figures represent the heroes of the Arcadia, the cousins Musidorus and Pyrocles, Princes of Macedon, the one dis-guised as a shepherd of Arcadia known as Dorus, the other as an Amazon with the name of Zelmane. Her costume corresponds closely

---

[1] Henry Willoby, *Willobie his Avisa*, 1594, McK. and F. no. 215.

[2] McK. and F., introduction, p. xxxviii

[3] Hind, I. Théodor de Bry, no. 6.

[4] *Icones animalium Qvadrvpedvm viviparorvm* . . ., Zürich, 1553, 'Qvadrvp. ferorvm. Ordo tertius', 87.

enough to the description of it in the story: the Amazon is wearing[1]

> a coronet . . . couered with feathers . . . that it was not vnlike to an helmet; . . . Vpon her bodie she ware a doublet . . . couered with plates of golde & as it were nailed with pretious stones, that in it she might seeme armed; the nether part of the garment was so full of stuffe, & cut after such a fashion, that though the length of it reached to the ankles, yet in her going one might sometimes discerne the small of her leg, which with the foot was dressed in a shorte paire of . . . buskins, in some places open (as the ancient manner was) to shew the fairnes of the skin. Ouer all this she ware a certaine mantell, made in such manner, that comming vnder her right arme, and couering most of that side, it had no fastning of the left side, but onley vpon the top of the shoulder: . . . On the same side, on her thigh she ware a sword, which as it witnessed her to be an *Amazon*, or one following that profession.

Amazons were of course known to have come from the lands beyond Asia Minor, then part of Turkey, so that she has been given a Turkish sword similar to that of the *miles turcus* in de Bruyn's costume book of 1581;[2] the decorated chape could also have been found in a costume book.[3]

Dorus who has slipped his disguise over his princely suit and donned a very stylish version of a shepherd's hat, is the 'poore shepherd' and expresses the meaning of this and all Arcadias: 'and I here . . . more proud of this estate, then of any kingdome: so manifest it is, that the highest point outward things can bring one vnto is the contentment of the mind'.[4]

The animals masquerading as supporters are in fact the victims of a dashing exploit carried out by the young princes to save the lives of their ladies, Philoclea and Pamela. It was on the occasion of 'the shepherdish pastimes'; the ladies were sitting down with Zelmane and Dorus near them, 'when sodainly there came out of a wood a monstrous Lion, with a she Beare not far from him, of little lesse fiercenes, . . . Zelmane . . . strake him such a blow vpon his chine' and 'gaue him such a thrust thorow his brest'. But 'there withall he fell downe, and gaue *Zelmane* leasure to take of his head, to carrie it for a present

---

[1] *Arcadia*, 1593, p. 22v.
[2] A. de Bruyn, *Omnivm pene Europae Asiae, . . . Gentivm habitvs*, 1581.
[3] *Habitvs Praecipvorvm Popvlorvm*, printed by H. Weigel, 1577, no. cxcix.
[4] *Arcadia*, 1593, p. 35v.

to her Ladie *Philoclea*.' Meanwhile the 'yong shepheard with a wonderfull courage hauing no other weapon, but that knife'[1] but with his hand guided by the god Pan, 'slew the bear' and presented its paws to Pamela.

The emblem of the pig and the marjoram bush occurs as no. XCIII in *Symbolorum et Emblematum de re herbaria* by Joachim Camerarius the Younger. The motto runs across the top of the page. The verse below the engraving reads:

> Pravis est animis virus doctrina salubris
> Sic lutulens fugitat porcus amaracinum.

(Wholesome teaching is poison to corrupt minds; so the filthy pig flies from the smell of marjoram.) Camerarius was a scholar and botanist and his compilation of an emblem book from botanical matter reflects the contemporary interest in the world of plants. Although the title-page bears the date 1590, the dedication is dated May 1593, at Nuremberg, which would seem to be too late for the book to have been used by the editor of the *Arcadia*. This was Hugh Sanford, secretary to the Earl of Pembroke and tutor to William Herbert, the *H.S.* who signed the address 'To the Reader' and who must have issued the instructions for the pictorial contents of the title-page. It is possible that part of the emblem book might have been communicated to Sanford before publication, the engravings perhaps, which might have been ready before the text. Sidney knew Camerarius well; he had offered to help with the cost of bringing out his father's works,[2] and links may have continued to exist after Sidney's death with the Countess of Pembroke and her circle. Moreover, Sanford was well known for his interest in unusual emblems and devices; when the young William Herbert was to show himself for the first time as a *Man at Armes*, it was feared that 'Mr *Sanford* will in his Humor, persuade my Lord to some pedantike Invention'.[3] But perhaps Sanford used an earlier continental source from which Camerarius also borrowed; that the church in the English emblem may be a foreign type suggests this. Alternatively he may have devised the emblem himself from the literary sources (see below), for pictorially the emblems are not very close; the attitude of the pig and the background

---

[1] Ibid., pp. 36ff.

[2] *The Complete Works of Sir Philip Sidney*, ed. A. Feuillerat, 1912–26, IV, p. 402. Letter from Sidney to J. Camerarius the Younger, 1 January 1578.

[3] *Letters and Memorials of State*, ed. Arthur Collins, 1746, II, p. 216.

scenery are different, and where Camerarius has an indeterminate plant in a pot, Sanford has taken an illustration of marjoram from a herbal.

Though the emblem complete with motto and moralising verse was hardly a novelty in 1593 the elements which go to make it up are even older and had been known to the learned for many generations. Horapollo states that 'when they [the Egyptians] wish to represent a pernicious man, they draw a pig, because the nature of the pig is of this sort.'[1] Erasmus in the *Adagia* enlarges on two classical sayings concerning the pig, 'sus per rosas'[2] (a pig among roses) attributed to the philosopher Crates, and 'Nihil cum Amaracino sui'[3] (pigs will have nothing to do with what is of marjoram), after Lucretius.[4] Pierio Valeriano in his great book on hieroglyphs draws all this material together; he connects Horapollo's original hieroglyph with the saying of Crates, and by finding a biblical meaning for the rose—'une syncerite de vie', gives the proverb a deeper moral significance. He then quotes the passage from Lucretius:[5]

> Le pourceau hait tout odeur qui sent bon,
> La mariolane: et luy semble poison
> Ce qui nous plaist.

Inset is a woodcut of a pig trampling a bush underfoot. If proof were needed that Pierio's work was familiar to those for whom the *Arcadia* was intended one might cite a book on emblems by Abraham Fraunce[6] who was the friend and protégé of Sidney; it appeared in 1588 and not only draws on Pierio extensively but mentions him by name. The emblem on the title-page would therefore be recognised as an illustration of the passage in Lucretius and it would be noted that the motto pointed the plant's unsuitability to the pig.

Further interpretation is contained in Sanford's address, 'To the Reader',[7] where it becomes apparent that the marjoram bush symbolises the ethical treasures of the *Arcadia*, a parallel to Camerarius' 'wholesome teaching'; these by implication are to be enjoyed only by the

[1] G. Boas, ed. and trans., *The Hieroglyphics of Horapollo*, New York, 1950, II, p. 37.
[2] Erasmus, *Adagia* . . ., Venice, 1508, III, lxi.
[3] Ibid., I, cccxxxv.
[4] Lucretius, VI, 973–4.
[5] Pierio Valeriano, *Commentaires Hieroglyphiques*, Basle, 1575, book 9, 160f.
[6] A. Fraunce, *Insignivm, Armorvm, Emblematvm . . . explicatio . . .* , 1588. For his relationship with Sidney see K. Duncan-Jones, 'Sidney's personal imprese', *JCWI*, xxxiii, 1970.
[7] *Arcadia*, 1593.

virtuous-minded. But while the emblem was directed generally against men whose thoughts were evil, so in accordance with the fierce literary polemics of the period, the writer could also use it to praise his friends and wound his critics. The first edition had appeared in 1590; in it 'the Division and Summing of the chapters had been adventured by the overseer of the print'. Sanford's edition had three books 'to end' it, taken from the Countess of Pembroke's own manuscript. Sanford opens his address with an apology for bringing out the new edition, which he commends to the favour of his well-wishers:

> though they finde not here what might be expected, they may finde neuerthelesse as much as was intended, the conclusion, not the perfection of Arcadia: and that no further then the Authours own writings, or knowen determinations could direct. Whereof who sees not the reason, must consider there may be a reason which hee sees not. Albeit I dare affirme hee either sees, or from wiser judgements then his owne may heare, that Sir Philip Sidneis writings can no more be perfected without Sir Philip Sidney, then Apelles pictures without Apelles.[1]

He then proceeds to a vicious attack on those who had dared to disagree with his judgment; 'There are that thinke the contrary: and no wonder. Neuer was Arcadia free from the comber of such Cattell,'—enter the animal motif—an oblique but obvious reference to the lowly pig on the title-page: 'To vs, say they, the pastures are not pleasaunt: and as for the flowers, such as we light on we take no delight in, but the greater part growe not within our reach. Poore soules! what talke they of flowers? They are Roses, not flowers, must doe them good, which if they finde not here, they shall doe well to go feed elsewhere.' With his allusion to roses Sanford reverts to the companion proverb of a 'pig among roses', as more fitting with what he had to say; but the switch would present no difficulties since the two proverbs had been placed together by Pierio. The next lines do not really concern us but should be included as they are complementary to what has gone before. 'Any place will better like them: For without Arcadia nothing growes in more plenty, then Lettuce sutable to their Lippes', a recollection of a saying allegedly of Marcus Crassus when he observed an ass eating thistles—'every lip finds a lettuce to its liking'. The theme of like attracts like enables Sanford to make a last appeal to the generous reader: 'the

---

[1] Apelles made a picture of Venus for the Coans which he left unfinished at his death and which no one could be found to complete. Cf. Pliny the Elder, XXXV, 36; Cicero, *ad Fam.*, I, 9, 4; *de Officiis*, III, 2.

noble, the wise, the vertuous, the curteous, as many as haue had any acquaintance with true learning and knowledge, will with all loue and dearnesse entertaine it, as well for affinity with themselues as being the child to such a father.'

The abuse which Sanford drew on himself by the inclusion of this barbed emblem is well known. Chief of his enemies was John Florio[1] who presumably saw Camerarius' book when it came out in 1593, with a second edition in 1595. A second edition of the *Arcadia* appeared in 1598, the same year in which Florio published his Dictionary. In his address 'To the Reader' he picks out from 'the leering curs' who had 'snarled' at him, the initials H.S. and attaches a whirl of epithets thereto:—'Horse Stealer, Hob Sowter, Hugh Sot, Humphrey Swineshead, Hodge Sowgelder. Now Master H.S.,' he goes on, 'if this doe gaule you, forebeare kicking hereafter, and in the meane time you may make a plaister of your dride Marioram'.[2] Five years later he returns to the attack in the address which precedes his *Essayes of Montaigne*. 'Why but pearles should not be cast to swine: yet are rings put in their noses: and a swine should know his stie, and will know his meate and his medicine, and as much beside, as any swine doth suppose it to be Marioram.'[3] Thomas Nashe, presumably involved in the quarrel,[4] puts forward a different reading of the emblem and broadly hints at some other feud: 'H.S. that in honour of Maid-marrian giues sweete Margerà for his Empresse [*impresa*—emblem] and puttes the Sowe most savcily uppon some great personage, what euer she bee, bidding her (as it runnes in the old song) Go from my Garden go, for there no flowers for thee dooth grow.'[5] The free rendering of the motto is rather felicitous. That Sanford perhaps chose marjoram in the first place in compliment to his Maid Marrian, that is Mary Sidney, Countess of Pembroke, may have some truth in it, for in the vernacular English of Gerard's *Herball* it is called 'Marierome'.

---

[1] *The Essayes ... of ... Montaigne*, trans. John Florio, 1603, dedication of *The Seconde Booke*, Sig. R3. For a study of the relationship between Florio and Sanford, see F. Yates, *John Florio*, 1934, ch. IX.

[2] John Florio, *A Worlde of Wordes*, 1598, 'Address to the Reader'.

[3] *The Essayes ... of ... Montaigne*, 1603, 'The Firste Booke. To the Curteous Reader', Sig. A₅.

[4] See Yates, op. cit., p. 194.

[5] Thomas Nashe, *Lenten Stuffe*, 1599, 'The Epistle Dedicatorie'. See also *The Works of Thomas Nashe*, ed. F. P. Wilson, 1958, III [147]. This title-border has been discussed in an article by R. L. Eagle in the *Library*, 5th series, iv, 1949, pp. 68–71, and by Jean Robertson in her edition of *The Countesse of Pembroke's Arcadia (The Old Arcadia)*, 1974, textual introduction, pp. xlvii f. It is included here because of its importance.

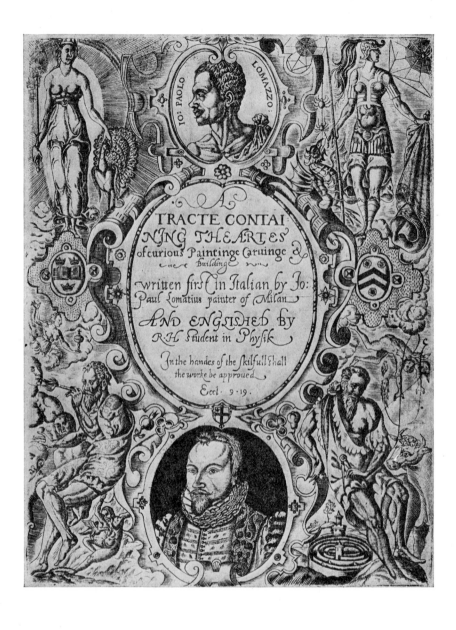

IO: PAOLO LOMAZZO.

A
TRACTE CONTAI
NING THEARTES
of curious Paintinge Caruinge &
Building

written first in Italian by Jo:
Paul Lomatius painter of Milan

AND ENGLISHED BY
R·H· student in Physik

In the handes of the skilfull shall
the worke be approued
Eccl. 9·19·

3

RICHARD HAYDOCKE

A tracte containing the Artes of curious Paintinge Caruinge & Buildinge

Oxford, 1598

(Hind, I. Richard Haydocke, no. 3)

Engraved title-page. Enclosed in a central oval scrollwork cartouche is the title: *A/*TRACTE CONTAI=*/NING THE ARTES/* of curious Paintinge Caruinge &*/Buildinge/written first in Italian by Jo:/Paul Lomatius painter of Milan/AND ENGLISHED BY/R.H student in Physik/*. Beneath is the biblical quotation: *In the handes of the skilfull shall/the worke be approued/Eccl. 9.19.* Above, the frame of the cartouche is opened to join it to a smaller cartouche in a scrolled frame on a second scrollwork cartouche frame. This encloses a medallion portrait of Lomazzo in profile to the left. He is shown bare-chested in the Roman manner with a robe knotted over his left shoulder: around him is the inscription IO: PAOLO/LOMAZZO. Below, the frame of the central cartouche is linked to a second smaller cartouche whose frame is set with studs and diamonds and which again is shown against a scrollwork frame. This contains a portrait, half-length and near full-face of Haydocke, wearing a ruff, doublet and a gown lined with flowered stuff. The junction between the central and lower cartouche shows the arms of Haydocke, 'argent, a cross sable, in the dexter chief quarter, a fleur-de-lis of the second', on a shield set on a shaped shield. Attached by diamond and round-headed studs to arms extending from centre right and left of the central carouche are oval shields with, l., the arms of the University of Oxford and, r., the arms of New College, Oxford. In each of the corners is a figure, with attributes or significant scenes.

The two upper figures, heavenly goddesses, are separated from the lower figures, earthly beings, by a bank of clouds which is seen rolling behind the arms of Oxford and New College. In the *top left-hand corner* is Juno, wearing a crown of antique type and holding a fleur-de-lys sceptre topped by an eye. Her left hand rests on a peacock. She is bare-breasted, and her ankle-length tunic is held by a girdle. She stands against a plain oval disk which radiates light. In the *top right-hand corner* is Pallas, her head turned in profile to the right, holding a lance in her right hand and a cloak or tapestry with a border of olive, the tree of Pallas, in her left. She wears a plumed helmet, a Roman corslet over a tunic which is girded up, and buskins. Behind her are webs illustrating the story of Arachne with two spiders on a thread hanging from the left one. A winged dragon leaps up at the bottom spider. In the *bottom left-hand corner* is Prometheus, bearded, wearing a leaf-edged cloak. Seated on the edge of the cartouche, he is breathing the fire of life into a man he is modelling from clay. Two other figures of men, already modelled, stand to left and right. Above is Pandora, bare-breasted, wearing a tunic held by a girdle, and holding a box (shaped like a ciborium). A half-length figure, she emerges from clouds. Below the legs of Prometheus is a scene showing him chained hand and foot to the rock, with the eagle plucking at his liver through his stomach, which is torn open. In the *right-hand bottom corner* is a parallel figure of Dae-dalus, bearded, with leaf-bordered tunic knotted on his right shoulder, resting his right hand on the cartouche frame as he reclines towards it and holding a pair of compasses in his left. He rests his feet on a rock. To the right is the figure of a cow, of wood covered with leather, which he made for Pasiphae in order that she could satisfy her lust for the bull: to the left is the labyrinth of Crete, shown as a coil of circular walls with a tower at the opening and a second tower in the centre. Above is the Fall of Icarus.

Richard Haydocke is the earliest English writer on art. Something can be added to the general biographical information about him given in the *DNB* and in Hind.[1] The arms on the title-page show that he belonged to the family of Haydocke of Greywell, in Hampshire. We can therefore identify him with the Richard who is listed among the younger sons of James Haydocke of Greywell and his wife Margaret

[1] Hind, I, pp. 32–3, 231–5.

Bill in the visitation of 1634.[1] Through his mother he had some connection with the court, for she was the niece of Dr William Bill, Dean of Westminster and Almoner to Queen Elizabeth. But essentially his family was one of small country gentry which had held the estate of Greywell for a century. It was sold by his eldest brother William in 1601. Richard was born c. 1570, and went to school at Winchester, where he was educated 'in grammar learning'. When he matriculated at New College, Oxford, in July 1588 his age is given as eighteen. On matriculation he was described as of Hampshire. In 1590 he was made a fellow of the College, on 16 January 1591/2 he took his BA and on 31 October 1595 he became an MA.[2] According to Anthony à Wood, he now 'travelled for some time beyond the seas'.[3] If this is true, he must have been back in England in 1597, if only because the dedication of his translation of Lomazzo is dated 24 August 1598 while we learn from his preface that he translated the book in England. By 1598 he had already entered on his medical studies at Oxford and on 14 June 1601 he took the degree of Bachelor of Medicine.

Haydocke first became acquainted with Giovanni Paolo Lomazzo's *Trattato dell'Arte de la Pittvra*, published at Milan in 1584,[4] through an imperfect copy obtained for him by his friend Thomas Allen. This 'could not bee matched in Paules Churchyard; vntill a most kind Gentleman, who had rather heare the name of a scholar, then his owne name, had procured mee a perfect coppie from Italy'. It is not generally realised that he did not translate all Lomazzo, but only the first five books, containing the theory, or as he terms it, the 'contemplative part' of the art. The last two books, containing the 'practicall' part, he purposed to translate and publish if the first part found acceptance. In the original Lomazzo has no illustrations, and Haydocke tells us in his Preface of the engraved title-page and illustrations he added to his translations:

> Howbeit in adding the Types and Pictures I may with modesty say, I haue bettered mine [original], or at the least made even for such other imperfections, as can hardly escape the best Translators, much more mee but a Novice in that tongue.

[1] See the pedigree of Haydocke in W. Berry, *County Genealogies: Hants*, 1833, p. 216: compare with the dates for the descent of the manor as given in the Victoria County History, *Hampshire and Isle of Wight*, IV, 1911, p. 77, from contemporary documents.

[2] J. Foster, *Alumni Oxonienses 1500–1714*, s.v.

[3] Anthony à Wood, *Athenae Oxonienses*, ed. P. Bliss, i, 1813, pp. 678–9.

[4] For Lomazzo see J. von Schlosser, *La letteratura artistica*, Florence, 1964, ed. O. Kurz, pp. 395–6, 402.

Which Pictures, if to the nicer of this more curious age, they
shall seeme meaner, then may stand with a tract of so rare precepts
of skill; yet the indifferent iudge will deeme them more, then
could bee expected from the vnexperienced hand of a student. Who
although he may better excuse his defects in dooing them, then
his rashnesse in attempting a matter beyond his power; yet is hee
not altogether deprived of patronage, for adventuring even therein.
For those which know any thing in these matters, cannot bee
ignorant, that Pictures cut in copper, beare an higher rate of
charge, then in probabilitie a professed schollar can undertake. And
as for Benefactors to anie such publique uses, former ages and
forraine countries, haue so far exceeded vs, that &c.

And heere if the wanton eie of the ordinarie beholder shall beare
with the defects of eie-pleasing delights, & the iudicious workeman
pardon the vnartificialnes of the shaddowing, I dare promise them
both truth of Delineation & Proportion, which was all I aimed at
in these Examples. The exact measuring, prooving, examining,
and comparing whereof, with the precepts and tables, what paines,
care, and circumspection it required, I refer to such as either haue
or shall meddle with the practise thereof. Which I must confesse, I
had never bin able to have gone through withall, had I not had
extraordinarie supplie of diuers exceeding rare bookes, both
Italian, French and Latine, from those two former most friendlie
Gentlemen, whose studies may well bee called the Libraries of all
the best and selected Auctors.

This passage reveals that Haydocke himself engraved the title-page
and plates of his Lomazzo. He also tells us that he was an amateur
painter, as well as an amateur engraver: already by 1598 he had spent
'7. yeares diligent and painfull practise in the Arte (though for my
meere pleasure and recreation)'. It has long been known that the source
of five of the plates, illustrating the proportions of the human figure,
are copies or versions from Dürer, whose treatise on the subject Haydocke evidently borrowed in one of its several sixteenth-century
versions. The sources of the others are untraced. The title-page is
clearly his own invention. Lomazzo's *Trattato dell'Arte de la Pittvra* has
no engraved or woodcut title-page, but Haydocke has borrowed for
his own title-page the woodcut oval medallion portrait of Lomazzo
which appears on the separate title-page to the first book (p. 17) of his
Trattato, and which was used again on the separate title-pages to each

of the seven books of his poems (*Rime*, Milan, 1587) and on the true title-page of his *Idea del Tempio della Pittvra* (Milan, 1590). He has added the inscription to the original.

Juno is figured with crown and sceptre as the Queen of Heaven. The eye on her sceptre was an Egyptian motif known to the Renaissance through the *Hieroglyphica* of Pierio Valeriano, and here is a symbol of universal rule.[1] Ordinarily it was given to Apollo, as being the sun-god and therefore the all-seeing eye of heaven, but Haydocke has given it to Juno to signalise her rank as queen of heaven. Juno is shown here because she placed the eyes of Argus, the guardian whom she had set over Io, on the tail feathers of her bird, the peacock, after Argus had been slain by Mercury. The story is told by Ovid (*Metamorphoses*, I, 722–3; II, 53). In this second passage Juno is said to have painted the peacock's feathers with the eyes of Argus.

> habili Saturnia curru
> ingreditur liquidum pavonibus aethera pictis
> tam nuper pictis caeso pavonibus Argo.

(Juno mounts into the liquid air on her smooth car, drawn by painted peacocks, peacocks painted but lately with the slain Argus.) These verses of Ovid, with their specific reference to 'painted peacocks' almost certainly explain why Haydocke shows Juno as an emblem of painting, with which no other source associates her.

Pallas appears as the goddess of tapestry, an art greatly esteemed in sixteenth-century England. The story of Arachne is recounted by Ovid (*Metamorphoses*, VI, 1–165) and summarised from Ovid by the mythographer Lactantius Placidus (VI, 1, 2) whose *argumenta* were frequently printed with the *Metamorphoses* in the sixteenth century. It tells how the Lydian maiden Arachne excelled all mortals in weaving and boasted that she excelled even her teacher Pallas. Pallas challenges her to a contest in which they both weave elaborate tapestries, and after both have finished, the goddess, envious of Arachne's flawless work, rends her web and strikes her with a shuttle. Arachne hangs herself, but is saved by Pallas who changes her into a spider. According to Lactantius, Ovid makes Arachne weave a richer work than Pallas in order to show that the goddess brought knowledge of the art to the contest, Arachne only labour.

The serpent in accord with ancient and mediaeval tradition is shown

---

[1] See Pierio Valeriano, *Commentaires Hieroglyphiques*, Basle, 1567, f. 234r & v: V. Cartari, *Le Imagini colla spositione de i dei de gli antichi*, Venice, 1556, f. xviiv.

as a winged dragon. A serpent is the emblem of Pallas and therefore fitly chases Arachne. Here in its act of leaping up at the spider there may also be an allusion to another ancient myth concerning Arachne. According to this story Arachne was the sister of Phalanx, who made her pregnant by incestuous intercourse. Minerva was furious, changed them both into serpents, and compelled Arachne to give birth at great risk to her life. After giving birth she was devoured by her children and according to legend it remained the custom of the young of serpents to devour their parent. This story is recorded with an attribution to Zenodotus by the Italian mythographer Natalis Comes (Natale Conti) in his very popular *Mythologiae* (VI, xxii), first published in 1568 and reprinted at least four times in Italy and northern Europe between 1581 and 1596. Conti, however, makes no other reference to Arachne and clearly Ovid was Haydocke's principal source.

The spider, though twice repeated on the thread and again on the top right web, must be Arachne, and the repetition indicates that she has been chased upwards to begin her untidy unornamental webs. The motif was probably suggested by Lactantius Placidus, who says that Arachne was changed into a spider so that she 'could make no effect of herself with such useless work'. A contrast is drawn between tapestries executed with art, like the cloak or tapestry held by Pallas, with its ornamental border of olive, the goddess's tree, and the unartificial webs of the spider.

The stories of Prometheus and Daedalus are related by Ovid, by the ancient mythographer Hyginus and in the sixteenth century most fully by Natale Conti. Prometheus represents the art of 'caruinge' or sculpture. It was he who first shaped men from clay in the image of the gods and breathed into them the fire of life. Haydocke represents him as blowing the fire of life through a tube into the mouth of his figure. In all probability he developed this motif from one of the sixteenth-century illustrated editions of Ovid in which Prometheus is shown giving the fire of life to man with a lighted torch.[1]

After Prometheus had made man, Jove commanded Vulcan to make the image of woman out of clay in order that she might betray and deceive man. To this Minerva gave a soul and each of the gods another gift, and the woman was then called Pandora. She was given in marriage

---

[1] The myth of Prometheus is recounted in Ovid, *Metamorphoses*, I, 82–8; Hyginus, *Fabulae*, cxlii, cxliv, and *Poeticon Astronomicon*, II, IV; Conti, *Mythologiae*, IV, c. vi. For a study of the myth and its representations see O. Raggio, 'The Myth of Prometheus', in *JWCI*, xxi, 1958, pp. 44–62.

to Epimetheus, the brother of Prometheus, and was sent by Jove to Prometheus with a gift of a jar that contained every evil enclosed within it. Haydocke has represented her descending from heaven to Prometheus on this errand from Jove. In his image the vessel she bears is shaped as a Renaissance covered cup or tazza of goldsmith's work. This motif goes back to Erasmus who described her as bringing a *pyxis* or box to Prometheus, thus converting her classical jar into the box now universally attributed to her. Its origin was traced by the Panofskys, who also found that Pandora was first represented holding a box-like object in a drawing by Rosso Fiorentino, made c. 1530–40. They did not realise that she is in fact represented holding a piece of plate—a motif chosen to suggest that the evils the box contained were concealed within a gift of tempting aspect. This tradition of representing her box as goldsmith's work originated in France. In one of the marks of the Parisian printer Gilles Courbin (working 1555–86) Pandora opens a box shaped as a covered drageoir, a vessel for handing sweetmeats. In the scene of Prometheus bound, Haydocke has followed the tradition which describes Prometheus as chained, rather than nailed, to the rocky slope of Caucasus.[1]

The motif of Daedalus represents his works in Crete. As his first work Daedalus made a cow of a wooden frame covered with leather for Pasiphae, wife of Minos, King of Crete, and this is shown beside him on the right. Although the figure of the cow represents this motif, the wooden frame was no doubt interpreted by Haydocke as a product of the art of carpentry, which in the Elizabethan age, as earlier and later, was considered a branch of architecture. And the compasses held by Daedalus indicate that he is here as the emblem of 'buildinge', that is architecture. Hyginus tells us that Daedalus was taught the art of architecture by Minerva, but was banished from his native Athens to Crete for having murdered a rival of whom he was jealous. After making a cow for Pasiphae, he built the inextricable maze of the labyrinth to house the Minotaur, her son by the bull. When Minos discovered these doings, he cast Daedalus into prison. He was freed by Pasiphae, and made feathered wings which he fitted to himself and his son Icarus with the help of wax. They then fled from Crete by flying over the sea, but Icarus flew too high and the sun melted the wax which held his wings, so that he fell into the sea. Daedalus escaped.

[1] For Pandora and her box see D. and E. Panofsky, *Pandora's Box*, 1956, where a number of Elizabethan and Jacobean literary references to Pandora are cited. Her story is also given by Giraldi (*De deis gentivm*, Basle, 1548, p. 571).

He was the type of the surpassingly skilful and ingenious architect and craftsman in antiquity. No doubt Haydocke also showed him with compasses to emphasise his mathematical skill as a designer of buildings.

The rather strained choice of Juno as the representative of painting, exceptional in Renaissance iconography, indicates that in devising his title-page Haydocke had rather more in mind than elegantly decorative allusions to classical myths. He shows us painting and its daughter art of tapestry, the woven picture, as arts that were practised by Juno, the Queen of Heaven, and by the goddess Minerva, mistress of all the arts. Prometheus was a Titan, and a divine or semi-divine being. In his scene we see him bringing sculpture from heaven and employing it on earth for the first time in the fashioning of man himself. And the figure of Pandora reminds us that sculpture was also practised by a much greater god, Vulcan, and at the command of Jove. Daedalus was taught architecture by Minerva, so that his art too is heaven-born.

The title-page, therefore, celebrates the divine origin of the three fine arts, an origin emphasised by the division of the title-page into an upper, heavenly region and a lower, earthly one. Since these arts were not disdained by the gods and goddesses of antiquity, they are not to be disdained in modern times by men and women of good birth or by the learned. Haydocke is justifying in visual form the claim of Renaissance humanist educators such as Castiglione and Sir Thomas Elyot, that painting, sculpture and architecture considered as a form of mathematical design are liberal arts and not mechanical arts, with which the Middle Ages had classed them. Elyot declared that they were suitable studies for children of noble or gentle birth who were naturally inclined to them, while Castiglione recommended that the ideal courtier should have 'cunning in drawing, and the knowledge of the verie art of painting'. And the great German scholar Cornelius Agrippa in his *De Vanitate Scientiarum* had commended them to the learned, as Haydocke, an Oxford scholar himself, points out in his preface.

For all the commendation of the arts and of the learned artist by these and other eminent authorities, for all the precedents that they cited from antiquity of emperors and noblemen who had practised the arts, there still persisted in England a general prejudice against them as base and mechanical and therefore unfitting a nobleman, a gentleman or a scholar. Dr John Dee dismissed the painter in 1570 as 'but the propre Mechanicien and Imitator sensible' of the mathematician. And in 1591 Harington says of the notes on ancient and modern painters which he inserted into the *Annotation* to Canto XXXIII of his version of Ariosto, a version used by Haydocke in his translation of Lomazzo:

> all which I have the more willinglie noted, and at more length . . .
> both because my selfe, I must confesse, take great pleasure in such
> workes (as pleasing ornaments of a house, and good remembrance
> of our friends) as also to show what great reckning that science
> hath been with Emperours and great Princes, and with Prelates and
> Religious persons, howsoever some austere (or rather vncivill
> persons) will seeme either to condemn it, or contemn it.

Haydocke, therefore, belongs to the group of cultivated Elizabethan gentlemen and scholars who sought to spread the new Renaissance doctrine that 'Learning is an essentiall part of nobilitie' and that a knowledge of the theory and practice of the fine arts is an essential part of learning. He himself declares that his object is the improvement of English art and English taste; in his own words,

> *the increase of the knowledge of the Arte*; which though it never
> attained to any great perfection among vs (saue in some very
> feawe of late) yet is it much decayed amongst the ordinarie sort,
> from the ancient mediocritie, for these 2. causes: First the Buyer
> refuseth to bestoew anie greate price on a peece of worke, because
> he thinkes it is not well done; And the Workemans answere is,
> that he therefore neither vseth all his skill, nor taketh all the paines
> that he could, because hee knoweth beforehand the slendernes of
> his reward. That both these obiections might be taken away, I
> haue taken the paines, to teach the one to *iudge* and the other to
> *worke*.

And he no doubt chose Lomazzo to translate not only because his book, unlike other Italian writings on art, is encyclopaedic in its treatment of the subject, but also because Lomazzo himself, in an endeavour to justify the claim of his art to be a liberal art, had deliberately made it as learned as he could. As such it was fit for an Oxford scholar to translate and well adapted to persuade the English audience for which Haydocke destined it.

The biblical quotation under the title is intended to justify the study and practice of art against the Puritans, all the more sincerely perhaps because Haydocke sympathised with some of their views. He omitted from Lomazzo's preface 'a large discourse of the vse of Images . . . because it crosseth the doctrine of the reformed Churches' and more than once he renders Catholics by 'Papistes', as well as protesting in a marginal note against representations of God the Father. A letter from Dr John Case (d. 1600), Aristotelian and Canon of Salisbury, which Haydocke prints after his own preface, reveals the response of one learned scholar to Haydocke's presentation of the case for the fine arts against the Elizabethan social and religious prejudice. Case wrote that he had at first wondered

> how so excellent a Booke could bee compiled vpon so meane a subiect; Meane I say in name, but not indeede: meane as we call a Gnatt, in whose life, parts, forme, voice and motion, Nature hath bestowed her best arte. . . . And truely had I not read this your Auctor and Translation, I had not fully vnderstoode what *Aristotle* meante in the sixth booke of his Ethickes, to call *Phidias* and *Polycletus* most wise men; as though any parte of wisedome did consist in Caruing and Painting; which now I see to be true: and more-ouer must needes confesse the same, because God himself filled *Bezaleel* the son of *Uri, with an excellent spirit of Wisedome and vnderstanding, to finde out curious workes, to worke in Golde, Siluer and Brasse, and in Grauing stones to set them, and in Caruing of wood, euen to make any manner of fine woorke.* In like manner hee indued the heart of *Aholiah with Wisedome* (as the Texte saith) *to worke all manner of cunning in embrodred and needle-worke.* And this he did for the making of his Arke, his Tabernacle, his Mercy-seate, his glorious Temple, which were the wonders of the Worlde, and only rare monumentes of this Arte.

Haydocke's praise of Nicholas Hilliard in his preface is a famous encomium of the great miniaturist. The two were on terms of friend-ship, perhaps of intimacy, for Haydocke says:

> his perfection in ingenuous *Illuminating* or *Limming*, the perfection of Painting, is (if I can iudge) so extraordinarie, that when I devised with my selfe the best argument to set it forth, I found none better, than to perswade him to doe it himselfe, to the viewe of all men by his pen; as hee had before vnto very many, by his learned pencell: which in the ende hee assented vnto; and by mee promiseth you a treatise of his owne Practise that way, with all convenient speede.

Hilliard's celebrated *Treatise on Limning*, which lay unpublished until 1910, was the result of Haydocke's request, and it is surely plausible that it was intended to be added to Haydocke's proposed translation of the 'Practicall' part of Lomazzo, who had not treated of limning (painting in miniature) which the Elizabethans themselves recognised as the only art in which they rivalled continental lands. If so, then Haydocke's abandonment of this project may be the principal reason why Hilliard never completed or issued his *Treatise*. The relationship between scholar and artist is of more than academic interest for the Lomazzo title-page. The portrait of Haydocke on it cannot be by Haydocke himself, since it is clearly much more accomplished in style than those parts which are his own invention. Its shape and its jewelled frame indicate that it is to be seen as a miniature, and there is a fairly strong presumption that it was copied from a miniature by an accomplished hand. From what Haydocke tells us of his relationship with Hilliard it seems a reasonable conjecture that we have here a portrait engraved after an original by Hilliard.

Hind found in the British Museum an impression and counterproof of a mural brass signed by Haydocke of Erasmus Williams (1552–1608) but was unable to identify either the sitter or the location of the mural brass. Erasmus Williams was a scholar of New College in 1570, and took his MA on 19 April 1578. He was presented to the college living of Tingewick, near Buckingham, in 1589 and was rector there until his death. Haydocke was his pupil and he is undoubtedly the helpful E.W. whom he thanks in his preface to Lomazzo, calling him

> a most learned Friend, so well knowne to the better and greater part of those, who haue at any time conversed with him, that he can bee no otherwise graced by mee, then by acknowledging his most sweete and commendable recreations in this kind, from his more graue, serious and weightie studies, to haue ministred no small helpe vnto this thy present delight.

The mural brass is on the north wall of the chancel of Tingewick church. Designed by Haydocke, as the inscription testifies, and probably engraved by him, it shows the emblems of music, painting, astronomy and geometry hanging behind him from a Corinthian column on the right. From the other side of the column are suspended volumes of Ptolemy, Livy, Pliny, Aristotle, Virgil and Cicero. The inscription explains

> His humane Artes behind his backe attende,
> Whereon spare howers he wisely chose to spende.

He is shown turned in prayer towards another, squatter column on the left, symbolising the Pillar of the Temple, with the Dove of the Holy Spirit on a ball resting on it. Above a rainbow arch signifies his hope of bliss at the Last Judgment which the angel beneath is sounding. A small portrait is shown on the emblem of painting suggesting what sort of pictures he painted. Williams must be one of the earliest recorded English amateur painters: he is also of considerable interest because he evidently encouraged in his Oxford pupils a taste for the theory and practice of painting, so introducing an important aspect of humanist culture into the University.[1]

[1] For Williams at Oxford see Foster, op. cit., s.v. His brass is reproduced in G. Lipscomb, *The History and Antiquities of the County of Buckingham*, iii, 1847, plate facing p. 124.

SEMPER EADEM

IOHN
HVIGHEN VAN
LINSCHOTEN.
his Difcours of Voyages
into y Easte & West
Indies .
Deuided into foure Bookes

Printed at London by
IOHN WOLFE
Printer to y Honorable Cittie of

THE KINGE
OF COCHI

THE KINGE
OF TANGIS

Willins Rogers
ciuis Londi

nenfis Inuentor
et fculptor.

I   W

4

JOHN HUYGEN VAN LINSCHOTEN

His Discours of Voyages into y^e Easte and West Indies

1598

(1st state not recorded. BL 212.d.g.
2nd state, Hind, I. William Rogers, no. 24)

We take this title-page to be the first state from the brilliance of the impression and from the literary evidence.

Within a central strapwork cartouche the title, followed by the imprint: Printed at London by/IOHN WOLFE/*Printer to ye Honorable Cittie of*/LONDON; this last line embellished with calligraphic flourishes. Across the top of the cartouche is the royal motto SEMPER EADEM running beneath the royal arms encircled by the Garter and with the supporters standing on the scrolled upper edge of the cartouche. Flanking the supporters are foliated scrolls on which are placed obelisks decorated with branches of pepper, l., and vine, r. To the right and left of the obelisks standing astride the scrollwork are Indians, one with a top-knot. They wear loin-cloths and brandish swords. To the outer l. and r., coiled serpents support celestial spheres which have at the top and centre of the central column tiny terrestrial spheres. On either side of the cartouche stand two figures framed by branches of scrollwork, l., THE KINGE/OF COCHIN, r., THE KINGE/OF TANGIL. The former has a top-knot of hair, an aquiline nose, curly-ended moustache, looped ear rings reaching to his shoulders and bracelets on his upper arms; he holds a bow in one hand and an arrow in the other. The King of Tangil also has a curly-ended moustache and

81

in addition a light beard, a rather broad nose and full lower lip; he has a stiff cloth round his body and his forearms are covered in bracelets; from his curly head protrude two animal horns. On the outer l. and r., suspended by knotted drapes from the scrollwork, hang two shields emblazoned with coats of arms. Within a circular strapwork cartouche beneath the title is a vignette of a Portuguese carrack riding at anchor; the flag and flagpole of the mainmast rise through the diamond- and pearl-studded circlet at the bottom of the central cartouche; a streamer flies from the main topcastle; a shore-going open boat is fastened at the stern; two seabirds disport themselves in the water. In oval strap-work cartouches are, l., a galley with a furled lateen sail and one bank of oars, and, r., a proa set with three sails; beyond the proa is a smaller vessel of the same kind. These cartouches rise from pedestals on each of which perches a bird picking at the berries of a plant. Bottom centre, the printer's mark, the Florentine lily, and his initials 'I.W.' Just above the margin, growing plants and grasses and standing amidst them, with their tails turned to the spectator, two fat-tailed Persian sheep. Signed on tablets affixed to the pedestals, *Willm̃s Rogers/ciuis Londi-/nensis Inuentor/et sculptor.*

This is an original engraving by William Rogers. The loose scrollwork of the design which may support or enclose subjects of interest is characteristic of him. The tendency of scrolls to finish in leaf or blossom into flower is also seen in the decorative work of Théodor de Bry.

The title-page fronts the English translation[1] from the original Dutch edition of Linschoten's book the *Itinerario . . .*[2] which appeared in three parts in 1595 and 1596. The representations of figures, of eastern craft and animals are taken from different sources, some from the engravings which are included in the Dutch publication of Linschoten and in complete copies of the English translation, others from illustrations to the *Verhael Vande Reyse by der Hollandtschepen ghedaen naer Oost Indien*, and another version of it, the *Journael . . .*[3] which appeared within a few months of each other, the first in late 1597, the other in 1598. The voyage these describe of four Dutch ships was made between 1595

[1] References to the *Discours* are from BL copy 212.d.g.
[2] *Itinerario Voyage ofte Schipvaert van Jan Huygen van Linschoten*, 1596.
[3] *Journael Vande Reyse der Hollandtsche Schepen ghedaen in Oost Indien . . .*, 1598.

and 1597 and was led by Cornelis Houtman. It was the first Dutch fleet to go to the East Indies; they stopped in Madagascar on their way and then sailed for Java where they engaged in trade in various places and fought the Portuguese. Historically, their enterprise was closely connected with the work of Linschoten. To go back a number of years—in 1580 the Portuguese succession failed, Philip II became King of Portugal and his enemies the Dutch (and the English) saw themselves increasingly cut off from Portuguese ports and so from the whole eastern Indian spice trade. It became imperative, therefore, to reach the eastern sources of supply themselves. Linschoten left Holland to join his brother in Seville in 1576; his desire, he says, was to see the world. In fact, by his endeavours he was to provide the knowledge indispensable to the Dutch and all future pilots who headed for the East. Though presumably a Catholic he was a patriot, hard-headed and far-seeing. While in Seville he made arrangements to join the suite of the newly appointed Archbishop of the Indies who was leaving to take up his office. The fleet of five Portuguese vessels sailed from Lisbon in April 1583 and the Archbishop's ship arrived in Goa on 30 September of that year, having made a two weeks' stay in Mozambique. Linschoten remained in the Indies for five and a half years and in his first book he describes all he saw in India and Africa. The second book contains translations of the sea routes to the East and West Indies taken from the logbooks of the Spanish and Portuguese pilots. This part was published in 1595 in time to be used by Houtman and his fellow admirals.

Both Linschoten's undertaking and the first Dutch voyage were naturally of intense interest to English merchants and seafarers and almost as soon as accounts of them appeared in Holland, arrangements were made to bring out translations in England. Some time in 1597 the *Itinerario* came into the hands of John Wolfe, the great printer and publisher. It was 'commended'[1] to him by Richard Hakluyt for whom in previous years he had brought out other books of travel.[2] Before his English edition was ready Wolfe published, early in 1598, a translation of the *Verhael...*, *The Description of a Voyage made by certaine Ships....*[3] Both were translated by William Phillip. The one was meant to whet the appetite for the other, for Phillip wrote in the address to Sir James

[1] *Discours*, address 'To the Reader'.
[2] E. G. R. Taylor, *Late Tudor and Early Stuart Geography. 1583–1650*, 1934, pp. 8f.
[3] *The Description of a Voyage made by certaine Ships into the East Indies*, 1598. *STC* 15193 under Langenes.

Scudamore, 'if it please your Worshippe to like and accept it,'[1] 'it may procure the proceeding in a more large and ample discourse of an East Indian voyage lately performed and set forth by one Iohn Hughen of Linschoten to your further delight'. Doubtless it was widely read; unlike its original it contained no illustrations but Wolfe and Rogers, perhaps because the matter of the two books was so closely connected, took the unusual step of putting some of the figures from the *Verhael* into the title-page of the Linschoten. With the *Journael* was an *Appendix* containing nautical information and Madagascan and Javanese vocabularies which Wolfe published, under the title of *An Addition to the Sea Journal or navigation of the Hollanders vnto Jaua . . .*,[2] putting into it woodcut reproductions of the set of etched illustrations[3] to the *Verhael*. This also came out in 1598.

Presumably with publication in view, Linschoten made careful and factual drawings, which he signed, of everything which interested him. They were engraved by the Doetecums, father and son; the father Joannes had been associated with the naval world through his work for Wagenaer's *Spiegel der Zeefaart*, 1585. We have not seen the unique copy of the *Verhael*. The etchings which illustrate the *Journael* are anonymous, nor is it known who was the draughtsman.

The *Kinge of Cochin* was adapted from the engraving of *Rex Cochini . . .*[4] by Joannes à Doetecum, in which he is seated on an elephant holding an arrow; Rogers has perhaps taken the bow from that held by an Arabian sailor on another plate.[5] Cochin, after Goa, was the richest possession of the Portuguese in India. It had a magnificent port and merchants came there from all over the eastern world. The king, once subject to the Samorin who held court at Calicut, had been favoured by the Portuguese and was now very rich. The two fierce little figures in the scrollwork above are 'Noblemen or Gentlemen, called, *Nayros*, which are souldiers';[6] they are seen as the king's guards in the original engraving. The top-knot is a characteristic of Nair costume: the weapons are typical of this military caste.

The Dutch fleet on its way to the East anchored in the Bay of

---

[1] Ibid., Sig. A$_{2v}$.

[2] *STC* 11747 under Geraldson.

[3] P. A. Tiele, *Mémoire bibliographique sur les journaux navigateurs néerlandais*. Tiele states, p. 118, that the illustrations in the *Journael* are 'dans la même manière' as those in the *Verhael*, so etched. He knew of only one copy of the *Verhael*, p. 122.

[4] *Discours*, plate between pp. 78 and 81.

[5] Ibid., plate between pp. 78 and 81.

[6] Ibid., p. 77.

Figure 1. Second state,
p. 86

Antongil on the north-east coast of Madagascar. A local king was friendly to them and came aboard one of their ships. On the title-page he is grandly called *The Kinge of Tangil* to match his peer *The Kinge of Cochin*. The representation of him showing the bull-like horns is from the illustration in the *Verhael*;[1] in this particular it does not correspond with the relevant passage in the text of *The Description*: 'The King . . . was as blacke as a Deuill, with two hornes made fast [note!] upon his heade.' Otherwise it tallies: 'his ornamentes were ten or twelve Copper Rings about his armes'; the modified negroid features are like those of his people, 'their hayre and beardes . . . not so much curled as the right Mores, nor their noses nor lippes so great and flat'; his robe with its stiff folds was made of 'the barke of a tree'[2] finely woven or possibly

[1] Tiele, op. cit., p. 117. Illustrations in the *Verhael*, plate (a), and at p. 118.
[2] *The Description*, pp. 7v. ff.

of cotton.[1] The figure shown in the German translation[2] of the *Verhael* of 1598 is very similar to that of Rogers which shows the curling hair and the cattle horns. However, it must very soon have been realised by the Dutch engraver that a mistake had been made, because when the *Journael* appeared the engraving of the king[3] shows him in a much less sensational headgear; a pointed cap with the 'horns' on either side made of some stiffened material 'hayr ende ander goet'[4]—hair and other stuff—ending in two curving points. This is the origin of the second state of the title-page in which Rogers has given the king a similar headdress to that just described, though his is more elegant. We do not know when the plate was altered; Wolfe would surely have obtained an early copy of the *Journael* since he had a professional interest in it, yet the significant alteration cannot have been noticed for some time since the first set of illustrations, which includes the one of the king with horns, appeared in the *Addition to the Journael*.[5] A further reason for taking this title-page to be the first state is the worn condition of all the impressions of the second state which we have seen, which suggests that the plate was already much used when the correction was made.

The celestial spheres at the top are perhaps to recall the flag worn by the Portuguese ships who sailed to the Indies; the celestial sphere with a cross at the top of the central column depicted on a white ground, came to be known as the white flag of Portugal.[6] The black pepper was the most important of the spices of the East to obtain which was the chief purpose of all the East India trade. The figure is probably adapted from that shown in Gerard's *Herball* of 1597, admitted by the author as probably not very like, but inserted 'untill further certaintie may be known thereof'. In fact, the confronting images of pepper and vine may well have been suggested by the passage in the *Herball* where the 'black Pepper' is described as growing up like a vine with its 'fruit clustered togither many set vpon a slender stem, like a little bunch of Grapes'.[7]

Serpents are mentioned in *The Description*; though so fancifully portrayed they may refer to those which came with the great floods in one region of Madagascar, so that the inhabitants had to build their

---

[1] Ibid., p. 6v.

[2] *Kurze Warhafftige Beschreibung der newen Reyse . . . so die Hollendischen Schiff in denn Orientalischen Indien*, L. Hulsius, 1598.

[3] *Journael*, plate 2. Tiele gives it as on plate 1.

[4] Ibid., Sig. B$_3$v.

[5] *An Addition*, Sig. D$_v$.

[6] *La connoissance des pavillons*, 1737, p. 21, plates LIX and LX.

[7] John Gerard, *The Herball*, 1597, pp. 1355f.

houses raised off the ground.[1] The birds are possibly crows of which Linschoten saw very many in India. Both Linschoten and the Dutch seamen were amazed by the fat-tailed sheep long since naturalised in eastern Africa and Madagascar. In Mozambique, Linschoten wrote, 'are found sheepe of five quarters in quantitie, for that their tayles are so broad and thicke, that there is as much flesh upon them, as upon a quarter of theirn body, and they are so fatte that men can hardlie brooke them'.[2] In *The Description* it says that 'Their sheepes tayles [in Madagascar] way at the least twelue pound, being of an elle long, & two and twentie inches thick.'[3] The sheep in the title-page are from a plate in the *Discours*.[4] The craft on the left is a galley, presumably such a one as went to fetch the Archbishop when his ship anchored in the river at Goa. Galleys were used by the Portuguese and the Indians for transporting merchandise and also for military expeditions.[5] The prow is shaped to form a ram and there are cannon at the bows on the raised central deck. On board are two Portuguese gentlemen, one at the stern with a sunshade in a stand beside him, another on the central deck carrying a sunshade; an Indian holding a stick and wearing only a loin-cloth, is also on deck and appears to be supervising the crew. The craft is flying at the masthead a flag showing diagonal stripes of the *Ordem da Christo*, the Portuguese military order, a survival of the Knights Templars, which was closely associated with the discoveries. The proa[6] was seen by the Dutch seamen in the waters round Java. They referred to it as a junk but this name now applies specifically to craft in the China seas. They learnt that it plied between Java, the Moluccas and other islands. Its design, with its two wide shallow sails which were said to roll up like *Sea Cards* (charts) *vpon a sticke*,[7] was peculiar to the Malay archipelago. It could carry a considerable cargo. The engraving shows prow and stern built high to withstand heavy seas; the keel curving round and up like a beak appearing below the prow; it is steered by an oar on each quarter; there is a short raised deck; two bands of decoration run along the sides. A seaman is attending to the rigging and two men are standing forward; another is seen through a square port, below decks. The little craft beyond is a fishing vessel.

[1] *The Description*, pp. 8f.
[2] *Discours*, p. 9.
[3] *The Description*, p. 6v.
[4] *Discours*, plate between pp. 54 and 61.
[5] Ibid., plate between pp. 54 and 61 and accompanying legend.
[6] Tiele, op. cit., p. 117. Illustrations to *Verhael*, plate (g).
[7] *An Addition*, Sig. E$_2$.

The great carrack should be the *San Salvator* in which the Arch-bishop and Linschoten sailed; all the ships in the fleet were between fourteen and sixteen hundred tons, therefore very large for the period. Linschoten states that two of the other vessels were newly built so the *San Salvator* may have dated from the 1570s or 1560s or even earlier; she has four masts with a characteristic enormous sail at the mainmast and lateen sail at the bonaventure mizzen; like all ships destined for the East Indian trade, well armed with two banks of four guns and possibly two at the stern; curved stem and rounded bow and broad-beamed hull; possibly a quarter gallery; fore and aft castles; top castles on three of the masts—in those on the mainmast and the mizzen spears stacked against an adversary; the flag, a cross on a white ground, may be that of the wealthy military order of San Salvator, whose members had originally been engaged in expelling the Moors from Aragon. No source has been found for this fine representation; possibly it was adapted from drawings of the huge carracks shown in the Portuguese rutter of João de Castro,[1] which had belonged to Raleigh; again Hakluyt or Petruccio Ubaldini,[2] who wrote the account of the Spanish Armada and had many ties with Wolfe, might have supplied a sketch. Certainly Rogers has understood the intricate design of body and superstructure, sails and rigging.

The coat of arms on the shield on the left is that of the City of London; that on the right belongs to the family of Hartwell. Abraham Hartwell the younger was secretary to the Archbishop of Canterbury; in the previous year he had translated for Wolfe, *A Report of the King-dome of Congo*, which is referred to in the address *To the Reader* of the *Discours* and acknowledged in the margin of the text[3] of *The Second Booke* which contains an account of this region of Africa. Hartwell dedicated his book to the Archbishop, whose concern in Africa and the Indies was for the conversion of the heathen. The presence of the two coats confronting each other may be meant to suggest the twin claims in these countries of Lambeth Palace and the City—of the Christian Faith and of trade. Hartwell expressed the hope in his dedication, that[4]

> such valiant English as do earnestly thirst and desire to atchieue the conquest of rude and barbarous Nations . . . doo not attempt those actions for commodity of Gold and Siluer and for other transitorie

---

[1] BL, Cotton MS. Tib. D.IX. f. 11v and f. 22.
[2] R. B. McKerrow, *Dictionary of Printers and Booksellers . . . 1557–1640*, 1910, pp. 297f.
[3] *Discours*, p. 209.
[4] Abraham Hartwell, *A Report of the Kingdom of Congo*, 1597, 'Epistle Dedicatory'.

or worldly respectes, but that they would first seeke the Kingdome of God & the Saluation of many thousand soules, which the common enemie of mankinde still detayneth in ignorance.

Wolfe took a more balanced view:[1]

> I . . . praye and wishe [he wrote], that this poore Translation may worke in our *English Nation* a further desire and increase of Honour ouer all *Countreys* of the *World*, . . . So it would employ the same [our ships] in forraine partes, as well for the dispersing and planting true Religion and Ciuill Conuersation therein: As also for the further benefitte and commodity of this Land by exportation of such thinges wherein we doe abound, and importation of those *Necessities* whereof we stand in Neede.

The royal arms and motto invite the patronage of the Queen for a book whose contents, if turned to good account, might bring both spiritual and material wealth to herself and her subjects. The pepper and the vine are here as the symbols of wealth and fruitfulness and the obelisks are monuments to the fame of the author.

---

[1] *Discours*, address 'To the Reader'.

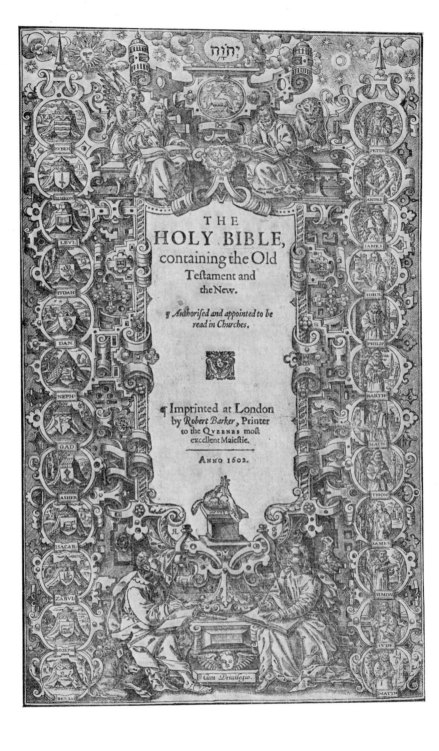

THE
HOLY BIBLE,
containing the Old
Testament and
the New.

¶ Authorised and appointed to be
read in Churches.

¶ Imprinted at London
by Robert Barker, Printer
to the Qveenes most
excellent Maiestie.

Anno 1602.

5

The Holy Bible . . .

The Bishops' Bible

Anno 1602

(McK. and F., no. 231. Rowland Lockey and Christopher Switzer)

An elaborate strapwork frame encloses the title: THE/HOLY BIBLE,/ containing the Old/Testament and/the New./ *Authorised and appointed to be/read in Churches.* Below a square printer's ornament showing a cherub, the imprint: Imprinted at London/by *Robert Barker*, Printer/ to the QVEENES most/excellent Maiestie./ANNO 1602. At the bottom of the title compartment a lamb trussed with its four legs tied together, lying on a plain altar. On the pinnacle above the compartment, the dove of the Holy Ghost surrounded by a nimbus, set on a cloud; next a band diamond ring showing a cut diamond; above again, the Paschal Lamb on a nimbus on clouds, in an oval medallion set on a cartouche terminating in a plain ledge; on the ledge is the Tetragrammaton on an oval, radiating light and surrounded by heavy billowing cloud. The starry sky extends across the top with the sun with human face left and right the moon. Right and left above the title compartment, St Matthew and St Mark sitting on a bench which has been slid into the scrollwork, each writing his gospel; their emblems are behind them, the angel pointing at his evangelist, the lion of St Mark with tail raised in the air. At the bottom of the design, also sitting, are St Luke with the bull beside him and St John with the eagle above his shoulder. They all wear a long garment with, over it, a long tunic and a cloak and are shod in classical sandals. Both Luke and John look up to the lamb on the altar. On the table which supports their gospels lie a pen-case and

91

an inkwell on a cloth. Below the table is a large cut stone, below again, a cherub head and finally a block bearing the inscription, *Cum Priuilegio.*

Running up either side of the scrollwork are twelve ovals; those on the left carry representations of the tents of the Sons of Israel; the tents are all of different design with elaborate canopies and decorated hangings. Before the opening of each tent is placed a shield showing the charge of its owner. From the top down, three barry wavy for RVBEN; a sword for SIMEON; an open book for LEVI; a lion rampant for IVDAH; a coiled snake for DAN; a hind for NEPH[t] (ali); on a flag, a lion rampant for GAD; a covered cup for ASHER; an ass statant for ISACAR; a ship for ZABVL(on); an ox for IOSEPH; a wolf passant for BENIA(min). Behind the tents, mostly open country with here and there a ruin, a tower or an arch. On the right are the twelve apostles each carrying the emblem of his vocation or the instrument of his martyrdom; PETER with the keys; ANDRE with his cross; IAMES (the Greater) with the wide-brimmed hat and staff of the pilgrim; IOHN with the goblet; PHILIP with book and staff; BARTH(olomew) with book and knife; MATH(ew) with set-square; THOM(as) with book and staff; IAMES (the Less) with long club; SIMON with book and hacksaw hanging from a nearby tree; IVDE with sword; MATTH(ias) with halberd. In the background are trees and buildings of Renaissance design; a small domed structure appears behind Matthew. Both tiers of ovals are surmounted by obelisks. Signed in the two bottom corners of the title compartment, 'RL' and 'CS'; beneath the latter a small shield bearing a coat of arms.

The intricate scrollwork design may have been taken from a pattern book or borrowed from a foreign title-page. It has been suggested that the initials 'RL' stand for Rowland Lockey,[1] who must have put the whole together as he was instructed, probably by a biblical scholar. Lockey[2] was known as a contemporary painter and miniaturist but no other woodcut design by him is recorded. We do not know whether Christopher Switzer was in England when he made the woodcut.[3] The minute coat of arms might be that of Zurich (in reverse) where he worked for many years and where he engraved the title-page to Du Bartas' *Deuine Weekes* (6).

This design owes some of its themes to a woodcut title-page for a

---

[1] See McK. and F., note to no. 231.
[2] See Erna Auerbach, *Nicholas Hilliard*, 1961, pp. 254ff.
[3] See p. 100.

Genevan Bible[1] published in London and in Amsterdam or Dort in 1599 and reissued many times in England and in Holland. It is considered to have been issued for the use of Puritans living in Holland and the spelling of some words has been adduced as evidence of a foreign printer. A short description will suffice: the title is in a heart-shaped compartment; on the left side in simple frames are the tents of Israel with their shields hanging before them as described above; on the right, the twelve apostles with their emblems; the dove of the Holy Ghost surrounded by cloud above the title and below the Paschal Lamb standing on a mound within a cartouche. A sabbath lamp hangs from the top of the framework enclosing the title. Set in oval frames the four evangelists MATHEW. MARC. LUKE. and IOHN. are placed two above and two below the title compartment. They are all seated at table writing their gospels. Mark and Luke are wearing hooded gowns while Matthew and John are in more or less contemporary dress, possibly academic. Just above the representations of Luke and John are two open books resting on branches of olive, inscribed, *ver/bum Dej Man:/et in Aeter/num.*

The 1599 design and its more elaborate and distinguished version of 1602 are a new departure in the series of pictorial title-pages to Elizabethan Bibles. The first Genevan Bible printed in 1560 shows on its title-page 'The Crossing of the Red Sea'; the 1561 edition of the Great Bible shows 'The Crucifixion' and 'The Labourers in the Vineyard'. By far the most important design during the Queen's reign was that for the first folio edition of the Bishops' Bible of 1568-9; the presence of the portrait of the young Queen proclaims her Head of the Church of England and Defender of the Faith. She is flanked by female figures representing Charity and Religion; in the title-page to the quarto edition the portrait is surrounded by the figures of the four cardinal Virtues. The title-border to the first large folio edition of the Genevan version, 1578, shows the figures of Justice and Mercy (?). A different type of design employed was purely decorative with scrollwork cartouches and so on. No doubt the abhorrence of 'idolatrous' images felt by the large Puritan wing of the Church of England was almost wholly responsible for this restraint, which was not infringed by the display of female personifications nor by the representation on a small scale of biblical scenes; but another factor must have been the great respect in which the Bishops' Bible was held. A new attitude of mind

[1] A. S. Herbert, *Historical Catalogue of Printed Editions of the English Bible 1525–1961,* 1968, p. 115.

may have been brought about by a desire to emulate the many glorious title-pages made for foreign bibles, Protestant as well as Catholic.

On a title-page to the Psalter in a Bible of 1579[1] the symbols of the four Evangelists appear. Now the figures of the Evangelists themselves are represented each with his gospel before him and his symbol alongside.

The twelve apostles confronting the emblems of the twelve tribes might have been suggested by the passage from Mat. 19.28: 'ye which have followed me, in the regeneration when the Son of man shall sit in the throne of his glory, ye also shall sit upon twelve thrones, judging the twelve tribes of Israel.' But this apocalyptic vision seems to be excluded by the unsophisticated nature of the design and the numerological parallel may simply have been a means of conveying the interrelationship of the Old and New Testaments and the dependence of the one on the other.

The Lord commanded Moses to see that 'Every man of the children of Israel shall pitch by his own standard, with the ensign of their father's house' (Numbers 2.2). Rabbinical commentators as early perhaps as the fifth century were of the opinion that the standards were emblazoned with the emblems of the twelve sons of Jacob drawn from his Blessing (Gen. 49). The Midrash Rabbah[2] which contains these commentaries was published in 1512, again in 1545 and in Salonika in 1593-4; it was therefore accessible to all Hebrew scholars and almost certainly known to the English hebraist Hugh Broughton. The description of the twelve princes of Israel was in itself a subject which attracted artists and various series were engraved[3] showing Reuben with an urn gushing water, Levi and Simeon with swords, Judah with a lion and so on. But the great Hebrew scholar, Arias Montanus, did not portray the standards when he included in the Royal Polyglot Bible[4] the engraving of the tents of Israel pitched 'far off about the tabernacle'. In it the tents have only the names plainly inscribed. It was not until later, perhaps for the first time in the Bible of 1599, that the blazons appear. To the sixteenth-century mind with its passionate interest in heraldry and in genealogy, so closely bound up with the coat

[1] McK. and F., no. 165.

[2] Midrash Rabbah, Numbers. 2 vols, trans. J. Slotki, 1939, I, pp. 28ff.

[3] By J. de Gheyn II after Karel van Mander. Hollstein, VII, nos 366-77 and Martin van Heemskerck. Hollstein, VIII, nos 56-67.

[4] Royal Polyglot Bible, Antwerp, 1569[1571]-73, vol. VIII, pl. 7. Signed I. Wierix; a version of Bernard Salomon's woodcut of the subject for La Sainte Bible, I. de Tournes, Lyon, 1551, p. 91.

of arms, it was an attractive exercise. The three wavy bars signify water for Reuben, 'unstable as water', the sword for Simeon 'instrument of cruelty', a lion's whelp for Judah, 'a serpent by the way' for Dan, Naphtali 'a hind let loose', Issacher 'a strong ass', Zebulon a ship, for 'he shall be for an haven of ships', Benjamin 'shall ravin as a wolf'. There are some differences from Jacob's Blessing and from the text of Numbers 1; the Levites were not numbered; they were appointed 'over the tabernacle of the testimony' (Numbers 1.50). As the progenitor of priests and scholars Levi has been given an open book as blazon. Gad shows a lion because he 'dwelleth as a lion' (Deut. 33.20), Asher the cup of plenty as an interpretation of the text of the Blessing, Joseph with the bullock, possibly referring to the well and ill favoured kine of Pharaoh's dream (Gen. 41.2–4).

The tents are similar to those used by contemporary commanders both for ceremonial occasions and on active service. With a separate top and flaps, they have a frame holding them together which is covered with an ornamental pelmet. The cloth may be woven or painted with a pattern. It was customary from an early period to place the emblazoned shield or banner on the tent of its owner. Examples may be seen in the *Bellifortis*,[1] in the fifteenth-century *Hausbuch* belonging to the Prince of Waldburg and Wolfegg[2] and in a painting by Melchoir Feselen of the *Siege of Rome by Porsena*.[3]

The Apostles as depicted suggest one of the Credo-series. These were separate engravings of the twelve apostles each named with an article of the Apostles' Creed inscribed in Latin below. The Creed was of equal importance to the Roman and Protestant churches and the series were extremely popular. Martin de Vos made the designs for a series engraved by A. Wierix, others exist by H. Goltzius, Crispin van de Passe, Ambrose Francken,[4] to name only a few. The order in which the apostles are placed was not always the same though Peter, Andrew, James the Greater and John come first. There is also some confusion about their attributes. Some of these go back only to the *Golden Legend* which first appeared in the thirteenth century. The older

---

[1] *Bellifortis*, Dusseldorf, 1967, f. 85.

[2] H. Th. Bossert u. W. F. Storck, *Das mittelalterliche Hausbuch. Nach dem Originale im Besitze des Fürsten von Waldburg Wolfegg-Waldsee . . .*, 1912, plate 61.

[3] Munich, *Bayerische staatsgemälde Sammlungen. Alte Pinakothek u. Neue Staatsgalerie*, 1953, catalogue no. 13.

[4] Hendrik Goltzius. Hollstein, VIII, nos H.34–47. Crispin van de Passe, D. Franken, *Oeuvre gravé des Van de Passe*, 1881, nos 211–24. A. Wierix, L. Alvin, *Catalogue raisonné de l'oeuvre gravé des trois frères J.J. et A. Wierix*, 1866, nos 669–82 and 684–97.

traditional stories were probably not consulted. Thomas was the patron saint of architects and should by rights carry the set-square, but this has been given to Matthew, who according to the Golden Legend commanded the erection of a 'great Church in Aethiopia' where he preached for thirty years.[1] Again, the dragon which symbolises the poison in John's cup has been omitted.

The presence of the sun and the moon recall the day on which the Lord made the sun and the moon stand still when He 'fought for Israel' (Joshua 10.12)—as He fights for Christendom, the spiritual heir of Israel (James 1.2). The three Persons of the Trinity had never before been represented on the title-page of an English Bible. The risen Christ is shown on the title-page to Coverdale's Bible,[2] and Christ as the Paschal Lamb is placed beside Christ crucified on Erhard Altdorfer's title-page to Matthew's Bible of 1537.[3] Much nearer in time, the title-page to the Bible of 1599 shows the Holy Ghost and the Paschal Lamb. It has been suggested[4] that this innovation springs from the need to meet the challenge posed by the growing strength of the anti-Trinitarian and Unitarian movements in the latter half of the sixteenth century. There were individuals and groups all over the Continent who held anti-Trinitarian views. In England, Francis Kett was burned in 1589 for denying the divinity of Christ. The stronghold of the anti-Trinitarians was however in eastern Europe and particularly in Poland. John Sigismund, from 1559 to 1571 ruler of Transylvania, was a Unitarian and there were many Unitarian churches all over Poland. Fausto Sozzini (Socinus), by birth a Sienese, was for some years in Transylvania and in 1579 took up residence in Poland. He was one of the most skilled polemicists of his day and his writings were being circulated in manuscript and in print from the late 1560s onward. In 1574 the Catechism of Krakow was published, the first Unitarian Confession of Faith. In Racov the anti-Trinitarians were in the ascendant and had their own school and printing press which published the Racovian Catechism in 1604.

In a title-page to a Louvain Bible of 1587,[5] the Persons of the Trinity appear as the Tetragrammaton, the Holy Ghost and Christ on

---

[1] Jacobus de Voragine, *The Golden Legend*, a reproduction from a copy in the Manchester Free Library, printed for the Holbein Society, 1878, p. cclxxxxvi.

[2] Hind, I, plate 5.

[3] McK. and F., no. 32.

[4] By the Reverend C. W. Dugmore, Emeritus Professor of Ecclesiastical History in the University of London.

[5] *La Saincte Bible. A Paris chez Jacques du Puys . . .*, 1587.

the Cross. Below the Cross, kneeling in adoration, are Henri III, his Queen and the Queen Mother. Henri had been elected King of Poland and ruled from 1573 to 1574. This title-page to a Catholic Bible need not have influenced those responsible for the English Bible since anti-Trinitarian views were a threat to all the established churches, Catholic and Protestant alike. By showing the Trinity *Ecclesia anglicana* was proclaiming its orthodoxy. The Trinity takes the form of a triangle on the title-page to Du Bartas' *Deuine Weekes* (6) and on the title-page to the Genevan version of 1607, with the form of the triangle reversed.[1] The three Persons of the Trinity appear again on the title-page to the Authorised Version.

Jesus Christ as *Agnus Dei*, 'the true lambe, the true sacrifice of the worlde',[2] is as important in the Roman rite as in the Protestant. But in the Protestant faith He figures as the Lamb in commemoration of the sacrifice of the first Passover. In the Missal[3] the Passover is recalled only in the Vigil Service before Easter Day but in the Church of England it is in the Communion Service on Easter day itself that the Priest says 'he is the very Paschal Lamb, which was offered for us'—Christ crucified as the Lamb of the Passover. On both title-pages He is represented as the Paschal Lamb, who carries the cross and the flag marked with a cross tied to it, the means of His death and the sign of His resurrection. In addition in the 1602 engraving, a lamb is shown on an altar, legs straight in the air, with no bones broken as it was ordered to the Jews in preparing for the Passover (Numbers 9.12). This prefigures the deposed Christ who had no bones broken (John 19.33).

Apart from the matter of the Trinity the fittingness of the themes of this design to contemporary Protestant thinking in England is proved by its inclusion without alteration other than the lettering, as the title-page to the New Testament in the first publication of the King James Bible, and again by the adoption of the themes of the Tribes and the Apostles by William Hole in his title-page for the 1607 edition of the Genevan Bible. Even more strikingly, these same themes were used in the main title-page to the King James Bible.

---

[1] Hind, II, p. 325.

[2] From 'The Summe . . . of all holy Scripture . . .' which first appeared in the Great Bible, 1559, then in many subsequent English Bibles, including the first edition of the Bishops' Bible, 1568.

[3] *Missale Romanum*, Antwerp, 1587, p. 211.

Vidit cuncta quæ fecerat · et erant valde bona gen.1.31.

יְהוָה

D. IACOBO MAGNÆ BRITANIÆ

FR. ET HIBERNIÆ REGI, SACRVM

BARTAS

HIS
Deuine WEEKES & Workes
Translated:
&
Dedicated
To the KINGS most excellent
MAIESTIE
by
IOSVAH SYLVESTER

6

GUILLAUME DE SALUSTE DU BARTAS

His Deuine Weekes & Workes

Translated by Joshuah Sylvester

1605–6

(Hind, I. Christopher Switzer, no. 3)

An arch supported on either side by walls and two Corinthian columns which rest on a deep plinth. The title in the opening of the arch: BARTAS/His/*Deuine WEEKES & Workes*/Translated:/&/Dedicated/ *To the KINGS most excellent*/MAIESTIE/by/IOSVAH SYLVESTER. Above, held by a swag of cloth, the royal arms encircled by the Garter and motto and surmounted by the crown. Inscribed on the architrave, D. IACOBO MAGNAE BRITANIAE/FR. ET HIBERNIAE REGI, SACRVM. Top centre, the Tetragrammaton within a triangle surrounded by rays; l. and r., cherubim placed on an outer triangle indicated by a white space interrupting the rays. Outer l. and r., the archangels Gabriel and Michael; Gabriel carrying an olive branch with a beam issuing from his mouth inscribed, *AVE*; Michael with a flaming sword and a beam inscribed *VE VE*. Beneath them the inscription, *Vidit cuncta quae fecerat—/et erant valde bona*. gen. 1.31. On top of the supporting walls, the celestial sphere, left, showing five signs of the zodiac along the line dividing the upper and lower hemispheres, and a number of constellations with the Great Bear top right, and the Ship Argo bottom right; stars as well as constellations are marked. On top of the right-hand wall is the terrestrial sphere with the names of the four continents inscribed. Between the spheres is a roundel showing The Creation of Eve. On the face of the left plinth The Fall is represented, shown on the right plinth is the ark on Mount Ararat with the drowned bodies of men and animals lying on the slopes. In the niche below the title, within a broad strapwork cartouche, is a scene representing the hills and valleys of the earth lit by the moon which is receiving its light from the sun; round the frame runs the motto, ACCEPTAM REFERO LVCEM: SINE LVCE SILESCO. Signed bottom right: *C. Swytzer Tiguri fec.*

The choice of Christopher Switzer as engraver may or may not be significant. He enjoyed a considerable reputation for in Francis Meres' *Palladis Tamia*, 1598 (p. 287), he is bracketed with William Rogers and Cure; this last is possibly Cornelius Cure, Master Mason to the Crown and future designer of Mary Queen of Scots' tomb. On the other hand, the engraving, though it displays much thought, is technically only average; nor does Switzer claim to be its inventor. He made it while in Zürich, 'Tiguri'.

Du Bartas published *La Sepmaine* in 1578 and part of *La seconde Semaine* in 1584; he died before he could complete it. This epic account of the Creation and the events which followed in the early days of the biblical world, had an immediate and prolonged popularity, both because of the felicity and ingenuity of the language and of the ease with which the poet moved in many branches of learning—the Bible and the classics, history and the natural sciences. It was translated into Dutch, German and English and even into Italian and Spanish, but its chief appeal was to his co-religionists, the Protestant laity in all countries. Sylvester brought out a first instalment of his translation in 1595; the edition of 1605–6 included the entire work and was the first to have an engraved title-page. It was dedicated to James I who had welcomed Du Bartas when he visited Scotland in 1586 and had himself translated a part of *The Second Week*.[1]

The Tetragrammaton represents God the Father as the form most acceptable to all Protestant thought.

The history of the triangle as a Christian symbol goes back to the fourth and fifth centuries. A few grave inscriptions have been found showing a triangle framing the monogram of Christ,[2] but throughout the Middle Ages it is an extremely rare motif. Its adoption in the fifteenth and sixteenth centuries may have been due to the influence of Platonic and Neo-platonic writings in which the idea of the divinity of numbers and of geometric figures is extensively developed. Reliefs

---

[1] See *His Maiesties poeticall exercises at vacant houres*, 1591, Sig. A 3ff, *The Exord, or Preface of the Second Week of Du Bartas* followed by *The Furies*.

[2] See G. Stuhlfauth, *Das Dreieck. Die Geschichte eines religiösen Symbols*, 1937.

on the pilasters on the façade of San Petronio in Bologna, made by Jacopo della Quercia between 1425 and 1428, show the Creation of Adam and the Creation of Eve, and in both scenes God has a triangular nimbus, so here the Trinity as the triangle is associated with the image of God as Creator—the Christian doctrine with the teaching of the Old Testament. Another example more concerned with the nature of the Trinity occurs in an engraving by Marc Antonio Raimondi[1]—the head of God is framed in a triangle, he holds a crucifix and the Holy Ghost is immediately above; no further clarification is needed, the three Persons of the Trinity are unified in the single figure of the Godhead. Much later, in 1589, the symbol and the Tetragrammaton are found combined in an engraving by Jacob de Gheyn[2] after a drawing by Karel van Mander. Top centre, the Tetragrammaton in rays enclosed by a first and second triangle; in the space between triangles the inscription, *DEVS CHARITAS EST*; below, adoring angels grouped on tiers of cloud. In the margin, Latin verses which refer to the design: 'Just as the third line gives to you the triangle which they say is the first and perfect figure, so the Father and the Word and also the Holy Spirit are one God Eternal, True and Divine, and the same the Divine volumes honour by various names. Let mankind acknowledge, venerate and adore Him.[3] This print may have been Switzer's source; it could have been seen either by him or by Sylvester if it was brought to England; or by Sylvester who spent much of his time in Holland where it was made. It may be surmised that the presence of the triangle as a symbol of the Trinity on this title-page is an affirmation of belief in orthodox Christianity against the powerful anti-Trinitarian movement whose activities have already been described (p. 96). Possibly with the same thoughts in mind Du Bartas had included lines which sum up the meaning of the Trinity according to the Athanasian Creed:[4]

> . . . in Essence vndeuided,
> Onely distinct in Persons, whose Diuinitie,
> All Three in One, makes One eternall Trinitie.

[1] Bartsch, XIV, 123, no. 138.

[2] Hollstein, VII, Jacob de Gheyn II, no. 380.

[3]
> Non secus, ac reddit tibi linea terna trianglum,
> Primam & perfectam quem tradunt esse figuram:
> Sic pater, & Verbum, sanctus quoque spiritus, Unus
> Sunt Deus, Aeternus, Verus, Divusq: & eundum
> Nominibus Variis divina Volumina honorant.
> Hunc genus humanum noscat, Veneretur, adoret.

[4] *Deuine Weekes*, p. 4.

The cherubim are placed on either side of the triangle in Switzer's title-page—in the making of the tabernacle God commanded Moses to make two cherubim of gold, 'in the two ends of the mercy seat' (Exodus 25.18), which was above the ark; and He is addressed in Psalm 80 as 'Thou that dwellest between the cherubims'. Their presence is therefore an allusion to God as lawgiver and protector of his people.

The archangels, 'Gods glorious Herralds',[1] the agents of His will, are described by Du Bartas in the course of the First Day. Gabriel is shown on the left,[2]

> In *Nazareth*, another rapt with ioy,
> Tells that a Virgine should bring forth a Boy.

On the right is Michael, the archangel who according to tradition, kept guard over Eden after Adam and Eve had been driven out. The motifs above together represent, half-symbolically, half-naturalistically, God surveying his creation, the Heavens, Earth and Man. The verse from Genesis recurs at the end of each day, and so alludes to the structure of Du Bartas' poem, which is divided into days.

The two globes are simulated; that is, the engraving of both the celestial and the terrestrial has been done from maps and not from actual globes. Hence they show much more than could be seen from a single viewpoint of the spherical object. The celestial globe may have been taken from *Two Planispheres*[3] engraved by Augustine Ryther and intended to accompany Thomas Hood's *The Use of the Celestial Globe* . . . of 1590. The engraver has taken the lower half of the North Polar Region and fitted it on to the upper half of the South Polar Region. He shows the whole of the arctic circle, the Great Bear and the Small Bear, the constellations most familiar to northern mariners, Cepheus, the Triangle, but has been forced to omit Andromeda for lack of space. The figures of the Zodiac from Aries, the first in the zodiacal year, to Leo, have been placed along a celestial equator added by the engraver. In the extreme south the Ship Argo can be seen with steering paddles at the stern, and Orion dressed as a huntsman. The terrestrial globe shows a representation similar to that of the left-hand hemisphere in the Drake and Cavendish Map of the World of 1592.[4] This map includes the western parts of Asia so that Switzer can

[1] Ibid., p. 29.
[2] Ibid., p. 26.
[3] Hind, I, p. 141.
[4] Ibid., I, p. 173.

inscribe the names of the four continents which at this period of course stood for the whole world. Though the manipulation of facts in the engraving would have been instantly realised by astronomers and geographers, it is completely in keeping with the spirit of Du Bartas that the Heavens and Earth should appear in as modern a guise as possible, and that the details should be clearly recognisable, for the poet himself speculates at length on the laws which govern heavenly bodies and he names the principal stars of the northern and southern hemispheres; he likewise describes all the countries of the world and gives up-to-date information about them. The inclusion of the celestial globe emphasises the part of astronomy in discovering God's work of creation and may well have been pleasing to the more learned members of the Church of England. George Hartgyll, astronomer and minister, shows on the title-page to his *Generall Callenders*,[1] a woodcut of *christianus philosophus* who is seen carrying a sphere and book lettered VERBUM DEI, and in his *Epistle Dedicatorie* he puts forward a plea for the 'Astronomer or Astrologian . . . [who makes] demonstration before all men, of the true and liuing God, *which by Astronomicall helps he may best performe of any man*'. James I, who was greatly interested in astronomy, would certainly have appreciated it.

The scenes in the roundel and on the plinths are possibly from a Flemish or French source. The creation of Eve is described as a contemporary surgical operation before which Adam is subjected to some form of anaesthetisation:[2]

> In briefe, so numb'd his Soules and Bodies sense,
> That (without paine) opening his side; from thence
> He tooke a Ribb, which rarely he refin'd
> And thereof made the Mother of Mankind:

The animals are witness to the Fall; among them, on the right of Eve, are a lion and a unicorn. The representation of the ark on Mount Ararat held a special significance for Du Bartas and Sylvester; after describing the Flood, 'He concludeth', as Sylvester says in a note in the margin, 'with a most godly praier, accommodated to the state of the Church in our time.'

> Lord, sinc't hath pleas'd thee, likewise, in our Age,
> To saue thy Ship from Tyrants stormie rage,

---

[1] George Hartgyll, *Generall Callenders*, . . ., 1594.
[2] *Deuine Weekes*, p. 226.

Increase in number (Lord) thy little Flocke;
But more in Faith, to build on Thee the Rocke.[1]

The scene in the cartouche is a pictorial representation of the astronomical truth that the lighted part of the moon reflects the sun's rays, a commonplace of ancient literature and also an observation which occurs in Pliny's *Natural History*.[2] Sylvester has adopted it as his emblem, most suitable to a translator, with an appropriate motto. The shortened form, 'Acceptam refero', without an emblem is found under his name on the printed title-page to *I Posthumus BARTAS. The Third Day of His* Second Weeke: .... 1606. For some of the sub-titles to *The Seconde Weeke*, in the edition of 1608, a different emblem has been selected, probably taken from an astronomical treatise. It resembles the illustration in Apianus' *Cosmographia*,[3] which shows the phases of the moon. The existence of these variants of Sylvester's personal emblem suggests that he himself undertook some research on it, and perhaps it is not too much to assume that it was he who got together the design for the whole title-page. Another version of the emblem found its way into a book of emblems by Julius Zincgreff first published in 1623.

---

[1] Ibid., p. 74.
[2] Pliny the Elder, *The Historie of the World* . . ., trans. Philemon Holland, 1601, I, bk 2, p. 9.
[3] Peter Apianus, *Cosmographia*, 1545, f. 50.

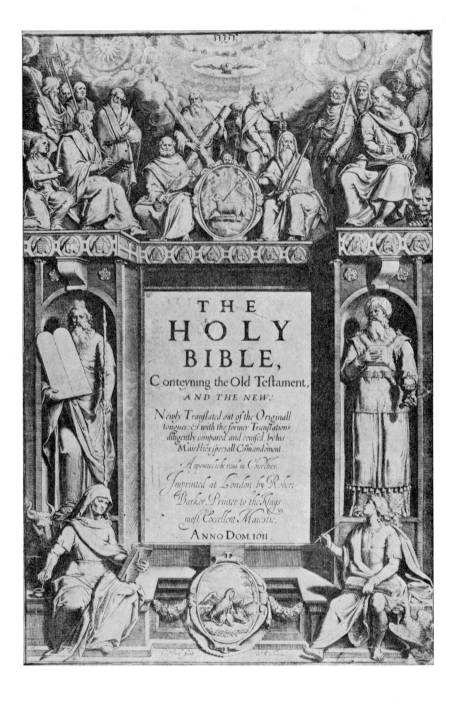

THE
HOLY
BIBLE,
Conteyning the Old Testament,
AND THE NEW:

Newly Translated out of the Originall
tongues: & with the former Translations
diligently compared and reuised, by his
Maiesties speciall Comandement.

Appointed to be read in Churches.

Imprinted at London by Robert
Barker, Printer to the Kings
most Excellent Maiestie.

ANNO DOM. 1611.

7

King James Bible
The Authorised Version

1611

(Hind, II. Cornelis Boel, no. 3)

The title-page shows a solid wall breaking forward on either side to enclose a recess where the title is inscribed on a plain slab: THE/HOLY/ BIBLE,/Conteyning the Old Testament,/*AND THE NEW:/Newly Translated out of the Originall/tongues: & with the former Translations/ diligently compared and reuised by his/Maiesties speciall Comandement./ Appointed to be read in Churches./Imprinted at London by Robert/Barker. Printer to the Kings/most Excellent Maiestie./*ANNO DOM. 1611. The central space is flanked by two arched niches; at the crown of each arch are consoles rising to support the cornices; the pilasters which frame the niches are also continued to the cornice. Two carved roses are placed on either side of each console. Within the niches are, left, Moses, bearded with two locks of hair raised on the top of his head; he wears a robe and a cloak and sandals and holds the tablets of the law in his right hand and a rod in his left. Right, Aaron, heavily bearded; he is dressed as the High Priest in the vestments and accoutrements described in Exodus 28.4–29. In addition he holds a knife and a covered cup in his left hand. At the top of the engraving, the Tetragrammaton within a segment of a circle of light; immediately below, the Holy Ghost also within an oval of light. Radiance spreads around the two Persons of the Trinity rolling back the heavy clouds. Below again, within a carved cartouche with a mask at the top and one on either side, the Paschal Lamb standing on a mound; rays emanate from the figure to meet the surrounding cloud which is pushed back to the frame. Peter and Paul sit on either side of the cartouche, each resting a hand on it. Both wear long robes and cloaks; Peter has a short beard, Paul a long one and his head is covered. Peter has the keys, Paul a sword. Sitting on the wall above, St Matthew with attendant angel holding the inkwell and St Mark with the lion, both old bearded men. On the plinth are St Luke, clean-shaven with covered head, dipping his pen in an inkwell with the bull beside him; opposite, St John, also clean-shaven, looking up, his eagle holding the inkwell in his beak. Standing along the top of the wall, against the dark sky, are the figures of eleven apostles each with his emblem. Under the title is another cartouche resting on a cloth, which encloses a representation of the pelican with young feeding from her blood. The cartouche, which has two carved masks, is secured to the wall of the plinth by heavy garlands of fruit and flowers. The sun with human face and the moon are shown on either side of the Tetragrammaton. Signed bottom centre, *C. Boel fecit in Richmont.*

Moses holds the tablets of the law by which God's covenant with Israel was established, and the children of Israel became God's chosen people; the rod is that by which, through the miracle of the rod and the serpent, he was made aware of his own authority. The locks of hair on his head glow with light, replacing the horns, which owing to a faulty interpretation of the text, appear in many representations from the twelfth to the sixteenth century. The figure of Aaron is adapted from the engraving in the Royal Polyglot Bible by Peter Huys, designed by the editor, Arias Montanus.[1] An earlier representation by Bernard Salomon, made for the de Tournes Bible of 1551,[2] gives him a tiara and a censer; but Montanus has replaced the tiara with a turban-like headdress; the knife, we may suppose, is for the slaughter of the bullock or goat, both of which are represented in the Royal Polyglot engraving; the cup is for the blood to be sprinkled on the altar, Lev. 16. Montanus gives a key to the identity of the garments and jewels, but there is none to these objects. Though Moses is represented on very many title-pages to the Bible, it is extremely rare to find one with Aaron; however, two French Bibles, both Louvain versions, that is Roman Catholic, the one discussed above (p. 96) of 1587, the other of 1609,[3] have title-pages which show Aaron confronting Moses. He is

[1] Royal Polyglot Bible, Antwerp, 1569[1571]–73, vol. VIII. *Aaron . . . [p. 5].*
[2] *La Sainte Bible*, Lyon, I. de Tournes, 1551.
[3] *La Saincte Bible*, Lyon, Thibaud Ancelin, 1609.

present as the High Priest, the appointed intermediary between man and God who alone offered the sacrifice in the temple.

Peter with the keys is the scourge of the heretic, whose entry into heaven he has the power to refuse; Paul's mission is the conversion of the heathen; seated on the right and left hand of the Saviour they guard and extend his dominion. Their features are traditional; Paul as an old man owes much to Holbein's figure in the New Testament of 1523. The sword is the instrument of his martyrdom.

The evangelists too are traditional in feature and gesture, though the loose cowl or cloth covering Luke's head is unusual. John is always depicted looking up as if at a vision, which sometimes is represented above him. In this engraving his eyes rest on the Paschal Lamb, recalling his report of the Baptist's words, 'Behold the Lamb of God' (John 1.29). The detail of the angel carrying the inkwell also occurs in Holbein's woodcut.[1]

We must presume that much the same reasons lie behind the representation of the Persons of the Trinity as have already been suggested for their appearance on the title-page to the Bishops' Bible of 1602; their presence was intended to affirm the main tenet of the Established Church against the heretical beliefs of the anti-Trinitarians of Poland. In 1609 the press in Racov issued a Latin version of the Racovian Catechism which was dedicated to James I without his permission. James was incensed at this unsolicited attention and the document was burned by order of Parliament in 1614. At this period similar heresies were current in England; Edward Wightman, burned at the stake in 1611, and Bartholemew Legate burned 1611–12, both held anti-Trinitarian views and denied the divinity of Christ.

The Apostles stand facing the Saviour. Since each carries his emblem perhaps they may be identified by the named series on the title-page to the New Testament in the same volume; from left to right, Jude, Thomas, Matthias, Bartholomew, Andrew, Matthew, John, Simon, James the Less, James the Greater, Philip. Such groups of apostles were common in engravings of the period; in a title-page by Stradanus to the *Acta Apostolorum* of 1582[2] they sit above and below the space on which the title is inscribed. Although as a whole they do not depart from their traditional aspect, Thomas, dark-eyed and youthful, John with his broad devout face and thick neck suggest Boel's acquaintance

[1] *Das neuw Testament,* Basle, 1523.
[2] *Acta Apostolorum,* ed. P. Galle. Martin Heemskerck and Ioh. Stradanus. Hollstein, VIII, Heemskerck, nos 306–40.

with Rubens' series of Apostles[1] for the Duke of Lerma. These were despatched from Antwerp some time between 1610 and 1612 and it is more than possible that Boel saw them, or sketches made for them, since he was working in 1610 and earlier for Otto van Vaen, who had been Rubens' first master.

Many title-pages to the Bibles of the period have an architectural structure as a framework, the grandest among them undoubtedly that to the Sixtine Bible of 1590.[2] But the conception of the structure itself having a religious meaning is new. The heavy main wall in this title-page stands for the world of the Old Testament; the impression of strength is increased by its being made to run out to the margin and by the supports to the projecting cornice. The Old Testament is the history of Israel; the tents of the Patriarchs along the cornice announce this central subject. They have been taken over from the title-page to the Bible of 1602 and only simplified by the omission of background scenery. Moses and Aaron, as the first founders of Israel's history, take their place logically in this context.

As Jesus based his teaching on that of the Old Testament so the Evangelists, Peter and Paul and the Apostles, are physically supported by the different parts of the wall. Released from the small compartments of the 1602 version they have assumed human stature, each endowed with the dedicated face of teacher and martyr.

The light from the sacred Name in the heavens rolls back the clouds of ignorance; the darkness against which the apostles appear will be pierced by the light of their preaching. Boel has given the theme an added significance—God's light outshines that of His creation, the sun and the moon, who have lesser confined circles of illumination. The engraver has also made manifest the doctrinal contrast between heaven and earth below. The order of the Persons of the Trinity in the 1602 title-page has been changed so that the figure of the Saviour, who for a time was of this world, is physically connected with the earthly structure. The cartouche enclosing the representation produces the architectural harmony.

The pelican with her young as a symbol of Christ's sacrifice can be traced back to the end of the second century.[3] Since the representation

---

[1] Prado Museum. See L. Burchard, *Corpus Rubenianum*, part VIII, *Saints*, vol. 1, Hans Vlieghe, 1972, nos 6–18.

[2] First edition of this revision of the Vulgate Bible.

[3] See *Physiologus*, ed. F. Sbordone, 1936, pp. 16ff. In the Middle Ages the representation of the pelican with her young is seen on paintings of the Crucifixion, on the doors of tabernacles for the Host and on monstrances.

is enclosed in a cartouche similar to that surrounding the Paschal Lamb, they may be read together to symbolise the body and blood of Christ and the sacrament of Holy Communion.

The impact of the design owes much to the brilliance with which the themes are stated and interwoven one with another; it is enhanced by the uniform dimensions of the figures, modified only by distance, and by the absence of small-scale detail.

The main purpose in undertaking a fresh translation at the beginning of the new reign had been to make a more accurate version than the Bishops' Bible which it was to replace. However, it was extremely important that continuity of tradition should be seen to be observed. The engraver was certainly given instructions by one or more of the body of compilers and it must have been their deliberate policy to adopt motifs for the new title-page from those which it considered suitable in the title-page to the last edition to the Bishops' version of 1602. That some of these were in turn represented on the title-page to a Genevan Bible printed for the use of Puritans abroad, would have been a matter of satisfaction to the Puritans in the Church of England. Probably only Roman Catholics and those with Roman leanings would have been acquainted with the title-pages to the Louvain Bibles; to those who were, it must have afforded a secret pleasure to discover the figure of Aaron possibly taken from it for the title-page to the new English version. But though the compilers neither wished to 'be traduced by those Popish Persons' nor 'maligned by self-conceited Brethren',[1] they sincerely hoped for conciliation of all branches of opinion, Puritan as well as Roman Catholic.

Quite apart from this question, it was necessary that the figure of the High Priest should appear in a pictorial statement of Anglicanism; for though in the statement of belief set out in 'The Summe of all holy Scripture',[2] Christ is said to be the only intermediary between God and man; as the Church of England was established, the priest and only the priest could administer the sacrament, the core of its doctrine. In this sense the title-page is an explicit rejection of Presbyterianism.

[1] 'The Epistle Dedicatory' to the Authorised Version.
[2] See p. 97 note 2.

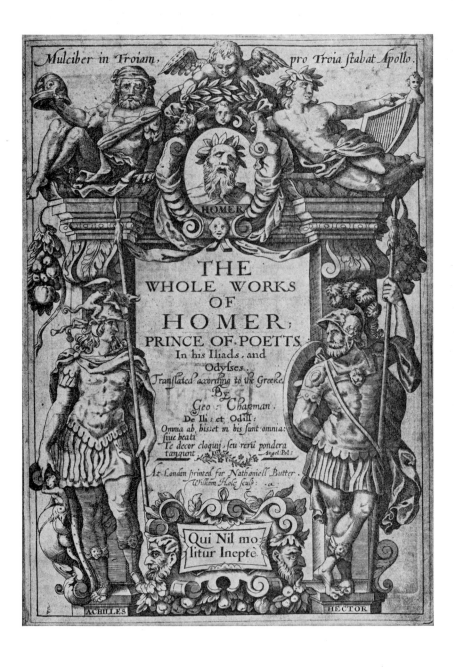

Mulciber in Troiam,   pro Troia stabat Apollo.

HOMER

THE
WHOLE·WORKS
OF
HOMER;
PRINCE·OF·POETTS.
In his Iliads, and
Odysses.
Translated according to the Greeke.
By
Geo: Chapman·

De Ili: et. Odill:
Omnia ab his:et in his sunt omnia:
siue beati
Te decor eloquij, seu rerü pondera
tanquit.   Angel:Pol:

At London printed for Nathaniell Butter.
William Hole sculp: ·a·

Qui Nil mo-
litur Inepte

ACHILLES   HECTOR

8

GEORGE CHAPMAN

The whole works of Homer; prince of poetts. In his Iliads, and Odysses

Translated according to the Greeke, By Geo: Chapman (1616)

Title-page engraved in 1611 (1612?), as used in 1616

(Hind, II. William Hole, no. 25)

The design of the title-page is in the form of an architectural monument; on either side square piers support capitals with square-cut and rounded mouldings with a deep cushion moulding at the top carved with acanthus leaf; beneath the capitals are consoles similarly decorated; swags of fruit depend from the capitals. The piers are joined by a horizontal member at the back of which rises a stone canopy. Within the space they enframe is the title followed by an epigram:

De Ili: et Odiss:
Omnia ab his: et in his sunt omnia:/siue beati/
Te decor eloquij, seu rerũ pondera/tangunt. Angel: Pol:

(All things descend from these works: in them are all things, whether the beauty of the divine eloquence touch you or the weightiness of the matter.) At the bottom, the imprint and the signature, *William Hole sculp:*. Immediately above the title is an oval cartouche, with, above, a winged cherub, at the bottom, a mask; on either side a herm, one male one female, their bodies terminating in spirals and their vestigial arms in scrolls; it is draped with cloth wound round the herms and falling in swags attached to the bases of the capitals. The cartouche frames a bust-length robed figure of HOMER as a bearded blind old man wearing a cloak with a hood and wreathed with bays. Above it a winged Cupid leans down holding a wreath of laurel. Along the top of the engraving the inscription, *Mulciber in Troiam,/pro Troia stabat Apollo.* (Vulcan was against, Apollo for Troy. Ovid, *Tristia,* I.II.3.) Below the inscription, reclining on top of the capitals, the figures of Vulcan (Mulciber) and Apollo, the former a bearded middle-aged man in cuirass and cloak, head covered with a cap knotted from a cloth, holding a helmet in his right hand. Apollo is a clean-shaven young man; he wears a laurel wreath. With his left hand he supports a harp whose frame terminates in a female bust, while with his right he appears to support and to display the cartouche containing the bust of Homer. Standing on a plinth in front of the left pilaster is ACHILLES, a youth with clean-shaven face and long, flowing hair; he wears a casque helmet with traces of an animal mask at the front, surmounted by a crest in the form of a dragon couchant; a classical cuirass with pendant lappets below worn over a tunic; a cloak fastened by a brooch on the right shoulder; buskins secured with lion's head buckles. In his left hand he holds a tasselled spear, while his right hand rests on his elaborate shield shaped in part as a shell, on which is seated a sea god whose body ends in a long curling tail. Opposite stands HECTOR shown as in the prime of manhood with beard and moustache. He too wears a cuirass with lion mask ornament at the neck and similar ornaments fastening his barely indicated buskins; a tasselled spear in his left hand and a round shield slung behind his right shoulder; a casque helmet with front in form of an animal mask and plumed crest; he wears a pleated tunic and a cloak. Below the title a cartouche of scrolls and fruit and leaves flanked by two bearded male grotesque masks, encloses a tablet which bears the inscription, *Qui Nil mo/litur Ineptè* (Horace, *Ars poetica,* II.140).

This title-page was first engraved for the edition of 1611 of *The Iliads of Homer.* It is an enlarged version of the title-page to *Homer . . . twelve Bookes of his Iliads,* 1610.[1] As we shall see, apart from the difference in size, there are interesting alterations in the design.

The phrase from the *Ars poetica* occurs in a passage in which Horace condemns bad methods of composing poetry and then goes on to consider the right way to set about it. The lines which follow—'Sing

[1] Hind, II, p. 332, plate 207a.

for me my Muse, the man who, after the time of the destruction of
Troy, surveyed the manners and cities of men'—are a Latin paraphrase
of the opening lines of the *Odyssey*. He is therefore referring directly
to Homer 'who attempts nothing improperly' or to put it more
strongly, 'who constructs nothing without due judgment'. The point
would have been taken by readers as their eyes glanced down the title-
page from 'Prince of Poetts' in large capitals, to the heavily engraved
quotation below. Chapman has chosen to include a commendatory
verse of Angelo Poliziano, the great fifteenth-century scholar and
humanist, because he was a translator and editor of the works of
Homer. In the second elegy of the *Tristia*, quoted across the head of the
page, Ovid invokes the help of the 'gods of sea and skies, for oft times
as one god harasses us, does another bring us assistance', and gives as an
example the opposing stands of Vulcan and Apollo in the Trojan War.
The short compact figures and broad faces of Vulcan and Apollo recall
those engraved by Goltzius for the Set of the Antique Gods[1] done after
frescoes by Polidoro da Caravaggio. The helmet which Vulcan holds
up to the spectator is surely part of the armour forged by him for
Achilles at the request of Thetis. In the 1610 version of the title-page
Apollo is shown with moustache and light beard. This is very unusual
both in antiquity and in the Renaissance,[2] and possibly it was altered in
1611 because the earlier type had been criticised as incorrect.

The bust of Homer is after the figure in Marc Antonio Raimondi's
engraving[3] of Raphael's *Parnassus*. There is also literary evidence for the
iconography of the poet going back to the eleventh century, which
Chapman cites in his essay *Of Homer* which precedes the *Iliads*:[4]

> at Constantinople . . . [in] the Bath of Seuerus . . . the workes of
> all Ages being conferred, and preserued there, of Marble . . .
> Amongst these master peeces, . . . stood Homer, as he was in his
> age; thoughtfull, and musing: . . . his beard vntrimmed, and
> hanging downe; the haire of his head in like sort thinne on both
> sides before; . . . his eyes fixt or turned vp to his eye browes, like
> one blind (as it is reported he was).

[1] Hollstein, VIII, Hendrik Goltzius, H. nos 296–303.

[2] In the title-page (see below) engraved by Willem van de Passe to Homer's *Batra-
chomyomachia* translated by Chapman [1624], Apollo is again shown bearded. Hind, II,
p. 299, plate 184.

[3] Bartsch, XIV, 200, 247.

[4] Chapman's *Homer*, 'The Preface to the Reader'. The work to which Chapman refers
is the *Annales* of G. Cedrenus, edited by Xylander, 1566.

Hector is the same in both the earlier and later title-pages. In the 1610 version Achilles resembles Hector, apart from the sword at his side and his body armour which is partly plated and richly engraved and embossed. There has been a complete change for the new title-page; he is youthful and elegant in direct contrast to Hector; the light cuirass reveals the lines of the body beneath; the round shield meant for battle has gone, the dragon replaces the plumed crest on the helmet, which resembles a parade helmet such as those worn in masques and tournaments. The prototype was possibly one engraved by Enea Vico in a design for a panel of ornaments,[1] in which the brim curves up and round to form the top lip of an animal mask; however, the motif is found in several engravings any one of which could have been used. Leaving these aside, a consideration of the style of the whole figure suggests a nearer source—Inigo Jones, Chapman's brilliant contemporary who was at this period engaged on designs for masques for the court. The graceful pose, the beautiful expressionless features, the tapering hands, so different from the heavy fist of Hector, are all typical of Jones' theatrical drawings. A comparison with particular sketches brings out further similarities; in one example now thought to be a design for a parade helmet[2] for Prince Henry possibly worn by him at the *Barriers*[3] there is a sphinx as plume holder and a brim which is curved at back and front; perhaps it is worth noting that the drawing for (?) Merlin[4] for the *Barriers* is taken from the same print by Marc Antonio as the Homer for the title-page. In another sketch for a knight masquer[5] in *Oberon the Faery Prince*, the helmet is very like though simpler, above a face in profile with straight nose, firm rounded chin and long locks. *Oberon* was performed on 1 January 1611, that is a few months before the engraving had to be ready.[6] Jones might have made a sketch for Chapman using ideas he had in his head at the time. Then again Chapman dedicated *The Iliads* to Prince Henry and he may have been admitted to his circle where he would have certainly encountered Jones. But in any case they were soon collaborating on the production of *The Memorable Maske of the two Honorable Houses or Inns of Court* . . ., written by Chapman, mounted and dressed by Jones and performed on 15 February 1613 in celebration of Princess Elizabeth's marriage. Their

---

[1] Bartsch, XV, 354, 443.

[2] S. Orgel and R. Strong, *Inigo Jones: The Theatre of the Stuart Court*, 1973, no. 52.

[3] Ben Jonson, *Workes*, 1616, pp. 295ff.

[4] Orgel and Strong, op. cit., no. 38.

[5] Ibid., no. 72.

[6] Entered for publication in the *Stationer's Register*, 8 April 1611, III, 457.

friendship continued, for in 1616 Chapman dedicated his translation of 'The divine poem of Musaeus' to Jones, 'Our only learned Architect'.[1] Jones may also have suggested a design for the shield of Achilles, made for him by Vulcan. It is in cartouche form like those commonly seen in masques or in allegorical representations—one similar though smaller appears in the engraving of *Queen Elizabeth* in classical dress, by Thomas Cecill.[2] It is viewed from the side with the front hidden, so avoiding the necessity of reproducing the myriad scenes of life on earth with which the original in the epic is decorated. The sea-being, set along the edge, must be a personification of Oceanus:[3]

> All this he circl'd in the shield, with pouring round about
> (In all his rage) the Ocean, that it might neuer out.

Homer is referring to ancient cosmography in which the earth was supposed to be entirely surrounded by water—the ocean.

The motif of the laurel-crown about to be placed on Homer's head is the keystone of the whole design. It recurs in Willem de Passe's engraved title-page to Chapman's translation of the other Homeric poems, published in 1624 as *The Crowne of all Homers Workes*. On this it is held by Apollo (left) and Apollo's sister Pallas (right) above the seated bard, while Mercury stands behind. The three gods form a trio symbolic of Homer's divine gifts of poetry and music (Apollo), eloquence (Mercury) and wisdom and learning (Pallas). On our title-page the crowning of Homer as 'Prince of Poetts' with a laurel wreath signifies the universal recognition of his supremacy as a poet. In the words of Chapman's introductory verses *To the Reader*:

> Whose vertues were so many, and so cround
> By all consents, Divine. . . .

For Chapman poetry was the supreme science. In his 'Preface to the Reader' he writes:

> no Artist being so strictly, and inextricably confined to all the lawes
> of learning, wisedome, and truth as a Poet. . . . To all sciences
> therefore, I must still . . . preferre it; as hauing a perpetuall
> commerce with the divine Majesty; embracing and illustrating al
> his most holy precepts; and enjoying continuall discourse with his
> thrice perfect, and most comfortable spirit.

[1] *The Divine Poem of Musaeus*, translated by George Chapman, 1616.
[2] Hind, III, p. 33, plate 19a.
[3] Chapman's *Homer*, 'Of Homers Iliads', pp. 265f.

In his eyes Homer was the first and greatest of all poets, and he is accordingly glorified as such on the title-page. This glorification of Homer as the 'prince of poetts' is continued on the separate engraved title-page to the *Odyssey* where his standing figure appears transfigured in an aureole against a background of lesser poets who appear as faint shades through his dazzling brightness.

The elements of the decoration, masks, swags and herms all occur in English woodcut title-pages[1] of the later sixteenth century. Combined with the massive masonry they make an impression of sombre magnificence.

---

[1] Herms occur in the title-page to *Institutio sev Ratio Grammatices . . .*, 1567. McK. and F., no. 124.

S. IOANNIS
CHRYSOSTOMI
OPERA GRÆCE,
Octo
Voluminibus,

ETONÆ,
In Collegio Regali,
Excudebat IOANNES
NORTON, *in Græcis etc.*
Regius Typographus. 1613.

NAZIAN.

ATHANASIVS

BASILIVS.

CYRILLVS.

9

ST JOHN CHRYSOSTOM

Opera Graecé

Edited by Sir Henry Savile

Eton, 1610–12

(Hind, II. Léonard Gaultier, no. 1)

A triumphal monument with an entablature breaking forward from the wall on either side into a wing supported by two fluted Corinthian columns which rest on a plinth. Above each wing rises an obelisk with ball feet and topped by a ball; it stands on a square moulded pedestal resting on a base of three steps. In the centre, supported by an incurved pedestal which rests on top of the plinth is the tablet on which is inscribed the title: S. IoANNIS/CHRYSOSTOMI/*OPERA GRAECÉ,*/ Octo / Voluminibus, / *ETONAE,* / In Collegio Regali, / *Excudebat IOANNES/NORTON, in Graecis etc./Regius Typographus. 1613.* (The Works in Greek of St John Chrysostom in eight volumes. At Eton in the Royal College, printed by John Norton, Royal Printer in Greek, etc., 1613.) The tablet in turn supports another pedestal with scrolled incurved sides with a carved cherub applied to its face, and above again another pedestal in the form of a squat T, decorated with a cartouche. Above it is another cartouche of strapwork lobate ornament and satyr-headed hermaphroditic herms whose heads support a table. At the top a cartouche encloses the royal arms surmounted by the crown and encircled by the Garter, from the clasp of which is suspended an oval framing the arms of Eton College. On the architrave of either wing is a horizontal shaped cartouche with grotesque animal heads with rams' horns in the top corners, to each of which is attached a garland made up of bows of ribbons and medallions enclosing a Tudor rose;

from the mouths of the two inner heads is strung another garland of laurel and roses. The obelisks are lettered, l., OXONIVM and r., CANTABRIGIA. The arms of the universities are shown on their pedestals; Oxford's motto reads *Sapientiae et/foelicitatis*. From behind each obelisk emerge banners showing, l., the arms of Merton, Christ Church, Magdalen and New College, and, r., King's, Trinity, St John's and Peterhouse. Pairs of putti are seated on the steps of the obelisks; the outer ones each hold a palm and a branch of bay, while the inner ones hold a palm and a branch of bay respectively and point with their right hands to the blazons above. Within niches on the rear walls of the two wings are seated nimbused figures of four Greek Fathers of the Church identified by inscriptions; l., St Gregory Nazianzen, NAZIAN. and St Athanasius, ATHANASIVS.; r., St Basil, BASILIVS. and St Cyril of Alexandria, CYRILLVS. They wear copes; the orphreys seen on the left are decorated with a large Greek cross alternating with two smaller ones, while those on the right show large crosses only. Gregory Nazianzen and Basil are expounding from open books, Athanasius and Cyril hold shut books. On the faces of the plinths are bird's-eye views of King's College, Cambridge, left, and of Eton College, right. Between the plinths a strapwork cartouche encloses an oval with the arms of Sir Henry Savile. The monument is placed before a landscape whose hills and woods appear on either side of it. Signed, bottom right: *Leonardus Gaultier sculpsit*.

Gaultier was attempting to render the effect of a painted monument. Hence the apparent softness of flesh in the putti and the cherubim, the liveliness of the stone statues and the darks and lights of the Tudor roses in the medallions.

During the late fifteenth and the whole of the sixteenth centuries the writings of the Fathers of the Church, both Latin and Greek, were being put into print, sometimes in the original tongue, sometimes Greek turned into Latin, sometimes in the vernacular. They were now eagerly searched by members of the reformed churches for guidance to the truth of doctrine, liturgy and church government. Queen Elizabeth herself read the Fathers, both Latin and Greek. They were equally important to the Roman Catholics and both sides used patristic writings as a theological arsenal from which to draw ammunition for their polemics.

By the end of the sixteenth century controversy was so bitter and scholarship had so far advanced that it became necessary and possible to make definitive editions of the works of the Fathers. Such projects were made effective partly through the revived strength of the Theological School of the Sorbonne in the reign of Henri IV, and much facilitated by the opening of the royal library under the enlightened librarianship of Jacques Auguste de Thou and Isaac Casaubon. This boon was extended not only to Frenchmen but to scholars of all nationalities. Through the collection of François I and that of Catherine de' Medici the library was particularly rich in Greek manuscripts.

Sir Henry Savile was the foremost Greek scholar in Elizabethan England. He had been tutor in Greek to the Queen. He held the wardenship of Merton College and in 1596 became Provost of Eton, thus realising his greatest ambition. Determined to make the College a seat of higher learning he set about collecting books for the library and during the first five years of his office the College purchased 302 books which included many writings of the Fathers.[1] For many years it had been his ambition to make an edition of the whole works of St John Chrysostom, a task which had never so far been attempted. The Liturgy of St John Chrysostom had a special place in the development of English spiritual life for Cranmer had incorporated parts of it, taken from the edition of Venice in 1528,[2] into the Litany in the Prayer Book of 1549.[3] Chrysostom had been one of the greatest preachers in antiquity, the 'golden mouth' (Greek *chryseon stoma*), and the reformers, with their emphasis on sermons, were naturally attracted to him. Where Savile could, he worked on the manuscripts himself and English ambassadors were instructed to obtain for his assistants the entry to continental libraries. Of these assistants Thomas Allen, 'an eminent Grecian', fellow of Merton, became a fellow of Eton in 1604, Richard Montagu a Kingsman, in 1613, and John Boys' appointment was only prevented by the death of Savile in 1622. Dudley Carleton helped with the collation of manuscripts during his stays in Paris in 1603 and 1610 and lived in Savile's house during the first year of marriage to his step-daughter in 1607, where he continued 'plodding at his Greek letters'. The College was therefore involved from the first in the enterprise.

Although it was said that Savile undertook the preparation of the edition at his own expense, he did in fact receive a loan from Merton College as early as 1602 of £50 on condition that it should be repaid out of the proceeds of sale.[4] When the time for printing drew near it

[1] Sir Robert Birley, *The History of College Library*, Eton, 1970, p. 19.

[2] ... *Divina missa Sancti Ioannis Chrysostomi*, Greek and Latin, Venice, 1528.

[3] F. E. Brightman, *The English Rite*, 1921, 2 vols, vol. I, pp. lxvi, lxviii.

[4] G. C. Broderick, *Memorials of Merton College, Oxford Historical Society Publications*, vol. 4, 1885, p. 167.

was decided to install a press at Eton. This was a practical necessity for 'when proof sheets could not be transmitted by rapid post, you could only print where you lived'.[1] The King's printer in Greek, Latin and Hebrew, John Norton, was invited to undertake the printing. As no suitable Greek type fount existed in England he tried to secure that known as the French royal type; this was not available but he was successful in obtaining one closely related to it, the famous 'silver Greek', from a Frankfurt firm.[2] The first engraved title-page printed by Norton for the Chrysostom was from a woodcut previously used by other printers which had appeared in an edition of the *Booke of Common Prayer* in 1607;[3] it shows pillars entwined with vine leaves, a cartouche framing the title and two confronting fantastic birds at the top. This volume also carried a dedication to King James within a border originally used for the title to a manual on embroidery, Federico di Vincioli's *Les Singuliers et Nouueaux Pourtraicts pour toutes sortes de Lingerie*;[4] a lady sits on either side, one embroidering, one making lace, two putti display a piece of embroidery across the top; above is the Tudor rose, below the Scottish thistle. Originally perhaps its design was intended as an allusion to Mary, Queen of Scots whose talents as a needlewoman were well known in court circles.[5] These two woodcuts were used once only, in 1610, for the first impression of Volume 1;[6] we do not know whether from the beginning their inclusion was temporary or whether they were found to be not sufficiently imposing or perhaps old-fashioned. At some stage Léonard Gaultier was engaged to make a title-page for the enterprise and must been have sent most careful instructions. The best known engraver of title-pages in France, he was an artist who worked mostly from his own designs and was at the same time an expert craftsman. He made the title-page for the first volume of *Historia sui Temporis*, 1606, by J. A. de Thou, whose help with the Chrysostom Savile acknowledged,[7] and that for the *Bibliotheca veterum Patrum et auctorum ecclesiasticorum* in 1609,[8] in which the Fathers of the Church and many ecclesiastical personages are carefully portrayed. The majestic title-page which he

---

[1] Mark Pattison, *Isaac Casaubon*, 1892, p. 112.
[2] R. A. Austen Leigh, 'The Savile Types', *Etoniana*, June 1905.
[3] McK. and F., no. 223.
[4] Ibid., no. 252.
[5] See G. Wingfield Digby, *Elizabethan Embroidery*, 1963, pp. 55ff.
[6] BL, 78.g.l.
[7] *S. Ioannis Chrysostomi Opera Graecé*, 1613, vol. I, *Henricus Savilius Lectori. S.*
[8] M. de la Bigne, 3rd edn., Paris, 1609.

engraved for the Chrysostom glorifies the saint, magnifies the Crown as the patron of learning, the founder of Eton and of colleges at the two universities, and celebrates the achievement of Eton College in bringing out this enormous work.

The presence of the three cherubim, one over the name of Chrysostom and one on either side over the statues of the Fathers, indicates their holiness by an allusion to the Old Testament, for cherubim spread their wings above the ark. On what grounds were the four Greek Fathers represented selected for portrayal? Cyril of Alexandria was of greater importance than his namesake of Jerusalem so that it may be taken that it is he who appears here. According to one authority Cyril,[1] who was an outstanding teacher, synthesised the Greek doctrine of the Trinity and of the Person of Christ on the basis of the works of St Athanasius and the Cappadocian Fathers, among whom are St Basil and St Gregory Nazianzen. Taken singly, at least two of them had as much significance as Chrysostom for Anglican theologians; Athanasius because of the Creed to which he had given his name, Basil because of his *Liturgy* which also had been used in the compilation of the Prayer Book.[2] Basil was much revered—'A Prologue of Saint Basil the Great' had been inserted before the Book of Psalms in the 1572 edition of the Great Bible. The answer may be, however, of a more mundane kind; the *Works* of Athanasius were published in Heidelberg in Greek and Latin in 1600,[3] the *editio princeps* of the Greek text of Basil in Latin in Paris, 1603;[4] of Cyril in Latin in Paris, 1605, 1604;[5] of Gregory Nazianzen in Greek and Latin edited by F. Morel in Paris, 1609, 1611.[6] It seems likely that the *Works* of Chrysostom were meant to take their place in the series of patristic publications emanating for the most part from Paris, Savile's scholarship, the beautiful type and fine title-page rivalling, if not out-topping, the French productions. This suggestion is supported by the fact that Savile had himself intended to produce an edition of St Gregory Nazianzen but abandoned the idea on the appearance of Morel's; a work by St Gregory, his *In Julianum invectivae duo*, had been printed on the Eton press while the Chrysostom was in preparation.[7]

[1] F. L. Cross, *The Oxford Dictionary of the Christian Church*, 1957, 'Cyril, St of Alexandria'.

[2] Brightman, op. cit., vol. I, p. lxvi.

[3] *Operum sancti patris nostri Athanasii . . . Heidelbergae, Ex officina Commeliniana*, 1600.

[4] *Diui Basilij Magni . . . opera . . . Apud M. Sonnium*, Paris, 1603.

[5] *Diui Cyrilli . . . Opera omnia . . . (Compagnie de la grand'navire)*, Paris, 1605, 1604.

[6] *Sancti Gregorii Nazianzeni . . . opera . . . Lutetiae Parisiorium.* 1609, 1611.

[7] Sir Robert Birley, *One Hundred Books in Eton College Library*, 1970, no. 63.

James I was extremely interested in patristic research; Savile stood high in his regard; he must surely have watched the progress of the work and he accepted the dedication. The royal coat of arms therefore takes pride of place on the title-page. Of the eight coats flanking it, four belong to the royal foundations—at Cambridge, King's, the sister foundation to Eton, St John's founded by Lady Margaret Beaufort, mother of Henry VII, Trinity by Henry VIII; at Oxford the House was refounded by Henry VIII. A variety of reasons explains the presence of the other coats; Peterhouse is there because of her antiquity, so that she comes first after the royal colleges in the traditional precedence still observed in University functions; Merton was effectively the oldest college in Oxford, William Waynflete, the founder of Magdalen had been Fellow and Provost of Eton and a great benefactor; New College appears in all probability because of the *amicabilis concordia*, a treaty of mutual help and friendship between the two Wykehamist and the two royal foundations made in July 1444. The garlands of Tudor roses suspended from the entablature are in compliment to the royal house. The royal foundation of Eton College is neatly conveyed by the pictorial device of hanging its coat of arms from the clasp of the Garter—again the Order of the Garter is very closely associated with Windsor.

The role of Eton is emphasised by the large capitals in which the imprint *Etonae* is engraved. The position of the coat of the College is immediately above the title while the coat of the Provost appears immediately below. The inclusion of the view of Eton with that of King's as its pendant, at a period when the representation of actual places is extremely rare on title-pages, is part of the same theme. This view of Eton must have been engraved from an original sketch. It is the first known of the College, though a part of it, the Chapel, while still under construction, appears in the manuscript copy of Higden's *Polychronicon*[1] owned by John Blacman, Fellow of the College between 1443 and 1453, and probably by him. The engraving shows School Yard, College, in a part of which wing was College Library in Savile's time, the Provost's Lodge, Lupton's Tower, another part of the Provost's Lodge, now College Library, the top of the Cloisters beyond, and the Chapel. Lupton's Chapel built in 1515, the vestry, the porch and the steps leading up to it have been omitted, possibly a simple error. The press was installed in the house in Weston's Yard, built between

---

[1] Ibid., no. 9.

1603 and 1604, now known as Savile House. It lies to the north of College on the Slough road.[1]

The view of King's is from the south; it shows the College buildings, the Old Court which then became the University Library, the south wall of the Chapel, the Fellows' Garden, and west of the Chapel, the little wooden belfrey. Gaultier has possibly adapted his engraving from the 'Birds-eye Plan of Cambridge' by Richard Lyne in John Caius' *De Antiquitate Cantabrigiensis Academiae*,[2] 1574 or from the 'View of Cambridge' (from a drawing by William Smith done c.1574) in the *Civitates orbis terrarum*,[3] though he has made the belfry rougher and shabbier than in either of these two representations and has failed to show that its pronounced concave steeple rose elegantly from hexagonal walls. This structure was built originally to house the peal of bells given by the Founder, pending the erection of a lofty bell-tower, and was sited some 70 feet from the Chapel.[4] David Loggan shows it with a different design towards the end of the century.[5] It was removed in 1739; the parched bands which revealed its outlines in dry weather were first observed in the Great Lawn in 1879.

Savile's coat of arms shows quarterings of his remote ancestors, two of them going back to c. 1300—sufficiently impressive in its own sphere to match other elements in the title-page.

[1] Information about Eton College kindly given by Mr Jeremy Potter, one time Deputy Librarian of Eton College Library.

[2] Hind, I, p. 83, plate 44.

[3] Braun and Hogenberg, 1572–1618. See 1966 edn, vol. I, part I, Introduction by R. A. Skelton, p. xv and Appendix B, p. xxviii.

[4] See John Harvey, *Gothic England*, 1948, plate 115, and J. Saltmarsh, *King's College. A Short History*, 1958, p. 35, note I and p. 94.

[5] David Loggan, *Cantabrigia Illustrata* . . . 1675–90, illustration XI. Information about the wooden belfry kindly given by the late Mr D. Loukes, Assistant Librarian, King's College Library, Cambridge.

SIR WALTER RALEIGH

The History of the World

1614

(the first edition published anonymously)

(Hind, II. Renold Elstrack, no. 86)

The title-page has an architectural design; four Corinthian columns standing on a deep plinth support a platform; along the frieze is the title: THE HISTORY OF THE WORLD. Below, the plinth breaks forward in a central step decorated with ball and diamond ornament on which is the imprint and date: At London Printed for WALTER BVRRE./1614. The central figure, MAGISTRA VITAE, History herself, is in classical dress with gown, belted tunic and cloak; her head with a laurel wreath has a nimbus of rays of light; she upholds the globe which shows the known world; her feet press down on two figures reclining on the step, MORS, a skeleton, and a sleeping youth, OBLIVIO. The columns are labelled on their bases, TESTIS TEMPORV̄, NVNCIA VETVSTATIS, LVX VERITATIS, VITA MEMORIAE; each is decorated, the first with books, the second with hieroglyphs, the third with flames, the fourth with laurel branches. The side niches, which are decorated above with cut diamonds, enclose, l., the figure of EXPERIENTIA holding rod and leadline, and, r., VERITAS, nude with a circle of light round her right hand. The two winged figures on the platform represent FAMA BONA and FAMA MALA; the former wearing a wreath like *Historia* of laurel, standing in an aura of light has ears, eyes and tongues on her wings; the latter has spots all over her garments, wings and body; both blow trumpets. Above the globe is an enormous eye, PROVIDENTIA, within a lighted circle of billowing cloud; the heavens are light

E*

behind Good Fame and dark and cloudy behind Evil Fame. Signed bottom left: 'Ren: Elstrack/sculpsit.'[1]

The frontispiece is explained by Ben Jonson's sonnet.

'The Minde of the Front'

From Death, and *darke* Obliuion, *(neere the same)*
The Mistresse of Mans Life, *graue Historie*,
Raising the World to good, or Evill *fame*,
Doth vindicate it to Æternitie.

High Prouidence *would so: that nor the good*
Might be defrauded, nor the Great secur'd,
But both might know their wayes are vnderstood,
And the reward, and punishment assur'd.

This makes, that lighted by the beamie hand
Of Truth, which searcheth the most hidden springs,
And guided by Experience, *whose streight wand*
Doth mete, whose Line *doth sound the depth of things:*

She chearefully supporteth what shee reares;
Assisted by no strengths, but are her owne,
Some note of which each varied Pillar beares,
By which as proper titles shee is knowne,

Times witnesse, Herald of Antiquitie,
The light of Truth, and life of Memorie.

The titles on the columns, together with *Magistra vitae* are the famous epithets from Cicero's *de Oratore*, II.xl.36. The books on the column far left stand for 'the evidence of past times'. Sidney in his *Defence of Poesie* speaks of the historian's 'old Mouser-eaten Records';[2] Raleigh had in his rooms in the Tower a library of more than five hundred volumes[3] as well as almost certainly being able to draw on the libraries of others. The hieroglyphs on the second column are 'the messenger from Antiquity'. There is a critical appraisal in the *History* of the place

---

[1] Sir Charles Firth discussed the themes of the title-page in 'Sir Walter Raleigh and the History of the World', *Proceedings of the British Academy*, no. 8, 1917–18. C. A. Patrides in his edition of *The History of the World*, 1971, has made certain observations on the title-page (pp. xv f) with which we do not entirely agree.

[2] Sir Philip Sidney, *The Countesse of Pembroke's Arcadia*, 1598. *The Defence of Poesie*, p. 497.

[3] Walter Oakeshott, 'Sir Walter Raleigh's Library', *Bibliographical Society*, 1968 [p. 285].

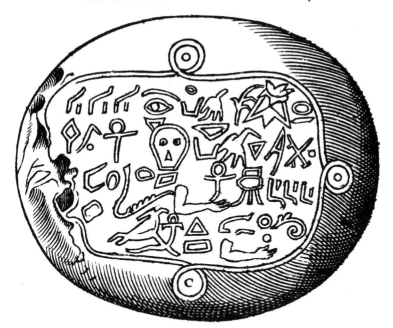

Figure II

of Egypt, with the conclusion that Egyptian monuments were the oldest surviving historical evidence: 'That Ægypt being peopled before the floud, and 200. or 300. yeares more or lesse after Adam, there might remaine . . . some monuments (in Pillers or Altars of stone or metal) of their former Kings or Governours'[1] and further, the conviction, 'that all the knowledge which the Greekes had, was transported out of Ægypt or Phoenicia'.[2] Elstrack has taken the signs from the illustration of an engraved gem[3] shown in a book, *Characteres Ægyptii* by Lorenzo Pignoria, who was an authority on hieroglyphs (see Figure II). Published only in 1608, it was the latest work on the subject. It deals specifically with the *tabula bembina*,[4] a copper slab richly engraved with figures and hieroglyphs. The learned reader would not have missed the allusion to one of the most famous Renaissance finds from antiquity. It was acquired in 1527 by Pietro Bembo,

[1] *History*, book I, ch. 8, p. 160.
[2] Ibid., book II, ch. 6, p. 319.
[3] The illustration of the engraved gem is on p. 9v.
[4] E. Scamuzzi, *La 'Mensa Isiaca'*, 1939, p. 30. *Pubblicazioni Egittologiche del R. Museo di Torino*, no. 5.

hence its name, and later passed to the collection of Vicenzo Gonzaga where it was at this time. The third column decorated with flames signifies 'the light of truth' and the last column 'memory preserved of past generations' shows the laurels which adorn the brows of the great heroes of the past.

The Ciceronian text was extremely popular; Sidney quotes it[1] and Pierre Matthieu paraphrases it in his dissertation on the meaning of history in his *Histoire de France*.[2] It encapsulates Cicero's teaching that a knowledge of past events was essential to the statesman, so that when similar things occur he might know what course to follow; or as Raleigh puts it, 'it being the end and scope of al Historie, to teach by example of times past, such wisdome as may guide our desires and actions. . . .'[3] Raleigh wrote of Cicero, 'than whom that world begat not a man of more reputed iudgement'.[4] The theme is exemplified in the title-page by the three allegorical figures of *Experientia*, *Magistra vitae* and *Veritas*. These are taken, with adaptations in the case of the two last, from Philippe de Galle's *Prosopographia*, published in Antwerp between 1585 and the beginning of 1601.[5] The author states that he has expressly included the less well-known personifications.[6] They are Christian, classical or contemporary inventions. Engravings after these plates are rare[7] and it is interesting that Elstrack could turn to them in his workshop. De Galle also says that he did not have to go to antiquity for his models but drew what he needed from Christian artists,[8] meaning in general probably the Dutch and Flemish Mannerists. Martin de Vos made a drawing[9] of *Experientia* with rod and leadline as in the *Prosopographia* but it is of a pretty girl, not de Galle's sombre mature woman.[10] Elstrack in his copy has accented the ageing lines in her face and neck. The historian, Sidney says, gives 'the experience of manie

---

[1] Sidney, op. cit., p. 497.

[2] Pierre Matthieu, *Histoire de France*, 1607-9, 'Avertissement . . .' [p. 9].

[3] *History*, book II, ch. 21, p. 537.

[4] Ibid., book I, ch. I, p. 21.

[5] The *Prosopographia* was dedicated to Marie de Melun, Comtesse de Ligne. She inherited the Melun titles listed in the dedication from Robert de Melun on his death in 1585. One of them is Marquise de Roubaix. In January 1601 her husband assumed the title of Marquis de Roubaix, presumably on her death. There is a copy in the British Museum Print Room.

[6] Philippe de Galle, *Prosopographia . . .*, 'Au Lecteur S.'

[7] B. Knipping, *De Iconografie van de contra-reformatie in de Nederlanden*, Hilversum, 1939, vol. I, p. 15.

[8] De Galle, op. cit., 'Au Lecteur S.'

[9] *Stedelijk Prentenkabinet*, Antwerp.

[10] *Prosopographia*, no. 9.

ages'.[1] These may act as a guide for the future, just as the mariner learns the depths of the sea from his instruments and is able to use them in steering his course. The rod had been used since time immemorial for measuring depth in shallow waters, but only since 1540[2] had the results of lead soundings taken in deep waters been marked on charts for the use of future navigators. *Magistra vitae* is adapted from de Galle's *Virtus*,[3] Righteousness, a Minerva-like figure in cuirass and helmet holding a lance and sword, her foot on the horned Pan. Elstrack has given her a laurel wreath to symbolise *Historia's* preservative eternising function and has of course omitted her armour and weapons. Minerva was the goddess of wisdom as well as of moral authority, so that the impact in her present guise of History, 'controller and instructor of human life', is indeed magisterial. Her other role as the recorder of the past, is indicated by her active suppression of Death and Oblivion. The importance of truth in recording history, already indicated by the flames on the column, is reiterated by the inclusion of the personification of Truth. She is traditionally naked; the only alteration from de Galle's figure[4] is the omission of the Holy Ghost probably because it had an exclusively Christian connotation. The emanation of light from the right hand is also seen in Ripa's personification.[5]

The map of the world is a rough copy from the *Theatrum orbis terrarum* of Ortelius, possibly from the edition published in London in 1606.[6] Centred on the north and south Atlantic, areas on the extreme right and left have been shorn off to fit it on the globe; the equator and lines of latitude and longitude are correctly shown; the three main islands of the Caribbean, Cuba, Hispaniola and Jamaica, are emphasised; the River Amazon is marked. There are relatively few symbols; the Fall —Adam and Eve and the Serpent—is wrongly placed north of the Black Sea. as Raleigh concludes that '*Paradise*' was 'seated in the lower part of the Region of *Eden* afterward called . . . *Mesopotamia*';[7] the cause of the mistake may only be that the engraver was pressed for space; the ark sits correctly on the eastern end of the Ararat range in the Caucausus; the warring phalanxes, in what was in Raleigh's time called

---

[1] Sidney, op. cit., p. 496 [498].

[2] Information kindly given me by the late Mr G. Naish of the National Maritime Museum, Greenwich.

[3] In the copy of the *Prosopographia* in the Stedelijk Prentenkabinet, Antwerp, no. R.62.

[4] *Prosopographia*, no. 3.

[5] Ripa, *Iconologia*, 1611, p. 529.

[6] *Theatrum orbis terrarum*, p. lv and unpaginated leaf.

[7] *History*, book I, ch. 3, p. 64.

Æthiopia, might represent the 'ten yeares warre that he [Moses] made against the Æthiopians',[1] or they may have been recognised as the symbol of the decisive battle in 1591 when the Moroccan army defeated that of the vast Songhai empire which was based on the regions of the Niger; north again Athens is shown and Rome; the considerable town in western Africa, north of the equator, one of the many fortified towns of the Portuguese in that area; the ship in the southern Atlantic is surely Drake's *Golden Hind*; in the northern Atlantic a battle is shown between eight armoured vessels, symbolising war between the English and the Spaniards; in southern Spain a town marks Cadiz or Seville at the mouth of the Guadalquivir—Seville and Cadiz controlled the West Indian trading fleet in the sixteenth century. Dublin is marked by a church, possibly to recall the years Raleigh spent in Ireland; in England, London is not marked, but a church and building in the west; it is unlikely that there would be an engraving slip here; could this be Winchester, the seat of his trial in 1603 and where he was condemned to captivity, wrily alluded to in the last sentence of his Preface?

The reason for choosing a contemporary map of the world for the title-page to the *History* as it stands, is not immediately obvious. The present volume ends in the second century B C. It might be that the design for the engraving was finished while Raleigh still intended to continue his vast work, possibly up to the end of the sixteenth century —that would be before 1612, the date of Prince Henry's death which, among other things, caused him to break off.[2] Or it may be explained by his treatment of the subject; his enrichment of the account of antiquity with material taken from all countries and periods; from the Americas, the east and west coasts of Africa, the East Indies, China and Russia, from Europe of the Middle Ages, the early sixteenth century and his own time.

The personification of Good and Evil Fame points to the historian as moralist who records the good and evil reputations which men make for themselves in the world. The *History* was 'directed' to Prince Henry and was at least in part for his edification. The wings of the two figures symbolise the speed with which their news travels; the trumpets (of fictional design) the enforced attention to their report; the eyes, ears and tongues on the feathers of Good Fame symbolise her vigilance,

[1] Ibid., book II, ch. 3, p. 251.
[2] Ibid., book V, ch. 6, p. 776.

awareness and mode of communication.[1] Evil Fame is covered with spots, a different concept altogether, signifying a spotted or blemished reputation.

The news of good and evil deeds is known to Providence, that is God, represented by the eye at the top of the engraving. In various editions of Horapollo published in the sixteenth century the woodcut of a great eye is shown, half surrounded by cloud and above a landscape with monuments. It was the symbol of the Divinity in distant times; by it 'they recognized God' according to the accompanying text, 'because just as the eye sees all that is presented to it, so God knows and sees all things'.[2] It is undoubtedly from this source that Raleigh selected the representation. At the beginning of the *History* Raleigh devotes a section to the meaning of Providence. 'God therefore, who is euery where present . . . *whose eyes are upon the righteous, and his countenance against them that doe evill,* . . . *an infinite eye,* beholding all things; and cannot therefore be esteemed as an idle looker on . . . God therefore who could onely be the cause of all, can onely prouide for all, and sustaine all.'[3] By making the eye dominate the title-page Raleigh emphasises the biblical and Christian theme of God as the supreme moral judge, of his constant vigilance and his intervention in human affairs.

Jonson's *Minde of the Front,* unsigned in the *History,* was included in *The Underwood* in the second volume of the Folio published in 1640 as *The Mind of the Frontispice to a Booke.* The *History* was banned by James I some months after it appeared. The ban was probably lifted when Raleigh came out of prison in 1616 and there were several editions between 1617 and 1640.[4] However, Jonson may have felt in the dangerous years before his death in 1637, that it was wiser not to avow his connection with it. The change of line 8 to 'When Vice alike in tune with vertue dur'd', relatively innocuous, may also have been prompted by caution.

---

[1] Ripa, op. cit., pp. 154f.

[2] *Ori Apollinis . . . de sacris notis . . .,* Paris, 1551, p. 222.
Ori Apollinis Niliaci, de sacris . . . notis, Paris, 1574, p. 104v.
Hori Apollinis. Selecta Hieroglyphica sive sacrae notae . . ., 1597, p. 262.

[3] *History,* book I, ch. 1, pp. 18f.

[4] J. Racin Jun, 'The Early Editions of Sir Walter Ralegh's *The History of the World*', *Studies in Bibliography,* vol. 17, 1964, pp. 199–209. *Papers of the Bibliographical Society of the University of Virginia,* Charlottesville, Virginia.

SVPER-EST

RELIGIO

PAX

THE
WORKES
OF THE MOST HIGH
AND MIGHTY PRINCE,
IAMES,
By the grace of God, Kinge
of Great Brittaine
France & Ireland
Defendor of ye
Faith &c;
Published by IAMES Bishop of
WINTON & Deane of his
Maᵗⁱᵉ Chappell Royall
1 Reg 3. 12 v. Loe I haue giuen thee
a wise and an vnderstanding heart.

LONDON
Printed by ROBERT
BARKER & Iohn Bill,
Printers to ÿ Kings moſt
excellent Maieſtie.
1616.

Renold Elstrack sculpsit

II

JAMES I

Workes

1616

(Hind, II. Renold Elstrack, no. 78)

The architectural design shows a central alcove enclosed by a rear wall and flanking wings. These are made up of substantial forward-breaking bases each supporting two columns framing arched niches and carrying the entablature. Within the alcove is a tabernacle-like structure on the panel of which is inscribed the title: THE/WORKES/OF THE MOST HIGH,/AND MIGHTY PRINCE,/IAMES,/*By the grace of God Kinge/of Great Brittaine/France & Ireland/Defendor of yᵉ/Faith etc:/*Published by IAMES, BISHOP of /WINTON & Deane of his/Ma: ᵗˢ Chappell Royall. Below, the text: *1 Reg: 3. 12 v. Loe I have giuen thee/a wise and an vnderstanding heart.* The structure is supported by a series of mouldings in baluster form and rests on the two lateral bases; as an additional support is a lower central bracket whose pendant moulding dovetails into the addorsed ornaments of the cartouche at the bottom of the alcove. This shows within an oval frame, the imprint: LONDON/*Printed by* ROBERT/BARKER & Iohn Bill./*Printers to yᵉ Kings most/excellent Maiestie./*1616. On a lower band of the cartouche, *Cum priuilegio.* Signed at the bottom left, *Renold Elstrack sculpsit.* Above the panel of the tabernacle rises a double scroll-ended cornice; this supports an arcaded base which carries two columns on top of which are candlestick-shaped pinnacles whose stems are pierced with vertical lobes; between them, resting on a bracket, is an obelisk carrying four crowns of diminishing size. The crowns are set with the crosses and fleur-de-lys of St Edward's crown. In the sky two flying angels hold aloft with their upper hands, a crown set with stars, while with their other hands they each hold the end of a wide riband bearing the inscription, SVPER: EST. Behind and above the angels and crown is the orb of the sun surrounded by rays. The main columns, surmounted by Roman Corinthian capitals, are decorated with royal devices, outside l. and r.. the rose and thistle, inside l. and r., the rose and fleur-de-lys. On the top of the entablature sit two pairs of the royal beasts; outer l. and r., the lion holding a shield in the form of a strapwork cartouche showing the royal coat of arms; inside l. and r., the unicorns with shields showing, l., the rose and r., the thistle, both surmounted by the St Edward's crown. The collars of the unicorns are of fleur-de-lys pattern. Between each pair rises a gothic baldachin or canopy, from the central boss of which hangs a lighted lamp of Renaissance design.

Projecting from the base between the two pairs of columns is a bracket baluster form on which stands a monumental female figure silhouetted against the frames of the niches; in scrolled cartouches, above the niches, are inscribed their names, l., RELIGIO and r. PAX. Religion, winged, rests her r. arm on the cross; and in her left, holds up a book. She wears a plain belted gown pinned with a square brooch at the neck; her head is covered with a coif from which a veil hangs down behind; from one arm of the cross hang reins and a bit; under her bare feet lies a skeleton; rays surround her head. Peace is clad in a semi-military leather or cloth corsage with a winged cherub motif on the breast; on her head is a coronet set with stars; with her right hand she holds an olive branch, with her left, a cornucopia filled with fruit and flowers; her booted feet tread on assorted military equipment—a pike, a halberd, swords, a shield and a standard.

Each architectural member is decorated; the plinths have panels showing a floral and foliage design; the mouldings making up the side brackets are each differently ornamented; the architrave and the cornice have rows of schematised classical mouldings including a row of dentils and one of egg and dart; the frieze has an arabesque design of shells and foliage. The central panel has a diamond ornament at the top of the curve enclosing the title, with arabesques in the spandrels; a diamond-cut stone acts as one of the mouldings holding the obelisk, and another four are part of the ornament in the widest of the mouldings which support the panel. The panel itself is framed on either side with a trefoil and leaf edging. The cartouche at the bottom is of pierced strapwork with bird and leaf motifs. The riband held by the angels is decorated with an arabesque design.

This title-page is one of the most elaborate and ornate of English examples, to be compared with the portrait frontispiece of Queen Elizabeth by Hogenberg in Saxton's *Atlas of England and Wales*, 1579.[1] It may be assumed that the wealth of ornament, which is chosen from a variety of sources, was to do honour to the exalted author, King James.

The four crowns are self-explanatory. A crown for a kingdom was an image used by James himself when speaking to the Lords and Commons, 'First, ye all know, that by the accession of more Crownes, which in my Person I haue brought vnto you, . . .'[2] The celestial crown to which James aspires is a royal model of the crown of glory which awaits the righteous in heaven. It has the shape of the British crown with stars instead of the usual symbols. This invention of the earthly and heavenly crowns may be compared with the emblem of Henri III, three crowns but of the same design, two representing his temporal kingdoms of France and Poland and a third place above, with the motto, 'manet ultima coelo'.[3] The sun, placed centrally directly above the tier of crowns, is a symbol for the Deity from whom the King derives his authority; in a similar, though much rougher, woodcut title-page to Bishop Mockett's *God and the King*, 1615, the King sits enthroned below the Tetragrammaton with a scroll extending across which reads, 'By mee kings raigne' 'Kings are called Gods by the propheticall King Dauid, because they sit vpon GOD his Throne in the earth';[4] they are 'his Lieutenants and Vice-regents on earth, and so adorned and furnished with some sparkles of the Diuinitie'.[5]

The doctrine of kingship which here finds expression is complemented by the belief in the hereditary principle; the King 'by birth, . . . commeth to his crowne, . . .'[6] In the engraving it is the unicorns who proclaim the hereditary right of James to his kingdoms, because the unicorn is the royal beast of the King of Scotland, which title he held by indisputable descent. On the left, the rose of the Tudors is from his great-grandmother twice over, Margaret Tudor, daughter of Henry VII, while the fleur-de-lys collar alludes to the title of King of

[1] Hind, I, p. 88, plate 39.
[2] *Workes*, 'A Speach to the Lords and Commons . . .', 1609, p. 541.
[3] F. Picinelli, *Il mondo simbolico*, 1669, libro XXV, capo vii, p. 830.
[4] *Workes*, 'The trew Law of free Monarchies', p. 194.
[5] Ibid., 'A Speach in the Parliament Hovse . . .', 1605, p. 500.
[6] Ibid., 'The trew Law . . .', p. 209.

France used by English kings until 1801 in consequence of the ancient claim to the Kingdom of France of Edward III, through his wife Isabella; on the right, the thistle is the emblem of the Scottish sovereign and the collar should be the reinforcement of the claim to France through his grandmother, Mary of Guise, the mother of Mary, Queen of Scots. The royal British coat of arms upheld by the lions sejant repeats in heraldic terms the claims of the title, of the four crowns, and of the roses, fleurs-de-lys and thistles decorating the columns.

There is no clear evidence for the meaning of the lamp under the baldachino, but its position on the entablature between the two royal beasts seems to imply a connection with James's titles, in fact the last otherwise here unrepresented, 'Defender of the Faith'. The deliberate choice of the gothic form for the baldachino, in striking contrast to the classical order below, suggests an ecclesiastical purpose, for at this period and until the 1630s, all churches were gothic except for minor modifications, the new architecture being used only for secular buildings. A lamp burning within a room is stated by Picinelli to be above all a symbol of Christ His Faith, with the text, 'That was the true Light' (John 1.9).[1] May not the invention stand for the Church, or more specifically the Church of England, with the lamp of the true faith burning within it?

The two allegorical figures of Religion and Peace represent the twin goals of James's policies, the ever-vigilant promotion of the true reformed religion and of the cause of peace. Peace was achieved at home by the union of the three kingdoms; in Europe he strove for it by his continuous attempts to reconcile the Catholic and Protestant powers. The figure of Religion first appeared, as far as is known, in *Icones*,[2] a volume containing a set of emblems published in 1580 by Théodore de Bèze, the great Calvinist divine and classical scholar. He dedicated it[3] to the young James I who was advised by friends and former colleagues of his, among them Peter Young who had been his pupil and in turn James's tutor. The allusion would certainly have been taken. The verses which accompany the figure explain in simple terms the meaning of her pose and attributes.

Who are you who walks in torn garments? Religion, true child of the highest Father.

[1] Picinelli, op. cit., libro XIV, capo viii, 'Strumenti di chiesa', pp. 604f.
[2] T. de Bèze, *Icones . . .*, 1580, emblemata XXXIX.
[3] G. F. Warner, ed., 'The Library of James VI. 1573–1583', *Publications of the Scottish History Society*, vol. 15, 1893.

Why so poor a dress? I scorn wealth that is perishable.
What book is this? The venerable Law of my Father.
Why the bare breast? This befits the friend of candour.
Why leaning on the Cross? The Cross is my only peace and rest.
Why winged? I teach men to fly above the stars.
Why radiant? I scatter the darkness of the mind.
What does this rein teach? To restrain the frenzies of the mind.
Why do you press down upon Death? Because I am the death of
   Death.

There is nothing controversial about her; or rather it is a comment on
the temper of the period that just as every church claimed to have the
true religion, 'most pure', the 'sureliest founded vpon the word of
God',[1] so could she make her appeal to different forms of religious
thought. She appears in Ripa's *Iconologia* as *Religione vera christiana*[2]
which was used all over Europe; Martin de Vos adopted her for a
broadsheet[3] with the verses loosely rendered into the German, Dutch,
Flemish and French vernaculars, probably for Protestant consumption;
Théodor de Bry engraved her in miniature[4] with *Christ/religio* inscribed on the book; the style of Elstrack's figure, the general heaviness,
the fact that the breast is covered, suggests a Dutch version as the
immediate source.

   The companion figure, overburdened with cornucopia and olive
branch, relentlessly treading on the weapons of war, is in fact the con-
flation of two emblematic representations of Peace. Bishop Mountague
alluding in the Preface to the text which follows the King's titles—
James, a second Solomon—says, '*GOD aboue all things gaue Solomon
Wisedome: Wisdome brought him Peace; Peace brought him Riches*',[5] therefore Peace and Abundance, that is with cornucopia; she first appears
in a book of emblems of Hadrianus Junius in 1565,[6] holding the child
Plutus with her right hand, here necessarily omitted. The clue to her
other attributes in the title-page is given by the portrait of James I[7]
which should face it in the *Workes*. This engraving by Simon van de
Passe carries the separate imprint of Bill and may have been sold as a

---

[1] *Workes*, 'A Speach in the Starre-chamber', 1616, p. 554.
[2] Ripa, *Iconologia*, 1611, p. 455.
[3] Hollstein, I., P. Baltens, no. 9.
[4] Hollstein, IV, T. de Bry, nos 187–90.
[5] *Workes*, 'The Preface to the Reader', e₂.
[6] Hadrianus Junius, *Emblemata*, 1565, emblem VI.
[7] Hind, II, pp. 259f, plate 154.

single sheet but Bill was one of the printers of the *Workes* and its inclusion was intentional as on the back of the engraving is printed the title. James is shown sitting enthroned with crown, orb and sceptre before a backcloth on which are inscribed the words, BEATI PACIFICI. Our figure repeats this theme; in addition to Peace and Plenty she represents the seventh Beatitude, 'Blessed are the Peacemakers. . . .' Ripa[1] describes the peacemaker as

> of those who are not content to live in peace and quiet . . . but know how peace may be restored through suffering when it is lost, both by their own means and with the help of others; not only by bodily force against external enemies, but on a higher plane, in the spirit, against the powers of Hell. So Peace shall be represented with arms under her feet, to show that it must be acquired and maintained by spiritual strength, so much the worthier of praise.

The olive is a sign of peace, as we read that 'Aeneas on disembarking in the land of Evander in Italy went forth with an olive branch in hand.' Her cuirass signifies her readiness for war, her star-set coronet shows her as the child of God, perhaps akin to the Virgin who as Queen of Heaven may have a crown of stars.

The message of spiritual self-discipline implicit in the representations of both Religion and Peace may have been addressed particularly to Prince Charles, to whom the *Workes* were dedicated; they were to lie before him '*as a Patterne, . . .*'[2].

[1] Ripa, op. cit., pp. 45f.
[2] *Workes*, 'The Epistle Dedicatorie'.

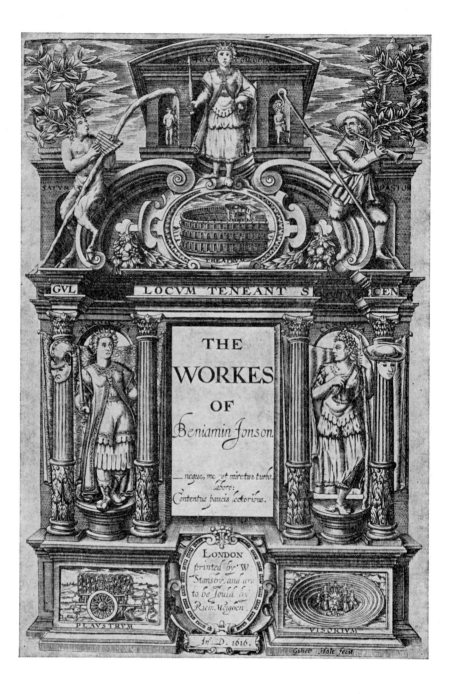

12

BEN JONSON

The Workes of Beniamin Jonson

1616

(Hind, II. William Hole, no. 27)

The architectural design shows four columns standing on a plinth which breaks forward on either side; they are carved with acanthus foliage at the bottom, continuing fluted, with Corinthian capitals; a central aperture and open arches r. and l.; above the cornice and frieze is a broken pediment enclosing a carved cartouche which is embellished with a swag of fruit and myrtle; behind the pediment is the rear wall with arched niches, r. and l; it is surmounted by a second, shrine-like structure with curved pediment, a central and two side niches; on either flank, standing on the rear wall, is an obelisk garlanded with laurel and topped with a ball and ornament in the shape of a flame (?). On a panel in the central aperture, the title, with the motto:

> —*neque, me ut miretur turba,*
> *laboro:*
> *Contentus paucis lectoribus.*

Directly below, in a cartouche, the imprint, LONDON/*printed by W:/ Stansby, and are/to be sould by/Rich: Meighen*; below again, the date, *An° D.1616.* Along the frieze the inscription, SI[N]GVLA QVAE-QV[E] LOCVM TENEANT S[O]RTITA DECEN[T]ER. Before the left arch a female figure representing the muse of TRAGOEDIA; she stands before a damask curtain and is wearing a crown, a jewelled and belted top tunic over another knee-length tunic, both finished with lappets, a robe edged with jewels, high boots with raised soles, and is holding a sceptre; hanging on the column l., is a helmeted mask. On the r. stands the muse of COMOEDIA before a plain curtain; she wears tunic and chiton and a cloak which she holds with her right hand; she has slippers on her feet and a stave in her left hand; a wreath crowns her hair; on the column r., hangs a mask surmounted by a wide-brimmed hat. In the upper central niche is the figure of TRAGI COMOEDIA with crown and sceptre, a cloak and jewelled robe, under it tunic and chiton and slippers on her feet. Astride the arch of the main pediment, l., is a SATYR holding a reed pipe with a clubbed stave over his arm. Opposite is a shepherd PASTOR in a jerkin and belt to which is attached his scrip, knee-length breeches, hose and boots; he wears a brimmed hat and is blowing a cornet; he keeps his crook in place with a leg. In the cartouche within the pediment is a Roman theatre, THEATRVM with three arcaded orders and stage with returning wings. On the face of the plinth l., is a wagon, PLAVSTRVM, drawn by a horse; a man in contemporary dress is gesticulating on its floor, a goat is tethered to it and a wine flask is tied to a support. R. is an amphitheatre, VISORIVM, sunk below ground level; round the altar, on which is a lighted sacrifice, dances the *Chorus* made up of men and women all in contemporary dress. Signed bottom r.: *Guliel° Hole fecit.*

The lines below the title are from Horace, *Sermones* 1.10. 73–4. 'I do not work so that the crowd may admire me, I am contented with a few readers.' The sentiment is echoed in the *Prologue to Cynthia's Revels*;[1] referring to the poet's muse, '*Nor hunts she after popular applause,/Or fomie praise, that drops from common iawes*', and by Francis Beaumont in the verse *Upon his Catiline*,[2]

> *If thou had'st itch'd after the wild applause*
> *Of common people, . . .*

Jonson, more than any other dramatist of the period, was deeply influenced by Horace; as well as his translation of the *Ars Poetica*, undertaken probably about 1604, there are other translations from Horace and many references to the poet in his works. In the complimentary poem by *I.C.* included in the 1640 edition of *The Art of Poetry*,[3] he is hailed as 'English *Horace*'. He was thought to have rivalled the Latin poet in his knowledge of Greek and Latin drama and to have conceived his own works in the spirit of the classical writers; he was the one who understood

[1] *Workes*, I, 186.
[2] Ibid., introductory poem, 'To my deare friend, M. BEN: IONSON.'
[3] B. Jonson, *Quintus Horatius Flaccus his Book of the Art of Poetry . . .*, 1640. Introductory poem, 'ODE to BEN JONSON/Upon his Ode to himselfe.'

> . . . the faith of ancient skill,
> Drawn from the Tragick, Comick, Lyrick qvill:
> The Greek and Roman denison'd by thee,
> And both made richer in thy Poetry.[1]

The hexameter on the frieze is from Horace's *Ars Poetica*, 'Let each particular variety hold the place properly allotted to it.'[2] Or, in Jonson's own translation . . .

> *Each subject should retaine*
> *The place allotted it, with decent praise.*[3]

It comes at the end of a passage on the different forms of poetic drama; it sums up the classical theory of decorum, that the characters in any given play should speak in the metre and wear the demeanour suited to it. Jonson was an authority on the subject as his friends testify (see *Conversations with Drummond of Hawthornden*[4] and Francis Beaumont *Upon his Foxe*[5]), so the quotation was aptly chosen as the chief theme of the title-page which is rather more a didactic exercise than a guide to the contents of the folio. The muse of Tragedy has the rich trappings of the noble and exalted personages with which she is concerned; the tunics are Roman in inspiration; the 'robe of State' and the buskins enhance her dignity. Comedy deals with people in ordinary life so, as Ripa,[6] following classical authors, stipulates, her muse wears slippers or *socci* (the sock of comedy) and carries a stave to show her humbler sphere and rustic origins. The chiton was also used by Inigo Jones.[7] Her mask with its travelling hat is in contrast to that of the warrior helm. The curtains before which these two figures stand are those which may be hung along the back of the stage—a further suggestion of theatre.

The three other main figures do not belong to the classical canon. The new forms of drama which were evolving in the sixteenth century gave rise to a prolonged debate; Sir Philip Sidney devotes a part of the *Defence of Poesie*[8] to the question and Polonius is of course alluding to it in his account of the players. Tragi-comedy, that is a play which takes

[1] Ibid., introductory poem 'To Mr. *Jonson*' by Zouch Tounley.
[2] Line 92.
[3] . . . *of the Art of Poetry*, 1640, p. 6.
[4] G. H. Herford and P. Simpson, *Ben Jonson*, 1925, vol. I, 132, 134.
[5] *Workes*, introductory poem 'To my deare friend, M. BEN: IONSON.'
[6] Ripa, *Iconologia*, 1611, p. 81.
[7] P. Simpson and C. F. Bell, *Designs by Inigo Jones . . . Walpole Society*, XII, 1923-4, plate xvii.
[8] Sir Philip Sidney, *Arcadia*, 1598. *The Defence of Poesie*, p. 503.

its *dramatis personae* from the ordinary as well as the exalted ranks of life, was known in antiquity, but the only work in which the word itself is used was the *Amphitryo* of Plautus (line 60) and it is this play which is commonly cited as an example of the genre. Jonson told Drummond[1] that he would like to have written an *Amphitryo* but that he could not find two actors sufficiently alike to fill the cast and there is no work of this kind in the folio. In the title-page Tragi-comedy declares her double allegiance by borrowing her wardrobe from Tragedy on the one hand and Comedy on the other and so combines crown and sceptre with simple gown and *socci*.

SATYR belongs to the world of the Entertainments which fill the last part of the first volume of the *Workes*. One of these, at p. 871, *A particvlar entertainment of the Queene and Prince . . . at Althrope . . . 1603* is called *A Satyre* and opens with '. . . *a Satyre lodged in a little Spinet*'; he is the inhabitant of the *Satiricall Scenes* of Serlio's theatre[2] '*where in you must place all those things that bee rude and rusticall*'. Like the fairies to whom he is mildly opposed, he emerges from the woods a supernatural creature whose role is to play and joke and make music on his pipes. There are satyrs too in one of the masques, OBERON, THE FAERY PRINCE A MASQVE OF PRINCE HENRIES.[3] They are the descendants, much tamed, of the Greek satyr, '. . . The rough rude Satyrs naked, . . .'[4] sent forth on to the stage by Aeschylus, as described in the *Art of Poetry*. But they have no connection, although the word is the same, with *A Comicall Satyre*, the sub-title given by Jonson in the *Workes* to *Euery Man out of his Humour*, *Cynthia's Revels* and *Poetaster*.[5] PASTOR, in contemporary costume, exemplifies the shepherd of pastoral poetry, of Theocritus and Virgil, and in the sixteenth century of Sannazaro, Guarini, Fletcher and Sidney and many others. Drummond[6] records that Jonson said he wanted to write a pastoral; he had been particularly critical of Guarini's lack of decorum in the genre, for he had committed the error of making the shepherds speak like himself, i.e. in polite not rustic speech. Later Jonson did write a pastoral comedy, but it was not completed. There is no work of this category in the folio.

The two scenes on the face of the plinth illustrate the earliest days of

[1] Herford and Simpson, op. cit., vol. I, 144.
[2] Sebastiano Serlio, *The first (-the fift) booke of Architecture . . .*, 1611. *The Second Booke The Third Chapter Fol. 26*.
[3] *Workes*, I, 975.
[4] *. . . of the Art of Poetry*, 1640, p. 13.
[5] *Workes*, I, 174, 177, 271.
[6] Herford and Simpson, op. cit., vol. I, 143.

the classical drama. Jonson drew his information for them from Greek and Latin authors and also from sixteenth-century and contemporary works such as the *Antiquitatum Romanarum Corpus*[1] of Rosinus to which he refers in the notes to *Sejanus* and elsewhere.[2] Rosinus includes a short history of the classical theatre.[3] R. is the chorus who dance and sing in honour of Bacchus. This is the traditional origin of drama; that men and women took part is deduced from the *Troades* of Seneca. On the altar must be the goat, won by the best of the contesting poets and to be sacrified to the god. The dance is taking place in the arena of an amphitheatre. Thomas Dempster, who published an amplified edition of the *Antiquitatum . . .* in 1613 gives *visorium* as the Latin for *amphitheatrum*;[4] this may have been Jonson's source. The fact that *amphitheatrum* derived from the Greek may have led him to believe that these structures existed in the Greek world; the oval shape was obviously most suitable for the round dance. Here it is shown dug out of the earth like a proper Greek theatre. The representation on the left illustrates the lines from Horace; the man in the wagon must be Thespis,

> . . . said to be the first, found out
> The Tragoedy, and carried it about,
> Till then unknowne, in Carts, wherein did ride
> Those that did sing and act: their faces dy'd
> With lees of Wine. . . .[5]

His innovation was to write a solo part for one member of the chorus, which perhaps was taken by himself. The wine barrel produces the lees for his make-up; the goat trotting along is perhaps the result of his success at a festival he has already attended. His wagon is of common English design. THEATRVM is a Roman theatre, possibly intended for the 'Theatre of Marcellus' of which there is a representation in Lafreri's *Speculum Romanae Magnificentiae*.[6] The auditorium is very like but the stage buildings are different; the *scaena* is shown but there is no proscenium with pediment. In addition it has substantial returning wings (one only being shown); this feature may have been put in to accord with the literary evidence,[7] or a design of some other Roman theatre

---

[1] Basle, 1583.
[2] Herford and Simpson, op. cit., vol. I, 252.
[3] Rosinus, op. cit., 187–94.
[4] Rosinus, *Antiquitatum Romanarum . . .*, ed. Thomas Dempster, 1613, p. 342.
[5] *. . . of the Art of Poetry*, 1640, p. 16.
[6] Published 1582–6 (?).
[7] Vitruvius, *De architectura*, Loeb Classical Library, 2 vols, vol. I, bk V, c. VI, 8.

(e.g. at Orange or in Crete) may have been known. In the l. top niche the tiny figure is Bacchus, the patron of the drama, and opposite him is Apollo, the leader of the muses.

In producing a collected edition of his works Jonson had engaged on an undertaking unprecedented in the world of contemporary drama. The presence of the obelisks, which are monuments, and the laurels, the traditional crown of the poet, is surely to signify the author's desire that the folio may bring him a poet's immortality. The pictures of the ancient theatre and the sentences from Horace proclaim the allegiance to the reverend models and precepts of the classical drama and classical poetry by which his works, too learned for the vulgar, have deserved eternal fame.

POLY-OLBION

GREAT BRI TAINE

By
Michaell Drayton.
Esqr:

London printed for { M Lownes. I Browne.
I Helme. I Busbie.

13

MICHAEL DRAYTON

Poly-olbion, or a chorographical Description of Great Britain

1612–22

(Hind, II. William Hole, no. 22)

The title-page has an architectural design in form of an arch springing from square pillars resting on a continuous plinth. The plinth breaks forward r. and l. and is decorated with a frieze of scallop shells. On either side walls pierced by arches and carrying a balustrade join the pillars; in front of them are Roman Doric columns surmounted by square capitals to form platforms. The main wall of the arch terminates in round-topped crenellations broken in the centre by a small arch enclosing a scalloped niche and flanked by obelisks. Behind the crenellations again, Doric columns support a square base from which rises a fluted ogival cupola; on either side of this base is a ball and flame ornament. Suspended from the obelisks by a wide riband is a carved cartouche bearing the title; in the centre left of the frame this cartouche is set with a diamond surrounded with four pearls. Attached to it are swags made up of shells, winkles and scallops, crabs and pieces of coral; two other similar swags hang from the top of the main columns. In another cartouche in the centre of the plinth is the inscription, *By/ Michaell Drayton/Esqr*: Branches of laurel rise on either side from the curved scroll-ends of the frame; in the scroll-end of the top is a loop for suspension. At the bottom of the engraving is the imprint: *London printed for M. Lownes. I. Browne/I.Helme. I. Busbie.* Signed: *Ingrauẽ/by W. Hole.*

    Seated under the central arch is the figure of Albion, a maiden with dressed flowing hair, draped in a cloak which exposes her left breast; the cloak is decorated with a map design featuring rivers, trees, mountains, churches, towns, etc. Round her neck is a triple row of pearls; pearl drops hang from her ears. In her right hand she holds a sceptre terminating in a fleur-de-lys, in her left a cornucopia filled with fruit and flowers. Above her head two cherubs hold a wreath of laurel; above them is a winged Fame blowing a trumpet. The rocky mound on which she sits is inscribed: GREAT BRITAINE; behind, the sea stretches to the horizon with ships and sea monsters moving across it. Standing on the capitals are, l., a beardless youth with long hair, in plate armour over which is a square-necked belted coat-armour; from the belt hangs a straight sword on which he rests his left hand. He wears a soft hat with a deep rolled brim and laced boots; suspended from his right arm is a shield showing a lion passant. R., a Roman emperor in armour and military cloak with wreath and diadem holding a staff and sword; his shield, hung up beside him, shows the lightly draped figure of Venus holding a flaming heart. On the left side of the plinth is a bearded man in helmet, scale armour bodice and leather or cloth skirt, holding a spetum; he has boots with wide turn-over tops. His shield which he holds with his left hand shows a horse rampant. Opposite him stands a man in plate armour and anime, holding an unsheathed sword in his right hand; he is wearing a crown with two arches, orb with cross rising in the centre and crosses at the base of each arch with intermediate crosses set in the circlet. He is booted and spurred and his shield shows leopards passant.

On the opposite page are the verses

Vpon the *Frontispice*

Through a *Triumphant Arch*, see *Albion* plas't,
In *Happy* site, in *Neptunes* armes embras't,
In *Power* and *Plenty*, on hir *Cleeuy* Throne
Circled with *Natures Ghirlands*, being alone
Stil'd *th'Oceans Island*. On the Columnes beene
(As Trophies raiz'd) what Princes Time hath seene
Ambitious of her. In hir yonger years,
Vast Earth-bred *Giants* woo'd her: but, who bears
In Golden field the Lion passant red,
Aeneas Nephew (*Brute*) them conquered.

Next, Laureat *Caesar*, as a Philtre, brings,
On's shield, his Grandame *Venus*: Him hir Kings
Withstood. At length, the *Roman*, by long sute,
Gain'd her (most Part) from th'ancient race of *Brute*.
Diuors't from Him, the *Saxon sable Horse*,
Borne by sterne *Hengist*, wins her: but through force
Garding the *Norman Leopards bath'd in Gules*,
She chang'd hir Loue to Him, whose Line yet rules.

The original design may have been larger as the tops of the cupola, the wreath and what should be the blade of the spear are cut off.

John Selden the great jurist and historian wrote the 'Illustrations' or notes to the first eighteen books of *Poly-olbion*. The influence of his learning and antiquarian fervour is apparent in the details of the title-page.

The central figure of Albion is inspired by personifications of Britannia on the reverse of certain Roman coins: William Camden, in his *Britannia*, 1586, discussing the origin of the first name of Great Britain, 'Albion', commented that on 'the coined pieces bearing the stampe of Antoninus Pius and Severus, Britaine is pourtraied sitting upon rocks in womans habit',[1] and in the 1600 edition he includes illustrations of the relevant coins[2] from the collection of Sir Robert Cotton. For this edition, William Rogers, presumably on instructions from Camden, placed on the engraved title-page in an oblong oval, the figure of Albion-Britannia seated on a rock holding standard and spear; beyond her lies a bay flanked by rocky shores. For this figure he has selected elements from the various personifications. For the edition of 1607 Hole himself made a copy of this title-page but modified it, for Britannia's spear is now reversed, to show, we may suppose, that her wars are over. It was probably also Hole who made fresh and better engravings of the coins. In the title-page to *Poly-olbion* the island nature of Britain is emphasised by the flow of sea around her rock; Britannia herself has assumed a different character from both the Roman and Rogers' representations; standard and spear have gone and the sceptre

[1] From the English translation of *Britannia*, 1610, p. 24.
[2] *Britannia*, 1600, p. 70, nos V (obverse), VI (obverse), p. 71, no. IX (obverse). See H. Mattingly, *Coins of the Roman Empire in the British Museum . . . Catalogue*, 1968, vol. IV, nos 1638 (?), 1640, 1977.

which she holds is based on one of several models carried by the kings and queens of England. She is prosperous and triumphant and for the only time in her long career, notably young and beautiful. She is shown indeed as a virgin nymph, with one breast exposed and the long, loose hair worn by unmarried girls. It may be assumed that the pearls she wears were found in British waters; '*In Rauenglasse, . . ./Comes Irt, . . ./* Her costly bosome strew'd with precious Orient Pearle,/Bred in her shining Shels. . . .'[1] The topographical signs on her cloak are not identifiable, but in the middle is a large town, probably London.

The armed figures represent the four successful conquerors whose descendants ruled over Britain. They are chosen to represent the history of England according to the favourite scheme of national historians in the Renaissance, by which the history of a race or country was conceived in terms of the succession and mutation of dynasties. They are placed in chronological order, and wear armour and carry shields which are carefully differentiated to indicate distance in time and with some attempt at antiquarian accuracy. Brutus, the first conqueror, gave his name to the British, who were the direct ancestors of the Welsh or Cambro-Britons. He was held to have been a Trojan, the great-grandson of Aeneas, most particularly by the Cambro-Britons because, as Selden remarks, of 'that vniuersall desire, bewitching our Europe, to deriue their bloud from Troians, . . .'[2] When Henry Tudor came to the throne his half-Welsh royal blood assumed great political significance for the claim of descent from the ancient British line strongly reinforced that through the House of Lancaster. Prophetic legends were discovered; an '*Eagle* . . . foretold of a reuerting of the crowne, after the *Britons, Saxons,* and *Normans* to the first againe, which in *Hen. VII.* sonne to *Owen Tyddour,* hath beene obserued, as fulfilled':[3] 'an Angelicall voyce' was 'giuen to *Cadwallader* . . . that restitution of the crowne to the *Britons* is promised, . . .'[4] Subsequent Tudor monarchs emphasised their British title. James I's main claim to the throne of England was through Margaret Tudor but he had a further claim to Welsh blood because Fleanch (Fleance), son of Banquo escaped to the court of Llewelyn, Prince of Wales and married his daughter. Their son who became 'L. high *Stewart* of *Scotland*'[5] was founder of the ruling Scottish dynasty.

[1] *Poly-olbion. The Second Part*, p. 163.
[2] Ibid., the first Song. Selden's notes, p. 18.
[3] Ibid., the second Song, p. 35.
[4] Ibid., p. 36.
[5] Ibid., the fifth Song, p. 83.

Drayton accepted the legend of Brutus on the faith of Geoffrey of Monmouth, Matthew of Westminster and Higden's *Polychronicon*, partly perhaps to please his friends the Welsh, to whom he addresses a special epistle at the beginning of *Poly-olbion*. But the story had already been disputed as a poetical fiction in the fifteenth century and was strenuously denied in the sixteenth, notably by Polydore Virgil and Camden. Selden emphatically disbelieved in it. In his preface to the poem he says, 'of their Traditions, for that one so much controuerted and by *Cambro-Britons* still maintayned, touching the *Troian Brute*, I haue (but as an Aduocat for the Muse) argued; disclaiming in it, if alledg'd for my own Opinion.'[1] In his note on Drayton's lines in the first Song defending the story, '*Which now the enuious world doth slander for a dreame*'[2] he again rejects it on his own behalf as a fiction, though citing in justification of his friend Drayton the oldest and best authorities he can find for the story.

The apparel of Brutus seems to be made up from different sources. Part of it may be from some representation of the early fifteenth century as the armour of the arms and the shape of the cuff suggest a date near 1400, and head-rolls such as his were worn on helmets and sometimes on the bare head at about this period;[3] perhaps it was eventually to support a crown as in the woodcut of Brutus in Godet's *Chronicle* of c. 1562.[4] The coat-armour seems to be a smartened version of the rough tunic worn by a 'more civill Britaine' shown in Speed's *History of Great Britaine*, 1611, p. 191. The reader may be meant to understand that Brutus introduced this fashion into Britain where it was generally adopted.

Drayton took the charge of *a lion passant gules* from the fifteenth-century herald Nicholas Upton (1400?–57) whose treatise *Libellus de officio militari* was still unpublished in 1622, but was well known to Selden, who owned two manuscripts of it, one of which he gave to Matthew Hale while the other he lent to Sir Edward Bysshe for his edition of 1654.[5] Upton cites the twelfth-century poet John de Hauteville, known to him as Archithorenius,[6] as his authority for giving the arms of Brutus as *Or, a lion passant gules*. Brutus, he says, later gave

---

[1] Ibid., Sig. A₂.
[2] Ibid., p. 17.
[3] Mr Vesey Norman very kindly gave us this information.
[4] Gyles Godet, . . . *the genealogie and race of all the Kynges of England* (1560–2).
[5] Nicholas Upton, *De Stvdio militari*, London, 1654, preface, *b*.v.
[6] Upton, ed. cit., pp. 126–7.

these arms to his eldest son Locrinus, by whose descendants they were borne to the eighth generation. In his *Illustrations*[1] Selden scornfully remarks of the historians who believe in Brutus that they speak 'so certainly of him, that they blazon his coat to you, *two Lions combatant, and crowned Or in a field gules*; others, *Or, a Lion passant gules*; and lastly, by Doctor *White* of *Basingstoke*, lately liuing at *Doway*, a *Count Palatinate*.'

Yet Selden, while disapproving of the fable of Brutus as unhistorical, loyally assisted Drayton to find an authority for the charge. In a note about it in the margin of the poem Drayton reveals himself impenitent: 'So *Hauillan* [*sic*. i.e. John de Hauteville] & *Vpton* anciently delivered. I iustifie it not; yet, as well as others can his other attributed Arms, I might.' The other version that Selden had in mind and therefore in all probability Drayton also, is that given by the fifteenth-century chronicler John Hardyng, as being borne by Brutus as the ancient arms of Troy:

> He bare of goulis, two liones of golde
> Countre rampant, with golde onely crowned
> Which kynges of Troie inbataill bare full bolde.

Hardyng's chronicle had been printed by Grafton in 1543,[2] but Selden owned a fine manuscript of it which is now in the Bodleian Library (MS. Arch. Selden. B.10).

The head of Caesar is clearly derived ultimately from an antique medal, probably through some literary source such as the *Promptuaire des medailles*. His armour presents no problems, being that of a Roman emperor as understood in the sixteenth and seventeenth centuries. The charge of Venus is explained by the fact that the Julian house claimed descent from the goddess through Aeneas her son. In the marginal note to his poem on the title-page Drayton justifies this blazon against possible critics.[3]

> Obiect not, that it should be the *Eagle*, because it is now borne by the Emperors; and that some Heralds ignorantly publish it, as I. *Caesars* Coat, *Double-headed*. They moue me not; for plainly the *Eagle* was single at that time . . . and but newly vs'd among the *Romans* (first by *Marius*) as their *Standard*, not otherwise, vntill afterward *Constantine* made it respect the two Empires: and since,

---

[1] *Poly-olbion*, p. 18.
[2] Hardyng, *Chronicle*, ed. Ellis, London, 1812, p. 39.
[3] Ibid., Drayton's notes to the verses, 'Vpon the *Frontispice*'.

it hath been borne on a Shield. I tooke *Venus* proper to him, for that the stamp of hir face (she being his Ancestor *Æneas* his mother) in his Coins is frequent, and can so maintaine it here fitter, then many of those inuented Coats (without colour of reason) attributed to the old Heroes. As for the matter of Armory, *Venus* being a Goddesse may be as good Bearing, if not better then *Atalanta*, which by expresse Authority of *Euripides*, was borne, in the Theban warre by *Parthenopaeus*.

Drayton may have learnt that Julius Caesar frequently used a profile head of Venus on his coins from Du Choul, who illustrates two examples in his *Discours de la religion des anciens Romains* (first edn, 1554). But the figure of Venus holding a flaming heart which he has chosen to show on Caesar's shield is not a classical image and must be a Renaissance invention from the tradition of courtly love. Gilles Corrozet in his *Hecatongraphie* of 1543 shows Venus holding a heart and wreath together with Eros; the motto reads, 'Amour accompaignée de vertu'.

The costume of Hengist may be based on an illustration in a manuscript in Cotton's collection, a copy of the *Psychomachia* by Prudentius[1] which contains Anglo-Saxon. If indeed this manuscript was used as a source, Drayton or his advisers assumed, correctly, that the armour represented was contemporary with the writing. The helmet with comb has been given a slight resemblance to a sixteenth-century morion by tilting up the brim in front and the javelin has been replaced by a spetum with simplified lateral blades. A horse is shown on his shield because, 'His name expresses a *Horse*, and the Dukes of *Saxony* are said to haue borne it anciently, before their Christianity, *Sable*.'[2] This information was probably gathered from Crantzius' history of the Saxons (*Saxonia* . . ., 1574, lib. II, p. 81) where he states that their insignia was a horse, black when they were heathen, changed to white on their conversion. Nevertheless the horse on the title-page is white, possibly due to a mistake by the engraver. Camden in the *Britannia* (p. 135) suggests that the Saxons who were very superstitious may have taken the neighing of horses as a portent and that Hengist and Horsa took their names from a horse as a token of their warlike prowess. He quotes the line from the *Aeneid*,

Bello armantur equi, bellum haec armenta minantur (III.540)

[1] BL, MS. Cleop. C.VIII, f. 30.
[2] Drayton's notes to the verses, 'Vpon the *Frontispice*'.

for which he gives the translation,

> For warre our horses armed are,
> These beasts also do threaten warre.

The verses 'Vpon the *Frontispice*' say of William the Conqueror that his 'Line yet rules'; this is a clear affirmation of Plantagenet rights. William wears an anime of the late sixteenth century—almost contemporary. His crown is a pastiche of St Edward's crown with which sovereigns of England have traditionally been crowned since the time of Edward the Confessor; but the fleurs-de-lys, originally trefoils, which alternate with crosses on St Edward's crown have been omitted, possibly because Drayton did not want to imply that William had a claim to the French throne. The unsheathed sword shows him prepared. The blazon of his arms as '*Norman Leopards bath'd in Gules*' Drayton justifies in a marginal note as, 'The common Blazon of the *Norman* Armes'[1] and in the *Illustrations* to the eleventh Song of *Poly-olbion* Selden has a long excursus on leopards as the ancient 'Coate of England' in annotation to Drayton's line, '*Our Leopards they so long and bravely did advance*'.[2] In this he refutes 'the common blazon of it, by name of Lions', and the statement of Polydore Virgil (book 9, at end) that William the Conqueror's arms were 'three *Fleurs de lis*, and *three lions*, as quartred for one Coat'.[3] To prove that the ancient coat of England was three leopards Selden cites Matthew Paris and a manuscript of Gower's *Confessio Amantis* as well as two grants of the right to bear royal arms made by Edward IV and Henry VI. From this note of Selden's it is clear that by Jacobean times the leopards of the Middle Ages had been replaced by lions,[4] and Drayton must have been guided by his friend's antiquarian learning in giving William a coat historically accurate, rather than that which the early seventeenth century popularly, but anachronistically, believed to be his.

The *delicacies of the Sea* which make up the swags are described in Song XX:[5]

> Of Currall of each kind, the blacke, the red, the white;
> With many sundry shels, the Scallop large, and faire;

---

[1] Drayton's notes to the verses, 'Vpon the *Frontispice*'.
[2] *Poly-olbion*, p. 172.
[3] Ibid., p. 181–2.
[4] See John Guillim, *A Displaye of Heraldrie*, 1610, p. 280.
[5] *Poly-olbion, The Second Part*, p. 13.

The Cockle small and round, the Periwinkle spare,
The Oyster, wherein oft the pearle is found to breed,
The Mussell, which retaines that daintie Orient seed:

The ball and flame ornament and the obelisks are monuments to posterity, likewise the sprigs of laurel on either side of the author's name.

Dum indico vol...

EXTRA

INTVS

THE
Compleat Gentleman
Fashioning him absolute in the
most necessary & commendable
Qualities concerning Minde or
Bodie that may be required
in a Noble Gentleman.

By
Henry Peacham,
Mr of Arts

Sometime of Trinity Coll:
in Cambridge.

— inutilis olim

Ne videar vixisse—

Anno 1622

Imprinted at London
for Francis Constable
and are to bee sold at
his shop at the white ho
in Paules churchyard

Ex Delaram.

Sculp. Anno 162

14

HENRY PEACHAM

The Compleat Gentleman

1622

(Hind, II. Francis Delaram, no. 42)

Within the aperture of an arch is the title THE/*Compleat Gentleman*/ *Fashioning him absolute in the/most necessary & commendable/Qualities concerning Minde or/Bodie that may be required/in a Noble Gentlemã./By/ Henry Peacham./Mr. of Arts/Sometime of Trinity Coll:/in Cambridge./— inutilis olim/Ne videar vixisse—/Anno 1622.* On the plinth of the arch to the left stands the figure of Nobility (identified by the inscription NOBILITAS on the cornice above). She wears an Earl's coronet and a long, sleeved robe under an ermine-bordered, short-sleeved robe of floral brocade cut to resemble a herald's tabard. Round her neck hangs the riband and Lesser George of the Order of the Garter. In her right hand, she holds a rod with black ends, in her left a shield blazoned with the arms of Howard, 'gules, a bend between 6 cross crosslets, fitchée, argent', and surmounted by an Earl's coronet. On the plinth to the right, raised on a small pedestal, stands Knowledge (identified by the inscription SCIENTIA on the cornice above). With her right hand she supports an open book and holds a branch of olive: in her left she holds a radiant sun. From a cloud above her head drops of rain are falling. Above Nobility's section of the arch flies a winged putto holding a scroll inscribed EXTRA ('without') above a military trophy— a banner, a partisan, a leading staff with a tassel, a cannon, helmet, breast-plate, drum, trumpet and cannon-balls. Above Learning's section a second putto holding a scroll inscribed INTUS ('within') flies above emblems of learning—a musical instrument (recorder or shawm?), a palette and brushes, a scale, a set-square, a globe, a pair of compasses standing point downwards on the books inscribed on the edge: PLVTARCH, THVCID:, TACITVS. Over the centre of the arch is an oval frame enclosing an emblem, a buoy with a rope floating in heaving waves of a narrow strait between high pointed rocks, with the device *Dum indico voluor* (while I indicate I am turned). In the recess of the plinth is an oblong with the imprint: *Imprinted at London/for Francis Constable/ and are to bee sold at/ his shop at the white liõ./ in Paules church-yard.* On the base of the plinth to left and right is the signature of the engraver *Er. (sic) Delaram. Sculp. Anno 1622.*

Henry Peacham[1] (1576–c. 1644) by profession a private tutor and schoolmaster, was also an enthusiastic amateur artist, a framer of devices and emblems, a poet and author. He is notable as the principal mouth-piece in Jacobean times of the Renaissance belief that 'Learning is an essentiall part of nobilitie' and as a writer of practical manuals on the arts and sciences necessary to a gentleman, most notably and frequently on the art of painting, in fulfilment of this ideal. Among his patrons were Prince Henry and Thomas Howard, Earl of Arundel, and his books voice attitudes current in their exceptionally cultivated circles. Peacham believed that a fit education for a nobleman and gentleman should comprise not only bodily exercise and military training, but also a knowledge of history and an 'in-sight into the most pleasing and admirable Sciences of the Mathematiques, Poetrie, Picture, Heraldrie, &c.' It was not necessary for a man of birth to know these arts with the thoroughness of those who professed them: it was enough to know as much as was useful and ornamental. He defends these doctrines with arguments that had become standard since their first appearance in Castiglione's *Cortegiano*: 'the Fountaine of all Counsell and Instruc-tion', he declares, 'next to the feare of God is the knowledge of good learning, whereby our affections are perswaded and our ill manners mollified.'[2] The ignorance of English gentlemen is a reproach to them, especially abroad, and he tells an anecdote of Monsieur de Ligny interrogating an impoverished young English gentleman who wanted to enter his household. Finding the young man knew nothing, the French nobleman turned to Peacham and said, 'See . . . how your Gentry of *England* are bred: that when they are distressed, or want means in a strange Countrey, they are brought up neither to any qualitie to preferre them, nor haue they so much as the Latine tongue

---

[1] For Peacham see the *DNB*, s.v., and the introduction by G. S. Gordon to the Clarendon Press reprint of *The Compleat Gentleman* (1906).

[2] These two quotations are from 'The Epistle Dedicatory' of *The Compleat Gentleman·*

to helpe themselues withall.' Peacham attributes the cause of this dis-creditable ignorance to 'the remissnesse of Parents, and the negligence of Masters'.[1]

The Compleat Gentleman, first published in 1622 and often reprinted until 1661, is dedicated to the eleven-year-old William Howard (1611–1680), later Lord Stafford, the second surviving son of Peacham's patron, Thomas Howard, Earl of Arundel and now Earl Marshal of England.[2] Originally, so Peacham says, it was written for Howard's private instruction. The book is a sort of schoolmaster's *Cortegiano*. In it Peacham explains with polished grace the kinds of knowledge that are proper to a young gentleman—history, cosmography, geometry, poetry, music, classical antiquities, drawing and painting, heraldry, exercise of the body and in the military arts. Each is defined, each has its usefulness explained and lauded, and each is made to sound as attractive as possible. Some rudiments of all these subjects are imparted, for as Peacham explains, the book is intended 'for a young and shallow capacity'. Some of the studies he recommends, especially painting, poetry and music, were generally disdained in England as either un-necessary or unbecoming to a gentleman, and Peacham is careful to remove such prejudices, usually by citing instances of great princes and noblemen who have not thought it beneath their dignity to practise them.

The theme of the title-page[3] is this necessary conjunction of nobility and knowledge. On it Nobility is assigned the place of honour on the left, as it is in the text, where Peacham gives it his first chapter. He defines nobility as

the Honour of blood in a Race or Linage, conferred formerly vpon some one or more of that Family, either by the Prince, the Lawes, customes of that Land or Place, whereby either out of knowledge, culture of the mind, or by some glorious Action performed, they haue been vsefull and beneficiall to the Common-wealths and places where they liue.

He explains that this last condition is essential, because 'all Vertue consisteth in Action' and those leading a contemplative, retired life are

---

[1] From the preface 'to my Reader'.

[2] For all matters connected with Thomas Howard and his office of Earl Marshal, see M. F. S. Hervey, *The Life, Correspondence and Collections of Thomas Howard Earl of Arundel*, Cambridge, 1921.

[3] The title-page is discussed in Hind, II, pp. 237–8, no. 42, with an account of altera-tions in later editions.

hardly 'to be admitted for noble'.[1] Hence those who fight valorously
for their country, even if born of mean parents, deserve the nobility
which they have earned for themselves, as do those who rise by means
of their studies, their knowledge of law, their magnificent gifts, or their
eloquence if these benefit their country.

Peacham was an experienced contriver of devices, having published
a whole volume of them in 1612, with explanatory verses, entitled
*Minerva Britanna or a Garden of Heroical Deuises, furnished, and adorned
with Emblemes and Impresa's of sundry natures, Newly devised, moralized,
and published.* Understanding well the possibilities of the form for
multiple meanings, he has given his figure of Nobility attributes which
are a compliment to his patron, Lord Arundel, as well as an illustration
of its principal meaning. She wears the coronet of an Earl and carries
a staff in allusion to Arundel's office of Earl Marshal, and on her left
arm carries the arms of Howard surmounted by a coronet in allusion
to his earldom of Arundel and Surrey.[2] Round her neck is the Lesser
George of the Garter. Arundel was given the baton of Earl Marshal on
21 July 1621: by a patent dated 29 August he formally received the
right to carry this 'golden stick engraved with the King's arms and his
own'.[3] Peacham and his engraver have correctly shown it with the
black ends that are proper to it. The title-page must therefore have been
designed after this date.

The upper dress of Nobility is an adaptation to woman's dress of the
tabard cut, enriched more than a real tabard would have been to suit
the dignity of Nobility. Its form is intended to suggest the importance
of heraldry to nobility. Peacham wrote more than once on heraldry, or
as he calls it 'Armorie or Blazon of Armes'.

> How should we giue Nobilitie her true value, respect and title,
> without notice of her Merit: and how may we guesse her merit,
> without these outward ensignes and badges of Vertue, which
> anciently haue beene accounted sacred and precious; withall,
> discerne and know an intruding vpstart, shot vp with the last
> nights Mushrome, from an ancient descended & deseruing
> Gentleman. . . .

And he praises the Earls Marshal of the last few years for having taken

---

[1] *The Compleat Gentleman*, 1622, p. 2.

[2] On the title-page the star on the bend, proper to Arundel's arms, is omitted, but it is
shown on the woodcut version of the arms in the 1622 edition, f.A2v.

[3] PRO, *Calendar of State Papers Domestic*, 1619–23, p. 281. For advice on the tabard
worn by *Nobilitas* we should like to thank Mr J. L. Nevinson.

steps to remedy the present 'intrusion by adding or diminishing into ancient families and houses'.[1] In giving his figure the attributes of Earl Marshal and a heraldic tabard, he may well have had in mind the role of the Earl Marshal as head of the Court of Chivalry and of the heralds of England, in other words, as guardian of authentic ancient nobility. Finally, Peacham's conception that it is the duty of a man of noble birth to lead an active life in the service of his country, above all as a soldier in the battlefield, is symbolised by the military trophy above. The winged putto with the motto EXTRA flying above indicates that such are the outward adornments of nobility.

Of knowledge, Peacham explains:[2]

Since learning then ioyned with the feare of God, is so faithfull a guide, that without it Princes vndergoe but lamely (as *Chrysostome* saith) their greatest affaires; they are blinde in discretion, ignorant in knowledge, rude and barbarous in manners and liuing: the necessitie of it in Princes and Nobilitie, may easily be gathered, who howsoeuer they flatter themselues, with the fauourable Sunshine of their great Estates and Fortunes, are indeede of no other account and reckoning with men of wisedome and vnderstanding than Glowormes that onely shine in the darke of Ignorance, and are admired of Ideots and the vulgar for the out-side; *Statues or Huge Colossos full of Lead and rubbish within* [in margin, *Plutarch, Alciat. in Emblem*], or the *Aegyptian* Asse, that thought himself worshipfull for bearing golden *Isis* vpon his backe.

And in the dedicatory epigram to Sir William Howard, he says of his book:

> *Ingenio, genio, dum vis Generosus haberi,*
> *Ingenua haec discas, ingeniose puer.*
> *Stemma nihil, cultis animum nisi moribus ornes,*
> *Et studeas studijs nobilitare genus.*

(If you wish to be regarded as one nobly born in wit and nature, learn these ingenuous things, ingenious boy. Noble ancestry is nothing, unless you adorn your mind with cultivated manners and study by your studies to ennoble your race.)[3]

[1] Edition of 1622, pp. 138–9.

[2] Ibid., p. 20.

[3] Ibid., A2v. The epigram is pointed by being placed below the woodcut of the Howard arms (cf. p. 166 note 2).

Peacham has devised his figure of SCIENTIA with the help of motifs drawn from Ripa, whose *Iconologia*, first published in 1593, and first reissued with illustrations in 1603, he certainly knew, if only because he draws on it, with and without acknowledgment, for both the text and the images of his *Minerva Brittanna*. In his 'heroicall devise' of *Doctrina* in this earlier book (p. 26) he has simply copied without acknowledgment the woodcut of *Dottrina* from the 1603 edition of Ripa, showing her as a middle-aged woman, seated with open book on her lap and with outspread arms, holding a sceptre topped by a sun in her right hand.[1] Upon her falls a shower of rain. In the verses beneath he embodies Ripa's explanation of his figure:

HEERE Learning sits, a comely Dame in yeares;
Vpon whose head, a heavenly dew doth fall:
Within her lap, an opened booke appeares:
Her right hand shewes, a sunne that shines to all;
   Blind Ignorance, expelling with that light:
   The Scepter shewes, her power and soveraigne might.

Her out spread Armes, and booke her readines,
T'imbrace all men, and entertaine their loue:
The shower, those sacred graces doth expresse
By Science, that do flow from heaven aboue.
   Her age declares the studie, and the paine;
   Of many yeares, ere we our knowledge gaine.

Peacham has devised a new figure of SCIENTIA for the frontispiece of *The Compleat Gentleman* by combining elements from Ripa's descriptions of *Sapienza* and *Dottrina*, so that the figure becomes a representation of both wisdom and learning. In herself the figure is Ripa's verbal personification of *Sapienza vera* as 'a woman almost naked', with her feet on a pedestal to represent Ripa's concept that *Sapienza vera* has her feet above the ground because she is absorbed in God and above earthly things. But instead of representing her like Ripa as looking upwards to a light shining down from above, Peacham has given her the olive-branch of Minerva. Ripa mentions this attribute under his last entry for *Sapienza* in discussing why the ancients took Minerva with an olive-branch as the type of wisdom, and explains that

---

[1] For the relevant passages and woodcut of *Dottrina* see C. Ripa, *Iconologia*, Rome, 1603 (reprinted with introduction by E. Mandowsky, 1970), p. 113. The emblem of *Doctrina* appears on p. 26 of *Minerva Brittanna*.

the olive-branch signifies the exterior and interior peace that springs from wisdom. Peacham has also given his figure the open book of Ripa's *Dottrina*, once more to show wisdom's readiness to 'entertaine' all men, and *Dottrina*'s radiant sun, the light with which she expels ignorance. And lastly he has set her beneath the shower of rain of *Dottrina* to display the 'sacred graces' which flow from Heaven 'by Science'. Ripa drew this last figure from Horapollo, who explains that the Egyptians used it to signify learning because dew softens young plants and hardens old ones: thus learning enriches those who incline to her and leaves the ignorant aside.[1]

The instruments above signify the various arts a gentleman should know—the recorder or shawm for music, the palette and brushes for painting, the scale, set-square and compasses for geometry, the globe for cosmography. Peacham recommends the study of geometry for its usefulness in surveying estates, in building, for supervising measures, and above all for military purposes.[2]

> Againe, should you follow the warres . . . you cannot without Geometry fortifie your selfe, take the aduantage of hill or leuell, fight, order your Battaglia in square, triangle, crosse . . . leuell, and plant your Ordinance, vndermine, raise your halfe Moones, Bulwarkes, Casamates, Rampires, Rauesins, with many other meanes as of offence and defence, by fortification. So that I cannot see how a Gentleman, especially a Souldier and Commander may be accomplished without Geometrie, though not to the heighth of perfection, yet at the least to be grounded and furnished with the principles and priuie rules heereof.

The three books are among the authors Peacham recommends in his chapter on good style in speaking and writing on history. Tacitus, in accordance with the admiration of his age for this author's powerful condensed style and penetrating analyses of character and statecraft, he ranks as 'the Prince of Historians . . . so copious in pleasing breuitie, each Sentence carrying with it a kind of loftie State and Maiestie, such as should (me think) proceed from the mouth of Greatnesse and Command; in sense retired, deepe, and not fordable to the ordinarie Reader'.[3] Tacitus is cited as an example of 'vniversall Historie . . .

[1] For *Sapienza* see Ripa, ed. cit., pp. 441–3.
[2] Edition of 1622, p. 77.
[3] Ibid., pp. 46–7.

which entreateth of the beginning, increase, gouernment, and altera-
tions of Monarchies, Kingdomes, and Common-wealths'. Thucydides,
called by Peacham 'Noble and eloquent', appears as an author of
'speciall Historie, that reporteth the affaires and gouernment of
particular Estates'.[1] Peacham attached special importance to the study
of history, both for pleasure and instruction by example:[2]

> No subiect affecteth vs with more delight then *Historie*, imprinting
> a thousand formes vpon our imaginations, from the circumstances
> of Place, Person, Time, Matter, manner and the like. And, *what can
> be more profitable* (saith an ancient Historian [in margin *Diodorus
> Sicula*]) *then sitting on the Stage of humane life, to be made wise by
> their example, who haue trod the path of error and danger before vs*?

In Plutarch, like all Renaissance moralists and educators, Peacham
saw a treasury of guidance and example for noble conduct.[3]

> For Moralitie and rules of well liuing, deliuered with such
> sententious grauitie, weight of reason, so sweetened with liuely &
> apt similitudes, entertaine *Plutarch*; whom according to the opinion
> of *Gaza* the world would preserue, (should it be put to the choice
> to receiue one onely Authour (the Sacred Scriptures excepted) and
> to burne all the rest) especially his *Liues* and *Morals*.

This extraordinary reverence for Plutarch is no doubt what is expressed
by his being set topmost on the other two. The winged putto with the
motto INTUS indicates that the arts and sciences below are to be the
inward adornments of the mind.

The emblem of a buoy in a stormy strait appears nowhere else in
emblem literature and seems to have been invented by Peacham
especially for the title-page of *The Compleat Gentleman*. The motto
indicates its meaning: the buoy marks the channel through a narrow
strait while tossed on the flood. The allusion must be to Peacham himself, since it clearly has no relation to his theme. Its likeliest explanation
is to be found in his circumstances when he wrote the book. He tells
us these in his preface *To my reader*. 'Being taken through change of
ayre with a Quartane Feuer, that leasure I had ἀπὸ παροξυσμοῦ (*in my
attacks*), as I may truly say, by fits I employed upon this Discourse.'
And in his chapter on style and history he remarks that[4]

[1] Ibid., p. 50.
[2] Ibid., pp. 51–2.
[3] Ibid., p. 52.
[4] Ibid., Sig. B$_2$, p. 52.

Bodin tells vs of some, who haue recouered their healthes by reading of Historie; and it is credibly affirmed of King *Alphonsus,* that the onely reading of *Quint. Curtius,* cured him of a very dangerous feuer. If I could haue beene so rid of my late quartane ague, I would haue said with the same good King: *Valeat Avicenna, viuat Curtius* [Farewell Avicenna, long live Curtius].

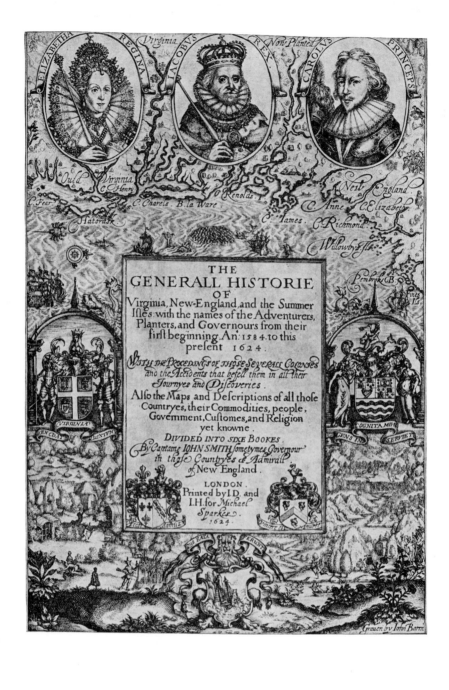

THE
GENERALL HISTORIE
OF
Virginia, New-England, and the Summer
Isles: with the names of the Adventurers,
Planters, and Governours from their
first beginning. An: 1584. to this
present 1624.

With the Proceedings of those Severall Colonies
and the Accidents that befell them in all their
Journyes and Discoveries.

Also the Maps and Descriptions of all those
Countryes, their Commodities, people,
Government, Customes, and Religion
yet knowne.

DIVIDED INTO SIXE BOOKES.

By Captaine IOHN SMITH sometymes Governour
in those Countryes & Admirall
of New England.

LONDON.
Printed by I.D. and
I.H. for Michael
Sparkes.
1624.

15

CAPTAIN JOHN SMITH

The Generall Historie of Virginia, New-England, and the Summer Isles . . .

1624

(Hind, III. Jan Barrà, no. 10)

At the top of the title-page[1] are the oval medallion portraits of Elizabeth, James and Charles; their titles on simple scrolls above, ELIZABETHA REGINA., IACOBVS REX., CAROLVS PRINCEPS. The three medallions are superimposed on a rough map of the eastern parts of North America, showing the coast of North Carolina to Maine. It is oriented with north on the right-hand side as indicated by the windrose, left. Two great rivers, the James and the Hudson, divide it vertically. At the centre top is the inscription, *Virginia Now Planted*; inland from the coast, l., *Ould Virginia* and r., *New England*. On the map are marked *C. Fear., Hatorask., C. Henry.*, and *C. Charels., B. la Ware., Renolds. I., C. Iames., C. Anne., C. Richmond., C. Elizabeth., Willowbys Ils., Pembroks B., Fines Ils.* On the headlands west of C. Fear are symbols marking the royal houses of the Indians and the houses of the common Indians;[2] along both sides of the James River, the habitations of the settlers, churches, halls and houses; on the upper reaches, two circular Indian villages and two houses surrounded by palisades; further north more Indian houses scattered about; along the banks of the Hudson, Indian houses, a circular village and two palisaded houses; in New England, Indian houses, one palisaded and a village; two symbols marking settlers' houses and a church. Extreme l., a tobacco

---

[1] *The Generall Historie of Virginia* . . . 1624, BL Grenville 7037 has been used, henceforth referred to as *Generall Historie*.

[2] *Generall Historie*; the map of Virginia marked 'Page 41', inserted before p. 1. The key.

plant with a parrot perched among its leaves; extreme r., perched on a tree, a bird with curved beak and broad square-ended tail, probably a falcon; a little lower on the right, a vine bearing bunches of grapes. West of *C. Iames*, a furry animal crouching low with head on the ground, and broad hairless tail, the American beaver. In the waters off the coast of *Ould Virginia* an Indian canoe with two men paddling, another smaller off *C. Iames*; wrecks off the coast round *Hatorask*, and under water, a King Crab and a Hammer-headed Shark. In the centre of the sea area a large shoal of fish with a sea monster on either side; further r., possibly a dolphin, lower down a large sea monster, and r., a whale with two spouts. Extreme l., a fleet of four merchant vessels all flying flags marked with St George's Cross; towards the centre, a pinnace set with foresail, one bank of three oars and a steering oar; r., a single merchant vessel showing the St George's Cross from the main mast; bottom r., another three-masted merchant vessel.

In the centre, on a simply framed panel, the title THE/ GENERALL HISTORIE/OF/Virginia, New-England, and the Summer/Isles: with the names of the Adventurers,/Planters, and Governours from their/first beginning An°:1584. to this/present 1624. /*WITH THE PROCEDINGS OF THOSE SEVERALL COLONIES* /*and the Accidents that befell them in all their/Journyes and Discoveries.*/ Also the Maps and Descriptions of all those/Countryes, their Commodities, people,/Government, Customes, and Religion/yet knowne./ *DIVIDED INTO SIXE BOOKES.*/By *Captaine IOHN SMITH some-tymes Governour/in those Countryes & Admirall/of* New England. Below, the imprint, LONDON./Printed by I.D. and/I.H. for *Michael/Sparkes.*/ *1624.* On either side of the imprint, a coat of arms; l., 'per pale three fleurs de lys, impaling arg. on a bend engrailed, three garbs'; crests, 'dexter a fleur de lys, sinister, out of a mural crown a talbot's head'; motto, *Accordamus*; r., 'arg. a chevron az. and or, between three Turks' heads'; crest, an ostrich with horse-shoe in its beak; motto, *Vincere est viuere.*

Flanking the tablet carrying the title are two arches surmounted by obelisks and supported by Corinthian columns. They enclose l., the coat of Virginia, 'az. St George's Cross quartering the arms of England, France, Scotland and Ireland'; crest, the bust of a maiden queen with flowing hair and eastern crown; supporters, two men in armour, beavers open, helmets ornamented with feathers, each holding a lance; motto, *EN DAT/VIRGINIA/QUINTVM* [regnum] (Lo, Virginia gives a fifth kingdom); r., the coat of the Council for New England, 'az. three barry wavy', the engraver's markings cut in imitation of waves; in chief, the coat of the royal house of Stuart; crest, Neptune on a hippocamp; supporters, two female figures, l., naked to the waist with classical garment draped round her body, carrying a large book under her right arm, a crested broad-tailed bird on her shoulder, symbolising Wisdom; r., swathed in a classical gown, carrying in her left hand dividers and a set-square, symbolising Architecture; motto, *GENS IN/COGNITA MIHI/SERVIET* (an unknown people shall serve me). Below, the coat of the Bermudas or Summer Isles, 'a lion sejant affronté' supporting between the fore-paws an antique shield, thereon a representation of the wreck of the ship the *Sea Venture*; motto, *QUO FATA FERUNT* (Whither the Fates carry us). Below the arches, a landscape with wooded hills and valleys, streams and pools; it is inhabited only by Indians several of whose royal houses[1] appear, left. They are seen hunting the deer, shooting duck from a canoe and fetching water; a warrior group with bows and arrows, extreme right, and the left towards the centre, beside a grove of palms, the solitary figure of a warrior with bow and arrow and quiver. A tobacco plant further to the left. Signed bottom r., *Grauen by Iohn Barrà*.

John Smith wrote several pamphlets about Virginia and New England, whose main purpose was to encourage people to become settlers in the young colonies. *The Generall Historie*, a far more ambitious work, appeared in 1624 at a time when the whole question of the government of Virginia was at issue. There had been a massacre by the Indians and a famine which was laid at the doors of those managing affairs. Smith was strongly of the opinion that the Crown should assume responsibility of government and testified to this effect before the Commissioners at the enquiry which was held in London. But in spite of the immediate crisis he never lost sight of the ultimate goal, the creation of great British colonies in North America. He lays out his thoughts in 'A Preface of foure Poynts'.[2]

> *This plaine History humbly sheweth the truth; that our most royall*
> *King* Iames *hath place and opportunitie to inlarge his ancient*
> *Dominions without wronging any; . . . and the Prince his* Highness *may*
> *see where to plant new* Colonies. *The gaining Prouinces addeth to the*
> *Kings Crown: but the reducing Heathen people to ciuilitie and true*

---

[1] T. de Bry, *America*, I, 1590. *A brief and true report of the new found land of Virginia . . .* by Thomas Hariot, facsimile reproduction, 1972, plates XIX, XX.

[2] Preface, following 'The Epistle Dedicatory'.

Religion, bringeth honour to the King of Heauen. If his Princely wisedome and powerfull hand, . . . please but to set these new Estates into order; their composure will be singular: . . . nothing but the touch of the Kings sacred hand can erect a Monarchy.

There is internal evidence to show that the *Historie* was rushed through publication in order that its influence might be felt in the days of decision.[1]

The engraved title-page gives pictorial expression to Smith's thesis. The royal portraits are at the top in their rightful position; the coats of arms of the three colonies are grouped below them. The backdrop is in two parts; the upper half a map, conveying what was known of the new countries; in contrast the lower half is a fictional landscape of valleys, groves and woods giving a romantic impression of them. Together they suggest the illimitable wealth in trade and land which lay waiting for development.

From the first the newly discovered territories were held to belong to the Crown; under the portrait of Elizabeth by Crispin van de Passe of 1592[2] runs the inscription '*Elizabet D.G. Ang. Fran. Hib. et Verg. [iniae] Regina . . .*' which occurs unabbreviated under the full-length portrait of 1596,[3] under the posthumous engraving of 1603,[4] which is the one adapted here by Barrà, and as late as 1632 under a version engraved by Hendrik Hondius II.[5] Neither James nor Charles adopted the royal style of King of Virginia. The portrait of James is taken from the engraved frontispiece to his *Workes* which carries the inscription, 'BEATI PACIFICI:'[6] and indeed under him matters were resolved. After a famous case the charter of the Virginia Company was terminated and in August 1624 Virginia became the royal colony. Prince Charles was already associated with New England which he named in 1614 at the request of Smith, who also entreated him to change the 'barbarous names [then in use] for such English, as posteritie might say [he] was their God-father, . . .'.[7] The portrait of him is not one of the standard types of this period, but it is certainly very up-to-date as he wears a beard which he is thought not to have grown until 1624.

---

[1] Philip Barbour, *The Three Worlds of Captain John Smith*, 1964, pp. 367f.
[2] Hind, I, plate 146a.
[3] Ibid., plate 144.
[4] Ibid., plate 141.
[5] Hollstein, IX, H. Hondius II, no. 44.
[6] Hind, II plate 154.
[7] *Generall Historie*, p. 205.

Possibly the source is a small drawing or miniature.[1] In state 4 (edition of 1626) he wears a crown and the inscription is *Carolus Rex*.

The impact of the coats of Virginia and the New England Council is enhanced by the gateways which frame them. These imposing structures topped by monumental obelisks imply stability and a building for posterity. Perhaps they are also intended to suggest the halls of government whether in England or America. The *State house in St. George Towne* in the Somer Isles had itself a Renaissance portal and gateway.[2] Smith was well aware of the significance of the other part of colonial rule, now in its very beginning. To the description of 'a generall Assembly', which was held in Jamestown in 1619, he adds the rubric 'Their time of Parliament';[3] again, 'A generall assemblie' held in 1620 in St George was 'in manner a Parliament'.[4] The sketch for the coat of Virginia is in existence.[5] It was made in 1619 or not much later, probably by Henry St George, Richmond Herald. Though never granted to the Company it was adopted by the Colony.[6] The engraving of it differs only in a few details from the sketch. Possibly this was the first time that the coat was reproduced in copper or woodcut. The figure of the crest has been variously interpreted; in the drawing the maiden wears a contemporary bodice; in Barrà's version she is naked to the waist and her hair hangs wildly about her; in the cut shown in Stow's *Survey of the cities of London and Westminster* . . .,[7] 1633, her breasts appear through her gown and her crown is entwined with berries; she seems to be a symbol of Virginia, a barbaric princess in her eastern crown. The supporters with their crusaders' crosses on their armour obviously express a missionary purpose; the charge of St George's cross may have the same meaning or it may be a complimentary allusion to the City of London which was necessarily involved in the affairs of the Company. The motto in the sketch has '*quintam*' [*coronam*] and this is the form in which the motto was most frequently used in the seventeenth century; after the Act of Union of 1707 it became '*quartum*'. In the coat of the Council for New England the 'three barry wavy' indicate the sea, so the blazon represents another

[1] Information kindly given by Sir Oliver Millar, KCVO, Keeper of the Queen's Pictures.

[2] *Generall Historie*, illustration between pp. 168 and 169.

[3] Ibid., p. 126.

[4] Ibid., p. 194.

[5] BL, MS. Harleian 6860, f. 7.

[6] Peter Walne, 'A Cote for Virginia', *Virginia Cavalcade*, summer 1959.

[7] Book 5, p. 268.

kingdom across the Atlantic. The motif of the sea is repeated in the crest. For the supporters the designer had presumably consulted Ripa's *Iconologia*[1] in which *Wisdom* is said to be nude except for a light covering—she has no need of ornament since she has every good in herself. This allegory of Wisdom corresponds to Faith and not to Learning and her being is directed towards the contemplation of God. Her book must therefore be the Bible. *Architecture* carries the dividers and set-square of geometry since from mathematics every craft derives its dignity. Her arms are bare and her sleeves rolled up to show the active nature of her craft. The bird perched on the shoulder of Wisdom, seen also on the larger version of the coat on the map of New England at p. 222, is recognisable by its profile as the Eastern Cardinal as represented in John White's famous drawings; it has the upstanding crest, square tail, though rather shorter than in the original, and broad-based short beak of these birds. The drawing had so far not been reproduced but the designer could have seen it in the original or in the copy made between 1593 and 1614.[2] The motto expresses the hope that the Indians would willingly become the subjects of the British crown, at this date within the bounds of possibility; indeed in 1621 nine chiefs put their marks to a document swearing loyalty to King James, the ceremony taking place in New Plymouth before the Governor. Until 1615 the Bermudas belonged to the Virginia Company. They were then sold to the 'Governour and Company of the City of London for the Plantacion of the Somer Islands'—the Somer Islands Company. The *Sea Venture* met disaster when she was carrying Sir George Somers, one of the commanders of a fleet of ships bound for Virginia; she was struck some miles out but Somers kept her afloat and 'by Gods Prouidence [she] escaped the rockes, till they gat within halfe a mile of the shoare, where shee stucke fast between two rockes.'[3] Her position is shown driving onto the rocks. The motto is adapted from Virgil's 'incerti quo fata ferant' (uncertain are we whither the fates may carry us). In the engraving[4] of the coat in Speed's *Prospect of the most famous Parts of the World*, 1627, the lion rests on a green mound, here replaced by the natural terrain depicted in the landscape.

The map of *Virginia Now Planted* combines features from the maps

---

[1] Ripa, *Iconologia*, 1611, pp. 26, 468f.

[2] Paul Hulton and David Beers Quinn, *The American Drawings of John White*, 1964, 2 vols. Vol. I, Introduction, pp. 24ff, no. 80 A.

[3] John Speed, *A Prospect of the most famous Parts of the World. . . . The Description of the Sommer Ilands . . .*, 1627, p. 41.

[4] Ibid., map following p. 41.

of Virginia and New England included in the book, with the Dutch
territories between roughed in. It is distorted to fit the exigencies of
the design. Only a few names appear, selected either for their notoriety,
like Cape Fear and Cape Hatorask; or because they commemorate the
names past and present of members of the royal house and the noblemen who were members of the Virginia Council or the Council for
New England; or are connected with Smith himself. *Ould Virginia*
includes that part of North Carolina where Raleigh's captains first
made attempts at colonisation; Cape Fear was a dreaded place to early
mariners; Hatorask, on the dangerous outer shoals of North Carolina,
was the scene of eight drownings in 1589; in John White's map showing
The arrival of the Englishmen in Virginia of 1590[1] there are the wrecks
shown off the coast which were copied by Barrà; Cape Henry and
Cape Charles, the promontories on either side of Chesapeake Bay were
named after the then Prince of Wales and the Duke of York; *B. La
Ware* after Thomas West, Lord De La Warr, Governor of Virginia in
1610 under whom Virginia first became a settled plantation; the name
reappears in a map of 1650[2]—*Delaware River*; the term 'State of Delaware' was first used in 1792. *Renolds I.* is a puzzle; it does not appear
on other maps of the period nor later; there was a Henry Reignolds
Esq. and a Iohn Reignolds listed among the 'Names of Adventurers,
1620'[3] and in Smith's will 'Mr Reynoldes the Say mr [assay Master] of
the Gouldsmiths Hall'[4] was left forty shillings. But still its inclusion
seems inappropriate in the context. It seems to be attached to 'an Iland
in forme of a triangle' which was discovered by Verrazano who compared it in size to 'the Iland of the Rhodes'—a passage well known of
course to Smith through Hakluyt. A credible explanation is the
misreading by Barrà of Smith's English secretary hand, and that *Rhodes
I* was written in the instructions for the design. In 1644 the General
Court of the eight-year-old colony ordered 'that the Ysland commonly
known as Aquethneck shall be henceforth called Isle of Rhodes, or
Rhode Island'; from the wording it is obvious that the name had been
established for some time. If Smith intended 'Rhodes I.' he was thereby
avoiding the inclusion of any Dutch name in the area and at the same

[1] T. de Bry, *America*, I, plate II.

[2] *Ould Virginia, 1584, now Carolina, 1650, New Virginia 1606*, by John Farrer, 1650.
New York Public Library. See W. P. Cummings, R. A. Skelton and D. B. Quinn, *The
Discovery of North America*, 1971, p. 269. We should like to thank Mr P. J. Hudson, BL
Department of Manuscripts, for his help.

[3] *Generall Historie*, p. 136.

[4] BL, Add. MSS. 28017, f. 170.

time was enabled to fill in what would have been an awkward gap in the string of names on the map. *C. Iames* was so christened by Prince Charles but its first name, Cape Cod, given it in 1602 by Captain Gosnold, reasserted itself; *C.Anne* and *C.Elizabeth* were named presumably after Charles's mother and sister; *C.Richmond*, not on the map of New England, was put in perhaps to commemorate the name of the Duke of Richmond, first on the list of original members of the Council for New England, who had died in February 1624; *Pembroke B.*, after William Henry, third Earl of Pembroke, member of the Council for New England; *Willowbys Ils.* named by Smith[1] after Robert Bertie, Lord Willoughby whose ancestor had taken his name from the village of Willoughby where Smith was born. On the map of Virginia only Jamestown is marked and on the illustration of '*the adventures of Cap: Smith in Virginia*'[2] there are no symbols for settlers' houses. In contrast on the map on the title-page there are symbols all the way up the James River indicating the many townships which had sprung into being. In New England, New Plymouth with its 'faire Watch-tower'[3] is marked —this must be one of its earliest appearances on a map since its settlement by the Puritans in 1621; the church to the north of it might be intended for London, where those governing the colony were 'knit together by a voluntary combination . . . aiming to doe good & to plant Religion'.[4] Again on the big map of Virginia there are Indian houses everywhere on the James River, and on the inset map the Indian villages which appear all over are palisaded, suggesting a state of war; on the title-page there are Indian villages only on the extreme upper reaches of the James River and very few palisades anywhere.

The figures of plants, birds, fish and animals: tobacco[5] was the most profitable crop in the South and was grown for export from 1614; grape-vines grew in Virginia[6] and were found in profusion by Smith in his voyage of exploration along the coasts of the north. Hawks of different kinds abounded; in de Bry's engraving in the 1619 publication of *America*[7] the settlers are shown hawking. The beaver, only of slightly different kind, was of course known in Europe but Smith gives a detailed description of it—'His forefeete like a dogs, his hinderfeet like

---

[1] *Generall Historie*, p. 205.
[2] Ibid., between pp. 40 and 41.
[3] Ibid., p. 247.
[4] Ibid., p. 247.
[5] T. de Bry, *America*, I, plate XX.
[6] Ibid., plate 11.
[7] T. de Bry, *America*, X, plate XI.

a Swans. His taile somewhat like the forme of a Racket, bare without haire, . . .'[1] It was trapped in its thousands by the Indians, the skins traded for trifles and shipped to Europe. Off the coast of North Carolina the King Crab and the Hammer-headed Shark are from White's drawings;[2] they are put in for their strangeness; the beaked head possibly belongs to a dolphin. The four enormous sea creatures have the three-pronged tails which are characteristic of the sea monsters which are regularly portrayed on maps; but the one on the left, in spite of its tail, is a whale, taken from the engraving by de Bry of the map of the coast of Virginia;[3] double-spouted and toothless with the black whalebone within the spoon-shaped mouth, it is surely the Atlantic Right Whale on which the colonial shore fishery was to be based; attempts at catching whales had been made by Smith and other settlers but the industry was not yet established in 1624. The shoal of fish in the centre is very likely cod. Cod, of which Captain Gosnold wrote that they 'saw more in 5 or 6 hours than they knew what to do with' was to be fished and salted and sent off from New England in enormous quantities. '. . . let not the meannesse of the word fish distaste you,' wrote Smith, 'for it will afford us as good gold as the Mines of *Guiana* or *Potassie*, with lesse hazard and charge, and more certainty and facility.'[4]

All the ships are heading for the coast of America, carrying settlers and their supplies. The fleet on the left is taken from the group represented on the map of New England. The pinnace is similar though not identical with that shown in de Bry's illustration making her way through the islands to find a suitable landing-place on the coast of Virginia.[5] Here she is sailing north towards Virginia and so might be intended to suggest the one built by Somers, together with a larger vessel, in which he and his companions sailed from the Bermudas for the mainland.

The map thus gives a heartening picture of the colonies, offering the assurance of settlement, with the Indians in retreat in Virginia; crops of tobacco, furs, plentiful fish and whale products to be got from the sea; the delights of hawking and perhaps the enjoyment of home-grown wine.

---

[1] *Generall Historie*, p. 27.
[2] T. de Bry, *America*, I, plate XIII.
[3] Ibid., plate I.
[4] *Generall Historie*, p. 248.
[5] T. de Bry, *America*, I, plate XI and letterpress below.

The landscape, laid out in steep perspective tapestry-wise, shows undiscovered America. It is only sparsely populated by Indians, who are shown engaged in their own pursuits; their domestic life is suggested by the two men drawing and carrying water. Down on the left, the palm trees and tobacco belong to the south and so does the warrior, John White's 'weroan, a great Lord of Virginia'.[1] The group of warriors, r., are ornamental rather than hostile—they are certainly not menacing enough to deter men and women from going out to claim these vast fertile lands.

The coats of arms on the tablet bearing the title both belong to Smith. On the left is the family coat; the Smiths of Lincolnshire were descended from the Smiths of Curdley, Lancashire, whose coat is shown dexter, impaling that of Richards, his mother's family.[2] The crest of the fleur-de-lys also belongs to the Smiths. The coat on the right is that granted to Smith himself in 1603 by Sigismund Batori, Prince of Transylvania, for killing three Turks in battle while in his service. It was recorded by Garter King-at-Arms only in 1625. The crest of the ostrich occurs as that of a Smith of Lancashire.

Jan Barrà, the accomplished engraver of the title-page, engraved a fine portrait of the Duke of Lennox and Richmond in 1624.[3] The *Generall Historie* is dedicated to the Duke's wife Frances, who also appears in another engraving by Barrà.[4] It may be through this connection that the artist came to be associated with Smith. The invention of the design must have been Smith's in the sense that he instructed Barrà what to include and where the emphasis was to be placed. He must have sought out the portraits most suitable for his purpose and given the artist copies of the coats of arms. From Part I of de Bry's *America*, published in 1590, he selected many of the details for the map and the exotic features for the landscape, whose ultimate source is in most instances John White. But the skilful combination of so many diverse elements into an engraving of considerable merit is due to the talent of Barrà.

---

[1] Ibid., plate I and Hulton and Quinn, op. cit., 1, no. 52 d.

[2] Granted to Charles Riccard, alias Richards, of Heek in South Yorkshire in 1595 (Harleian Society, *Grantees of Arms*, ed. Rylands, 1915, p. 213). Smith named Rickards cliffes after his mother.

[3] Hind, III, Jan Barrà, no. 7.

[4] Hind, III, Jan Barrà, no. 11(4).

יְהוָה

Et vidit Deus lucem quod esset bona

Mundus Intellectualis

SYLVA SYLVARVM
or
A NATVRALL HISTORY
In ten Centuries.
Written by the right Honble Francis
Lo: Verulam Viscount St Alban.
Published after ye Authors Death
by W: RAWLEY Dr of Diui-
nity. &c

Tho: Cecill sculp:

LONDON
Printed for W: Lee and are to be sould at
the Great Turks head next to the Mytre
Taurne in Fleetstreet.

Anno   1627

16

FRANCIS BACON

Sylva Sylvarum

1627

(Hind, III. Thomas Cecill, no. 21)

At the top the Tetragrammaton is inscribed on the centre of a glory from which emanate rays. These are cut off on either side by banks of cloud. Within the rays are two cherubim, the one on the left looking down while that on the right gazes at the sacred Name. One ray longer than the others descends towards a huge globe which it illumines. This ray divides the inscription across the sky, *Et vidit Deus lucem/quod esset bona.* Across the globe is inscribed, *Mundus Intellectualis.* Beneath the lettering are the dotted outlines of the countries of the world; the lower part is enshrouded in darkness. It rests on the sea which extends to the horizon. Two pillars with square bases stand on the strip of land in the foreground bordering the sea; they flank the globe. They have simplified Corinthian capitals and are fluted for two-thirds of their height, the remaining third being decorated with a design of acanthus leaves surmounted by ogival mouldings, with above them a band carrying medallions and tassels. Below the globe, within a simple cartouche, the title: Sylva Sylvarvm/or/*A NATURALL HISTORY*/In ten Centuries./*Written by the right* Honble *Francis*/*Lo: Verulam Viscount S^{ct} Alban.*/Published after ye Autho^{rs} Death/by W. RAWLEY D^{r} of Diui:/nity. &c. In the margin within ovals, r. and l., *Anno*/*1627*; centre, within a cartouche, the imprint, LONDON/*Printed for W. Lee and are to be sould at*/*the Great Turks head next to the Mytre*/*Tau^{e}rne in Fleetstreet.* Signed l. above the margin, *Tho: Cecill sculp:.*

Although the 'Natural History' is not among the titles listed in the table of the *Instauratio Magna*, William Rawley, who was Bacon's chaplain and amanuensis and the editor of many of his writings, believed that it was intended to form a part of it. He wrote in the address 'To the Reader': 'Besides, this *Naturall History* was a Debt of his, being Designed and set down for a third part of the *Instauration*.'[1] An appropriate means of showing that this work had an essential place in the other was to use the design for the title-page to the *Instauratio* as the basis for that to the *Sylva*. The former is very well known. It has been described by Sir Peter Medawar[2] who used it as an illustration of the new attitude of mind to science and philosophy which was dawning in the early decades of the seventeenth century. It shows two columns rising from opposite points of land; between them is a channel of sea leading to the ocean beyond—a ship sails forth from the narrow passage and another, far out, approaches the horizon. This was a brilliant adaptation of the emblem of the Emperor Charles V, invented for him by the humanist Marliano about 1517 to symbolise his rule, which extended from Spain over the vast unknown territories in the New World beyond the Atlantic Ocean. The flanking columns in this device are the Pillars of Hercules which marked the boundaries of the Ancient World, the *ne plus ultra*. They are often shown capped with the imperial bonnet, while the imperial double-headed eagle is placed over the seas. A riband carries the motto 'plus ultra'.[3] To Bacon, Hercules' columns represented 'a fewe receiued Authors . . . beyond which, there should be no sayling, or discouering'[4]—a defiant reference to Aristotle as interpreted by the Schoolmen and so to the whole body of an intellectual discipline which stood in the way of progress. The ships in his title-page symbolise human understanding going out to discover new territories for the empire of knowledge. 'Plus ultra' was to be the rallying cry for the intellects of the seventeenth century. The inscription just below the ships reads, 'Multi pertransibunt et augebitur scientia' (Many shall go to and fro and knowledge shall be increased. Dan. 12.4). This 'prophecy of Daniel' was to be understood in the geographical sense, since geographical discovery was the indisputable basis for the growth of knowledge. He declares that the text clearly intimates 'that the thorough passage of the world (which by now so many distant

---

[1] *Sylva Sylvarum*, Sig. A$_v$.

[2] Sir Peter Medawar, 'The Effecting of all Things Possible', *Listener*, 2 October 1969.

[3] For example in the *Portrait of Charles V* by Cornelis Teunissen, c. 1548.

[4] *The Twoo Bookes of Francis Bacon. Of the proficience and aduancement of learning*, . . . 1605. *The second booke*, f. 1$_v$.

voyages seems to be accomplished, or in the course of accomplishment), and the advancement of the sciences, are destined by fate, that is by Divine Providence, to meet in the same age.'[1]

Some strongly-voiced religious opinions were as great an obstacle to the new learning as outmoded ways of thought. Bacon attacked them: 'in every age Natural philosophy has had a troublesome adversary and hard to deal with; namely, superstition, and the blind and immoderate zeal of religion.'[2] It was feared that the ignorant might be corrupted: 'And others again appear apprehensive that in the investigation of nature something may be found to subvert or at least shake the authority of religion, especially with the unlearned.'[3]

The opposition continued for several more decades; Thomas Sprat deals with it in his *History of the Royal Society*[4] and so does Joseph Glanvill in his book written in 1668, which was presented to the Royal Society and was a supplement to Sprat's work.[5] In fact, the new philosophy, or, as it was called, the true philosophy, was firmly based on religion, on the profound belief that a knowledge of God's works must 'magnifie and discover their *Author*'.[6] The *New Atlantis* was published in the same volume as the *Naturall History* on Bacon's wishes, because it had 'so neare Affinity' to it '(in one Part of it)'.[7] Its famous college had as an alternative name '*the* Colledge *of the Six Daies Workes*;—God's creation'; its purpose was '. . . *the finding out of the true Nature of all Things (whereby* GOD *mought haue the more Glory in the Workemaneship of them). . . .*'[8] Bacon knew that the 'Illumination of the *Understanding*' could only come from a systematic approach—'the Scope which his Lordship intendeth', wrote Rawley, 'is to write such a *Naturall History*, as may be Fundamentall to the Erecting and Building of a true *Philosophy*:'[9] But from the theological standpoint it was first necessary to demonstrate how God operated to make a knowledge of his work accessible to the mind of man. This is the subject of Rawley's title-page, which is a modification of the earlier one, giving it a different meaning.

---

[1] *The Philosophical Works of Francis Bacon*, reprinted from the texts and translations of R. Ellis and J. Spedding, ed. J. M. Robertson, 1905. *Novum Organum*, p. 287.

[2] Ibid., p. 285.

[3] Ibid., p. 286.

[4] Thomas Sprat, *History of the Royal Society*, 1667, pp. 345ff.

[5] Joseph Glanvill, *Plus Ultra: Or the Progress and Advancement of Knowledge*, 1668, pp. 130f.

[6] Ibid., preface.

[7] *Sylva Sylvarum*, 'The New Atlantis', 'To the Reader', Sig. A₂v.

[8] Ibid., p. 19.

[9] *Sylva Sylvarum*, 'To the Reader', Sig. Aᵥ.

'Doctor of Divinity' appears after Rawley's name both on the engraved and printed title-pages, so that it should be clear that his views were those of the orthodox Church of England. There was material enough in Bacon's works from which to draw a text. 'GODS *first Creature*', Bacon wrote in the *New Atlantis*, '*which was* Light:'[1] light is knowledge.[2] From God to the angels: 'as farre as credite is to bee giuen to the celestiall Hierarchye, of that supposed Dionysius, the Senator of Athens . . . the second [place is to be given] to the Angels of light, which are tearmed *Cherubim*' who are 'the Angels of knowledge and illumination'.[3] Light in nature corresponds to knowledge in spirits (angels) and incorporall thinges.[4] It follows therefore that the inscription from Genesis 1.4. 'And God saw the light that it was good' is the divine sanction for human knowledge. 'Concerning the Celestial Hierarchy' to which Bacon refers, was written by Dionysius the Pseudo-Areopagite in the fifth century; that he was not the 'senator of Athens' of Acts 17.34 was known to contemporary scholars. It had enormous influence on religious thought throughout the Middle Ages and the Renaissance.

In the pictorial scheme God as the source of light is indicated by the great radiant glory round his Name. The cherubim, whose name denotes 'their knowledge and their vision of God'[5] are placed on the second darker sphere which surrounds the first and brightest, but very near to the source of light because of 'their readiness to receive the highest gift of light, and their power of contemplating the Divine comeliness in its first revealed power'.[6] The direction of their glances, the one fixed on the Name of God, the other on the globe below, shows that they are aware of the divine light as it proceeds to man, falling on the *Mundus Intellectualis*, the world of human understanding. The figure may have been taken from the literary image adopted by Bacon in his title to his work on the character and scope of the human understanding, the *Descriptio Globi Intellectualis*.[7] Rawley used the term *Mundus* perhaps because he had in mind the source of the religious ideas

[1] 'New Atlantis', p. 20.

[2] Ibid. The passage continues '*To have* Light *(I say) of the Growth of the Parts of the World.*'

[3] *Of the proficience and aduancement of Learning* . . ., 1605. *The first booke*, 27vf.

[4] Ibid., p. 28.

[5] St Dionysius called the Areopagite, *The Celestial and Ecclesiastical Hierarchy* . . . Now first translated into English by Rev. John Parker, 1894, p. 28.

[6] Ibid.

[7] This tract was written about 1612. It was published by I. Gruter in *F. Baconi Scripta in naturali et universali philosophia*, 1653.

embodied in the title-page. Those derived from the Neo-platonic concept of a 'universal hierarchy of God, the Angelic Mind, the Rational Soul (*mundus intellectualis*) . . . and Body'[1]—the scheme originated by Marsilio Ficino whose writings nourished the minds of sixteenth- and seventeenth-century poets and philosophers. However, the purpose of God's light and the relationship of the two worlds suggested by the design—the corporeal world as the object of enquiry by the world of reason—is not Neo-platonic; rather it is Bacon's grand innovation for which Rawley has here found so apt an expression. *Mundus Intellectualis*, the 'Intellectual Globe' is shown as co-terminous with the corporeal world, the whole material of natural history.[2] Where divine knowledge illumines the mind, the contours are defined clearly; where the divine light ceases the world is in shadow thickening to obscurity, the mind in a state of ignorance. The geographical outlay is not to be taken literally.

The meaning of the symbol is made plainer by the design of a later title-page to Bacon's philosophical works, that to the 1640 edition of 'Of the Advancement and Proficience of Learning'.[3] Here there are two globes, *Mundus Visibilis* and *Mundus Intellectualis*. The former is the material world lit by a physical light with hard outlines, trees, rivers, a sea creature, a ship and so on, the factual world of the senses and of experience. The latter is identical with that in Rawley's device, even to the dotting of the contours which was done originally perhaps to suggest that they rendered the truth *almost* corporeal. These conceptions of the divine light and its relation to man were very widespread. Thomas Stanley, in interpreting 'The Chaldaick Philosophy', says the Chaldeans held that 'God being . . . an Intellectual Light . . . he communicated it to all Creatures'.[4] Rawley saw the divine light fall directly upon Bacon—'I have been induced to think, that if there were a beam of knowledge derived from God upon any man, in these modern times, it was upon him.'[5]

---

[1] P. O. Kristeller, *Studies in Renaissance Thought and Letters*, 1956, p. 268.

[2] For a full discussion of this aspect of Bacon's philosophy, see Paolo Rossi, *Francis Bacon, From Magic to Science*, 1968, pp. 186ff.

[3] *Of the Advancement and Proficience of Learning* . . . Interpreted by Gilbert Wats, 1640. The title-page is by William Marshall. Hind, III, p. 140.

[4] Thomas Stanley, *The History of Philosophy*, 1655-6. *The History of the Chaldaick Philosophy*, p. 18.

[5] *The Works of Francis Bacon*, collected and edited by R. Ellis and J. Spedding, 1857, p. 1. Dr Rawley's *Life of Bacon*, p. 6.

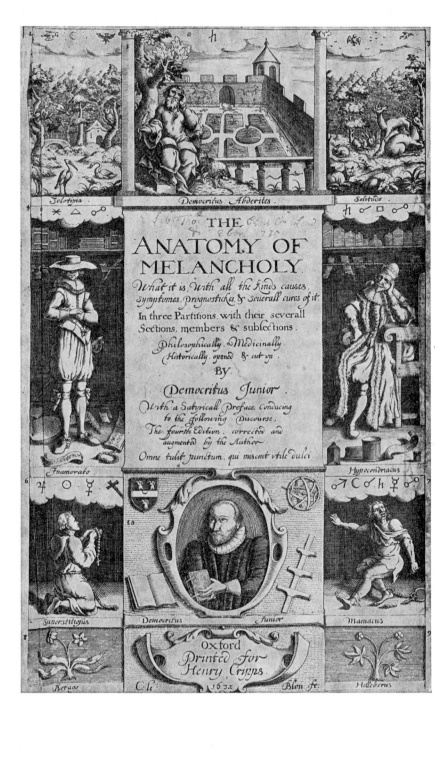

17

ROBERT BURTON

The Anatomy of Melancholy

4th edition, 1632

(Hind, III. C. Le Blon, no. 1)

The engraving is divided into three bands or panels; the middle panel is formed as a plinth and pedestal supporting a balcony. On the central tablet is the title THE/ANATOMY OF/MELANCHOLY./ *What it is, With all the kinds causes,/symptomes, prognostickes, & severall cures of it/. . ./Philosophically, Medicinally,/Historically, opened & cut vp./ By/Democritus Junior./With a Satyricall Preface, Conducing/to the following Discourse./. . ./Omne tulit punctum, qui miscuit vtile dulci.* (He who has mixed the sweet with the useful has carried every vote. Horace, *Ars Poetica*, 1.343). Immediately above is a scene enclosed by the two columns of the balcony numbered '1' on the left column; it shows *Democritus: Abderites* barefoot in a rough classical gown with a bearded face sitting on some rocks beneath a tree. He meditates, his left hand on his cheek with an open book on his knee and a pen in hand. By him a lizard; behind a balustrade is a formal garden; on the walls are the skins of animals hung up and along the paths flayed skins and bodies, including that of a snake. Beyond the walls is a windowed tower and in the sky the sign of Saturn. L. a wooded scene entitled *Zelotipia* (Jealousy), a bridge over a stream, a small hut; in the sky an owl, the crescent moon and a bat; in the middle distance two fighting cocks; in the branches of the tree on the left a pair of birds and in that on the right an owl; in the foreground a pair of herons, a kingfisher and a swan; '2' marked in the margin. On the right side of the engraving a comparable scene numbered '3' in the margin, illustrates *Solitudo*; an owl and another bird in the sky; a stag and a doe, a sleeping hare and a rabbit, and in the foreground, a sleeping dog and cat. Left of the title a scene entitled *Inamorato*, numbered '4' in the margin; it shows a standing youth in a falling ruff, belted jerkin and pear-shaped hose; garters and shoes tied with bows; a wide-brimmed hat pulled over his eye; his arms folded; on the floor a lute, two folded notes, scrolls of music and a wreath; above, books on a shelf and in a rack a quill pen, a paper and a holder; in the sky the sign of Venus with aspects sextile, trigone and opposition. Right of the title a scene numbered '5' in the margin, showing an elderly man in an armchair, *Hypocondriacus*; he wears a lace-trimmed cap, a falling ruff, a fur-lined gown over his buttoned jerkin and hose. He rests his face on his hand; on a shelf, many bottles, and folded papers in a rack; another bottle on the floor, pill-boxes, a scroll; in the sky the sign of Saturn in the ascendant, and the aspects quartile and opposition. Under *Inamorato*, numbered '6', is *Superstitiosus*, a monk or friar telling his beads as he kneels below the sign of the cross; in the sky alongside to the left the signs of Jupiter, Sol and Mercury. Under *Hypocondriacus*, numbered '7' in the margin, is *Maniacus*, a madman in rags shackled to the floor; in the sky Mars and Luna in conjunction, Saturn and Mercury in opposition. At the foot, l., borage, a flowering herb, labelled *Borago,* numbered '8', and, r., hellebore, another flowering herb, labelled *Helleborus*, numbered '9'. Below the title within a scrollwork cartouche is Burton's portrait with his book; l. above, his coat of arms and below an open book; r., a sphere and below a cross-staff; the portrait is entitled *Democritus Junior*; '10' marked on the left. Beneath the portrait the imprint within another cartouche: Oxford/*Printed for*/Henry *Cripps*/*1632*. Signed: *C. le Blon fe:*[1]

The compartments have been numbered to correspond with the verses of Burton's 'Argument of the Frontispiece' which first appeared with the engraved title-page in the third edition, 1628.

The Argument of the Frontispiece.

TEn distinct Squares heere seene apart,
Are ioyn'd in one by Cutters art.

1 *Old* Democritus *vnder a tree,*
Sittes on a stone with booke on knee,
About him hang there many features,
Of Cattes, Dogges and such like creatures,

[1] Page references to the *Anatomy* are to the 4th edition, 1632.

Of which he makes Anatomy,
The seat of blacke choler to see.
Ouer his head appeares the skye,
And Saturne *Lord of Melancholy.*

2 *Toth' left a Landskip of* Iealousye,
Presents it selfe vnto thine eye.
A Kingfisher, a Swan, an Herne,
Two fighting Cockes you may decerne,
Two roareing Bulles each other high,
To assault concerning Venery.
Symboles are these, I say no more,
Conceaue the rest by that's afore.

3 *The next of* Solitarinesse,
A portrature doth well expresse,
By sleeping dog, cat: Bucke and Doe
Hares, Conies in the desart goe:
Battes, Owles the shady bowers ouer,
In melancholy darknesse houer,
Marke well: if't be not as' should be,
Blame the bad Cutter and not me.

4 *Ith' vnder Columne there doth stand,*
Inamorato *with folded hande.*
Downe hanges his head, terse and polite
Some Dittie sure he dote endite.
His lute and bookes about him lye,
As symptomes of his vanity.
If this doe not enough disclose,
To paint him, take thy selfe byth' nose.

5 Hypocondriacus *leanes on his arme,*
Winde in his side doth him much harme,
And troubles him full sore God knowes,
Much paine he hath and many woes.
About him pottes and glasses lye,
Newly brought from's Apothecary,
This Saturnes *aspect signify,*
You see them portraid in the skye.

6   *Beneath them kneeling on his knee,*
A Superstitious *man you see:*
He fastes, prayes, on's Idole fixt,
Tormented hope and feare betwixt:
For hell perhaps he takes more paine,
Then thou dost, Heauen it selfe to gaine.
Alas poore Soule, I pittie thee,
What starres inclin'd thee so to be.

7   *But see the* Madman *rage downe right*
With furious lookes, a gastly sight.
Naked in chaines bound doth he lye,
And roares amaine he knowes not why?
Obserue him, for as in a glasse,
Thine angry portraiture it was.
His picture keepe still in thy presence,
Twixt him and thee, ther's no difference.

8.9   Borage *and* Hellebor *fill two sceanes,*
Soveraigne plants to purge the veines,
Of melancholy, and cheare the heart,
Of those blacke fumes which make it smart.
To cleare the Braine of misty fogges,
Which dull our sences and Soule clogges.
The best medicines that ere God made
For this malady, if well essaid.

10   *Now last of all to fill a place,*
Presented is the Authors *face;*
And in that habit which he weares,
His Image to the world appeares.
His minde no art can well expresse,
That by his writings you may guesse.
It was not pride, nor yet vaine glory,
(Though others doe it commonly)

Made him doe this: if you must know,
The Printer would needs haue it so,
Then doe not frowne or scoffe at it,
Deride not, or detract a whit,

For surely as thou dost by him,
He will doe the same againe.
Then looke vpon't, behold and see,
As thou likest it, so it likes thee.

And I for it will stand in view,
Thine to commande, Reader *Adew.*

There are various discrepancies between the engraving and 'The Argument'; the bulls specified in the verses in scene 2 and the column in scene 4 are omitted; the bats specified in 3 are wrongly included in 2; the verse about 6 does not prescribe a monk nor friar; the representation of the madman does not tally very faithfully with the poem. The poem makes it clear that the title-page was devised by Burton but in view of the differences noted it would seem that he was not able to supervise the engraver, who evidently worked on the basis of indications sent from Oxford, where Burton, unaware that his instructions were not being followed to the letter, wrote the explanatory verses without having seen the finished work.

The first scene shows Democritus the ancient philosopher as Hippocrates found him when he came to visit him in his garden in the suburbs of Abdera in Thrace, '*sitting upon a stone under a plane Tree, without hose or shooes, . . . busie at his studie, . . .*'[1] Hippocrates describes him as 'a little wearish old man, very melancholy by nature, averse from company in his latter dayes, . . . a famous Philosopher in his age, ...'[2] The pose in which the artist has placed him, with his hand under his cheek, goes back to early antiquity.[3] It can signify grief, weariness or meditation. After the appearance of Dürer's *Melencolia* it is frequently used in symbolic representations of Melancholy[4] and may express one or all of these states of mind. It is difficult to say from where Le Blon took it since it was so generally diffused; possibly from a print by Jacob de Gheyn II in which Melancholy is personified in the figure of an old bearded man, head in hand.[5] Or the source may have been a literary one, such as Lomazzo's *Trattato della Pittura*.[6] As the sign in the sky

[1] *Anatomy*, 'Democritvs to the Reader', p. 23.

[2] Ibid., p. 2.

[3] See R. Klibansky, E. Panofsky and F. Saxl, *Saturn and Melancholy*, 1964, pp. 286f.

[4] Ibid., illustrations nos 114, 122, 131.

[5] Hollstein, Jacob de Gheyn II, no. 127.

[6] G. B. Lomazzo, *Trattato dell'arte de la Pittura*, 1584, Lib. Secondo cap, ix, 128. Cited by B. G. Lyons in *Voices of Melancholy*, 1971. We wish to acknowledge our debt to this author both for her text and valuable references.

indicates, Democritus was born under Saturn the tutelary planet of melancholics. Burton says elsewhere that he was among those sufferers from a special kind of melancholy, 'which causeth many times a diuine ravishment, . . . which stirreth them vp to bee excellent Philosophers, ...'[1]

He is portrayed in the act of writing.

> The subiect of his booke was Melancholy and madnesse, about him lay the carcasses of many seuerall beasts, newly by him cut vp and anatomized, . . . to finde out the seat of this *atra bilis* or Melancholy, whence it proceeds, and how it is engendered in mens bodies, to the intent he might better cure it in himselfe, by his writings and observations teach others how to prevent & avoid it.[2]

In the first half of the seventeenth century pathology was still dominated by the theory of the four humours, which derived from antiquity. Their seats were in four different parts of the body, the spleen being the source of black bile and therefore the chief seat of melancholy. Anatomy was the branch of medicine which had made most strides during the Renaissance, many illustrated books having been published on it, so that Democritus' operations were readily acceptable to the contemporary mind. The only animal corpse which is identifiable is that of the snake with the forked tongue, the adder, one of the animals belonging to Saturn because she is 'so full of poyson'.[3] The tower perhaps belongs to the city of Abdera. It is recorded in the *Epistolae Hippocratis*, the source from which Burton obtained his information about Hippocrates' visit to Democritus.[4]

Burton refers to himself in the title as 'Democritus Junior' because his intention was 'to reviue againe' the work of the Greek philosopher now lost, and to 'prosecute and finish [it] in this Treatise'.[5] He was drawn to the work possibly because, as he says, '*Saturne* was Lord of my geniture',[6] a fact he also recorded in his horoscope shown on his tomb in the Cathedral, Oxford. Although his work was to be scientific and thorough, the line from Horace under the title shows his desire to sugar the pill, beginning with the pun on dissection in the

---

[1] *Anatomy*, p. 192.

[2] *Anatomy*, 'Democritvs to the Reader', p. 4.

[3] John Maplet, *The Diall of Destiny*, 1581, 66v.

[4] *Epistolae Hippocratis*, 1601, letter to Damagetus, p. 28.

[5] *Anatomy*, 'Democritvs to the Reader', p. 5.

[6] Ibid., p. 3.

title. 'By my profession a Divine, and by mine inclination a Physitian',[1] Burton was well placed to study melancholy as 'a common infirmitie of Body and Soule'[2] and the different scenes in the title-page show both spiritual and corporal examples of the disease.

Scenes 2 and 3 are concerned only with the animal kingdom, possibly to validate the experiments of Democritus by pointing to the then universally accepted truth that animals have the same temperaments and qualities of character as men. The scene on the left, 2, shows animals who suffer particularly from jealousy. The verse in 'The Argument' says that we should see '*Two roareing Bulles each other high*' but, as pointed out above, these have been omitted; the two fighting cocks explain themselves. Burton quotes an anecdote from another author about a 'Swanne about *Windsore*, that finding a strange Cocke with his mate, did swimme I know not how many miles after to kill him, and when he had so done, came backe and killed his henne';[3] kingfishers are said to bear a natural grudge to eagles; the 'Hearne when shee fishes, still prying on all sides'[4] through jealous fear of what her mate may be doing. The owl belongs to Saturn—her presence in the day time in ancient Athens was an omen of sorrow to come.

The desire for solitariness is a primary cause of melancholy, perhaps voluntary at first, at a later stage compulsive. In the last paragraph of his book Burton advises his readers. '*Be not solitary, be not idle.*'[5] In the third scene he has grouped the cat and the dog whose habit it is to seek out a quiet place to sleep, the deer, who timidly flee from the multitude, and the hare, another animal under Saturn, used by the Egyptians 'in their *Hieroglyphicks*' 'as being a most timorous and solitary creature'.[6] Both this scene and its companion show dark groves in the background and on the left, water, the surroundings sought out by those of a melancholy nature. Burton himself liked to wander 'By a brookeside or wood so greene'.[7]

'The Argument' tells us that the young man in love, a victim of Love-Melancholy, is composing a love song: 'Amongst other good qualities an amorous fellow is endowed with, he must learne to sing

[1] Ibid., p. 16.
[2] Ibid., p. 16.
[3] Ibid., p. 598.
[4] Ibid., p. 613.
[5] Ibid., p. 722.
[6] Ibid., p. 188.
[7] Ibid., 'The Authors Abstract of Melancholy'.

and dance, play vpon some instrument or other';[1] the books may be volumes or ballads and poetry for 'aboue all the Symptomes of Louers . . . they turne to their ability, Rimers, Ballet-makers, and Poets'.[2] His pose and above all, his hat pulled down over his eyes betray his unhappy condition. It is a special 'melancholy hat' worn in Jacobean times on melancholy occasions, or to express a melancholy mood, as we know from the famous satirical couplet about the dramatist John Ford:[3]

> Deep in a dump John Ford was alone got
> With folded arms and melancholy hat.

Le Blon seems to have taken as a model for *Inamorato* the little woodcut figure on the title-page to Samuel Rowlands *The Melancholie Knight* of 1615.[4]

> His face being masked with his hat pull'd downe,
> And in french doublet without gowne or cloake,
> His hose the largest euer came to towne, . . .
> Garters would make two ensignes for a neede,
> And shoo-ties that for circle did exceede.
> His head hung downe, his armes were held acrosse.

But rather than copy the original which was intended to portray a world-weary gallant, he has changed it to suit Burton's requirements— by elongating the body and widening the hat he has made a caricature of love-sick youth. Astrologically, Venus is in a conspicuous position in the lover's constellation; sextile and trigone are harmonious aspects; opposition signifies conflict and antagonism. All the astrological signs in the title-page except those in scene 6 should be read as passages from the subject's horoscope. Although Burton considers the claims of astrology to determine men's lives, he finally rejects them: 'let no man then be terrified or molested with such Astrologicall Aphorismes', he says, for 'the starres encline, but not enforce';[5] they cannot bind the rational mind, for that is under the control of God.

Hypocondriacus is in the same pose of melancholy as Democritus. He is suffering from a disease of the spleen, which is situated on the left in the hypochondries, that is below the costal cartilages. This organ is ruled by Saturn; the section of his horoscope shown contains

---

[1] Ibid., p. 540.

[2] Ibid., p. 541.

[3] *Choyce drollery* by J. G. 1656. *Songs and Sonnets* . . . now first printed from the Edition of 1656 . . . Edited by J. W. E. [Ebsworth], 1876, p. 6, *On the Time-Poets*.

[4] Introduction; taken from the edition of 1841 in which the woodcut is reproduced.

[5] *Anatomy*, pp. 586 and 585.

only maleficent aspects which suggests that his condition is predestined. His cheek bulges over his hand as if he had toothache, which would not be unexpected since those born under Saturn are said to have bad teeth. He wears a thick gown perhaps because of an 'unseasonable sweat all ouer the body' or he may have 'cold ioynts'.[1]

Superstitiosus is portrayed as a monk or friar; as noted above he is not so described in 'The Argument' so that this may well be an additional touch of satire on the part of the Protestant engraver. He has fallen into a religious melancholy. He belongs to '*Rome* . . . wherein *Antichrist* himselfe now sits'.[2] He believes in 'Images, Oblations, Pendants, Adorations . . . creeping to Crosses'.[3] He is seen worshipping the cross, emphatically engraved in black. The practices of his religion, despised by the Church of England as superstitious and idolatrous, lead him to fasting, solitariness, melancholy. 'You may guesse', says Burton, 'at the Prognostickes by the Symptomes. What can these signes foretell otherwise then folly, dotage, madnesse, . . . despaire . . . a bad end?'[4] The astrological signs are those which take their names from pagan gods, Jupiter and Mercury of ancient Rome, Sol, the Sun of ancient Egypt; it is these false idols which have influenced believers to follow their melancholy paths in antiquity.

The madman or maniac is shown on the title-page although Burton decided to treat madness apart from melancholy, and, following the most advanced thought on the subject, as a disease of the mind best cured by the attention of the most approved physicians. He defines it as 'a vehement *Dotage*, or rauing without a feaver, farre more violent then *Melancholy*, full of anger and clamor, horrible lookes, actions, gestures, troubling the Patients with farre greater vehenency both of body and Mind . . . that sometimes three or foure men cannot hold them.'[5] And so he is portrayed. The astrological signs follow the authorities cited by the author. '*If the Moone be in coniunction . . . at the birth time with . . . Mars . . . many diseases are signified, especially the Head and Braine is like to bee misaffected with pernitious humors,* to be melancholy, lunatick, or mad, . . .'[6] Such as haue . . . *Saturne, Mercury* misaffected in their genitures, . . . are most subiect to Melancholy.'[7]

[1] Ibid., p. 199.
[2] Ibid., p. 673.
[3] Ibid., p. 675.
[4] Ibid., p. 679.
[5] Ibid., p. 9.
[6] Ibid., p. 57.
[7] Ibid., p. 33.

The chief medicinal cure for melancholy lay in the administration of concoctions of herbs, foremost among them being 'Black *Hellebor*, . . . famous purger of melancholy'.[1] 'Black Hellebor purgeth downwardes flegme, choler, and also black choler especially, and all melancholicke humours, . . . it is good for mad and furious men, for melancholicke, dull and heavie persons.'[2] Borage not being a medicinal herb was to be taken as a tonic:[3]

> Borage bring alwaies courage. Those of our time do vse the flowers in sallads, to exhilarate and make the minde glad, C The leaues and flowere of Borage put into wine, maketh men and women glad and merrie, and driueth away all sadnesse, dulnesse, and melancholie, . . . D Syrupe made of the iuce of Borage, comforteth the hart, . . . is good . . . against melancholly.

In the portrait of Burton by Gilbert Jackson[4] painted in 1635 he is wearing a skullcap and for the edition of the *Anatomy* of 1638 the engraved portrait has been altered to show him also with this headgear which was intended to give protection from draughts. Burton was now elderly and perhaps had taken to it more or less permanently. He was obviously concerned that the title-page should not lose its impact by appearing in any way out-of-date. He is seen holding a copy of the *Anatomy*. The coat of arms is that recorded for the Burtons of Leicestershire in the latter half of the seventeenth century, showing its owner as the second son. The open book speaks for itself—Burton was one of the best-read men of his generation and owned a large library; the sphere and the cross-staff are symbols of the study of cosmography in which he delighted.[5]

---

[1] Ibid., p. 384.

[2] John Gerard, *The Herball*, 1597, p. 827.

[3] Ibid., p. 654.

[4] Mrs R. L. Poole, *Catalogue of Portraits in the possession of the University, Colleges . . . of Oxford*, II, 1925, p. 251.

[5] *Anatomy*, 'Democritvs to the Reader', p. 3.

18

JOHN BULWER

Chirologia

1644

(Hind, III. William Marshall, no. 150)

The background is a landscape of hills. In front of it is a breakfront plinth. Standing on the plinth, l., six-breasted Nature with one hand pressed to her bosom from which gushes milk; the other hand stretches out towards the centre; long, unkempt hair falls down her back; she wears a rough skirt, her feet are bare; her right foot is placed on a wheel. Behind her is an oak tree with inscription alongside *Quercus Dodon.* Inscribed on the moulding below, NATURA LOQVENS (speaking Nature). On the right is a female figure wearing a wreath of palm and clad in a loose short-sleeved robe with buskins on her feet; behind her a palm tree with a fruit hanging down, with five dates protruding from the sheath; below her the inscription, POLIHYMNIA. Her right arm and hand are extended; her left hand is held towards the spectator with thumb and fingers opened upwards. In the centre the square head of a cistern, with, on the plinth below, the inscription, CISTERNA CHIROSOPHIAE. Above the cistern an enormous hand with all fingers extended protrudes from a cuff; on the palm of the hand a head with flowing locks covered by a plumed helmet; an animal head (perhaps that of a cock?) as crest. From the mouth issues a stream of liquid which falls into the cistern. Two vertical curls of cloud fall towards the mouth, linking it with the outstretched hands of the figures; that on the left carries the inscription, *Hinc latices!* (Hence the liquid); on the right, *Digitisque loquor Gestumque decoro* (I speak both with my fingers and with aptness of gesture).

A cartouche carrying the title, CHIROLOGIA is placed above

the trees. The head and shoulders of Mercury appear over the top with his hands resting on the scrollwork. He holds the caduceus and wears a flat-topped petasus. At the top of the engraving banks of cloud, from which project, l., a hand with the two first fingers extended, the last two bent in, and, r., another with thumb and fingers extended. Immediately below, rising behind the cartouche, l., a pair of hands clasped in prayer, r., a pair expanded; a comet shoots from the clouds just above the latter pair; the inscription reads, *Sic Manus alloquitur hominem,Sic Deum* (Thus the hand [of God] speaks to man, thus [the hand of man] speaks to God).

On the faces of the plinth are diagrams of hands; on the left face, a hand represented with extended fingers with a pair of lips on the palm inscribed, *Elocutio Manualis.*; beside it a hand with thumb and fingers numbered *1/2/3/4/5* inscribed, *Arith:Nat:*. On the left side face of the recess is a hand extended with an ear on the palm; on the right side face, a hand with an eye on the palm; on the right front face, a hand extended with a tongue on the palm *Eloquen:/tia,* and a hand with fingers clenched and thumb outside, *Logica.* On the rear wall of the recess four oval frames showing hands, top l., with all fingers extended, *Intel/lectus.*, bottom l., with all fingers closed over the thumb, *Memo/ria;* top r., with fingers and thumb bent inwards, *Volun/tas.*; last, with fingers closed tight and thumb set over all the fingers, *Scien/tia.* Signed at the bottom, *Will:Marshall sculp:*

Following the *Chirologia* is a second part entitled *Chironomia;* although our frontispiece bears only the title to the *Chirologia,* the printed title-page reads, *Chirologia: or the Natvrall language of the Hand . . . whereunto is added Chironomia: or the Art of Manvall Rhetoricke;* that is, the art of gesture as employed by the trained speaker. In fact, the representation is concerned with the subjects of both parts. Bulwer was a philosopher and a doctor of medicine. In his address to the reader,[1] he acknowledges the inspiration of Bacon who had pointed out that Aristotle, though he had dealt with the making of the body, had given no systematic account of its movements. Bulwer was certainly acquainted with a passage in the *De Augmentis . . .*:[2]

I must speak concerning the Organ of Transmission in general. For it seems that the art of transmission has some other children besides Words and Letters. This then may be laid down as a rule;

---

[1] *Chirologia,* 'To the Candid and Ingenious Reader'.
[2] Francis Bacon, *The Philosophical Works,* reprinted from the texts of R. Ellis and J. Spedding, edited by J. M. Robertson, 1905.

that whatever can be divided into differences sufficiently numerous to explain the variety of notions (provided those differences be perceptible to the sense) may be a vehicle to convey the thoughts of one man to another. For we see that nations which understand not another's language carry on their commerce well enough by means of gestures. And in the practice of some who had been deaf and dumb from birth and were otherwise clever, I have seen wonderful dialogues carried on between them and their friends who had learned to understand their gestures.

In an era when merchants travelled all over the world it is not surprising that the impetus which led to a study of 'The naturall Language of the Hand' came from reflections that this was a way in 'which, without teaching, men in all regions of the habitable world doe at first sight most easily understand';[1] that there were those that drive 'a rich and silent Trade, by signes';[2] 'In this garbe long ago/We spake with th'Indian Apochankano.'[3] The benefit of a sign language to the deaf and dumb also attracts his notice; it was not his chief interest at this time, but only four years later he was to publish the *Philocophus* (see p. 211).

In the seventeenth century Ciceronian rhetoric which included persuasive gesture or manual rhetoric, was taught at the university and practised in the 'Schooles, Theaters, and the Mansions of the Muses, ... Churches, Courts of Common pleas, and the Councell-Table'.[4] It was still a part of western culture which Bulwer believed he could extend to enable all peoples to converse with one another without the spoken word. He has observed that there are many spontaneous gestures common to all human beings. He searches for these gestures of his 'Naturall Language' mainly in the Bible and the classical authors, though he also gives examples drawn from the works of Donne,[5] Lancelot Andrewes[6] and other contemporary writers. He refers to 'the civill rites and ceremonious customes and fashions of divers Nations in their nationall expressions by Gesture'[7] and nearer home he describes a gesture belonging to the 'loud naturall Rhetorique of those who

[1] *Chirologia*, p. 3.
[2] Ibid., p. 4.
[3] Ibid., Commendatory poem, 'Ad eundem. Jo. Harmarus'.
[4] *Chironomia*, 'Praeludium'. See W. E. Howell, *Logic and Rhetoric in England, 1500–1700*, 1956.
[5] *Chirologia*, p. 25.
[6] Ibid., p. 27.
[7] Ibid., 'To the Candid and Ingenious Reader'.

declame at Billingsgate'.[1] For the art of manual rhetoric he has used the signs taken from the authorities on rhetoric and added a commentary.

The engraving sets out the mythology of the language of the hand and envelops it with a religious sanction. The mixture of classical and biblical matter crammed into it is reminiscent of another title-page by Marshall, that to Wither's *Emblemes*; though not 'Beyond . . . their understanding'[2] readers must have found it over-elaborate and even puzzling. The author obviously gave his instructions but we do not know how far Marshall adhered to them, since unlike Wither, Bulwer has left no comment.[3] The theme, however, is clear: the contrast between Natural Language, left, unkempt and without the graces, and right, Language rendered comely by gesture and deportment. The two combine in the Well of Chirosophy, the wisdom of the hand.

Nature speaking, as mother of natural language, is portrayed as Ephesian Artemis, her common form from the sixteenth century onward. She bends towards the well, into which she pours her untutored words. Her foot, placed on the wheel of Fate or Fortune, is intended to signify that the gifts of fortune are the same as the gifts of nature or may supplement them. This idea often occurs in the literature of the time; in an emblem of Alciati's[4] to which the engraver may have turned, Nature and Fortune are seemingly interchangeable terms, for the title reads, *Ars Naturam adiuuans* while the verses relate only to *Fortuna* and the accompanying illustration shows the figure of Fortune on her sphere with Mercury beside her. In combining the attributes of Nature and Fortune, Marshall may have invented the image of Nature-Fortune. The presence of the tree behind her is explained by the tradition that the oracle at Dodona gave her answers by rustling the leaves of an old oak tree, 'Dodona's Oak', and thus spoke in the words of Nature.

The chiselled features and splendid helmet of the head in the centre can only belong to Minerva; this identification is borne out by the presence of the cock, one of the birds associated with Minerva. She is goddess of the liberal arts and the words of her divine rhetoric stream from her mouth into the Well of Chirosophy. The Well is placed under her protection, for the gesture of the hand backing her head is that in which 'Wisdome . . . cloathes her words'.[5] Mercury occupies the place of prominence as god of eloquence. He is patron of the art of rhetoric.

[1] Ibid., p. 34.
[2] Hind, III, pp. 187f.
[3] Ibid.
[4] Alciati, *Emblemata*, 1551, p. 107.
[5] *Chirologia*, pp. 42f.

Both Mercury and Minerva may be concerned with *Natura Loquens*, Mercury as a civiliser of mankind in its rough beginnings (Horace, *Odes*, 1.10.) may help to discipline untamed nature—hence his presence in Alciati's emblem. Minerva, too, is a trainer of nature; in one of Vaenius' *Emblemata Horatiana*,[1] probably familiar to Marshall, she is portrayed opposite Ephesian Artemis with a young pupil kneeling below them. The verses tell us that teaching is necessary to perfect the gifts of nature, which, in the context of the title-page, implies that natural gesture requires expert tuition before it can form part of the '*generall language of Humane Nature*'.[2]

Polyhymnia is the muse presiding over rhetoric and also singing—hence the buskins which show her connection with the drama. Her wreath of palm recalls the palm branches which were laid on the hands of the victors in the Olympian Games. But, asks Bulwer, 'why the Palme?' This is explained by the fact that 'the fruit of the Palme doth resemble the Hand and fingers, and are thereof by the Greekes named *dactili*, that is, *digiti*, fingers: . . . It seemed therefore right, the Palm should be given to them whose Hands were skilfull in Arts, and Fingers cunning in battail'.[3] The palm-tree behind Polyhymnia shows a fruit with five dates, while to emphasise the point, the left hand of the muse is opened in the gesture which is one of making clear,[4] a happy coincidence for the designer. Her right hand directs the flow of eloquent language towards the well. The legend refers to the classical teaching described in the *Chironomia*, that fittingness of expression depends on the art of gesture and on 'motions of the *Hand* and *Body*'.[5] It is possible that *gestum* is a misliteration of *gestu* but the sense is the same.

Above, emerging from the clouds, right, the hand of God which sets the comet in motion. The human hands immediately below are shown in 'a signe of amazement, 'tis an appeale unto the Deity from whose secret operation all those wonders proceed which so transcend our reasons, [this is a reference to the comet, one having been seen in England in 1618] which while wee cannot comprehend, . . . wee RAISE OUR HANDS TO HEAVEN, thereby acknowledging the Hand and Finger of God.'[6] On the left, again the hand of God, *manus dextera dei*

---

[1] Otto Vaenius, *Q. Horati Flacci Emblemata*, 1607, p. 12.

[2] *Chirologia*, p. 3.

[3] *Chironomia*, p. 23.

[4] Ibid., p. 53.

[5] Ibid., 'Praeludium'.

[6] *Chirologia*, p. 30.

of traditional iconography: by most passages of holy Writ this gesture signifies '. . . the powerfull . . . protection of God'.[1] The human hands on the left are lifted in prayer to invoke that protection.[2]

The series of six diagrams on the faces of the plinth may be explained thus: the lips on the open palm signify that gestures speak, the five fingers enumerate, the hand is used for counting, the ear on the palm indicates that gestures take the place of the sound of the voice, the eye on the palm that gestures are caught by the eye, the tongue on the open palm, that the hand is 'another Tongue', the clenched fist, 'the first invention of the Art of Logique, to note the moods and brevity of argumentation'.[3] The image of the tongue on the palm illustrates a statement of Pierio Valeriano which Bulwer cites: the Egyptians who 'used to decypher a distinct and articulate voyce by a Tongue, adde a *Hande* comprehending the same, to note out eloquence'.[4] It is therefore a hieroglyph as understood in the Renaissance, as are also the other five. The hands without Bulwer's additions may of course be conventional rhetorical gestures, such as the open hand expressing eloquence, which like the clenched fist of logic, goes back to ancient Greece.

The four gestures of the hand on the back wall of the plinth are not referred to specifically in either part of the book but surely they illustrate Bulwer's thesis that 'the *Hand* being the *Substitute* and *Vice-regerent* of the Tongue, in a full, and majestique way of expression, presents the *signifying faculties* of the soule, and the inward discourse of Reason.'[5] They are easily understood: the open hand, readiness to receive whatever feeds the intellect; the half-clenched fist, the will; the closed hand, knowledge held in the mind; the hand clasping fingers over the thumb, the mind's power to retain in the memory what it learns.

---

[1] Ibid., p. 44.
[2] Ibid., p. 14.
[3] *Chironomia*, p. 15.
[4] Ibid.; Pierio Valeriano, *Ieroglifici*, 1625, LIV, xxxiii, pp. 424f.
[5] *Chirologia*, p. 2.

19

JOHN BULWER

Philocophvs: or, the Deafe and dumbe mans friend

1648

(Hind, III. William Marshall, no. 152)

Springing from low walls, l. and r., a large transverse arch is coffered and pierced by two circular apertures; from these is suspended a drape bearing the title, PHILOCOPHVS. Beyond the arch stretches a long hall covered by a vaulted and coffered ceiling; its walls are carried on four square piers, there is a clerestory above them with round-headed windows; it ends in a curved apse-like structure with a round-headed doorway flanked by two columns and surmounted by two rows of windows. At the top of the design, rolling cloud in a dark sky; on a bank of cloud in front of the arch floats the figure of Nature. She is six-breasted, wears a loose skirt and has a scarf round her head and shoulders which forms a swathe above her head. She holds one hand of each of the youths who stand on her either side. They are clad in fancy Roman costume and each holds a shield displaying a spider in its web. Descending along the outer sides of the arch are two sets of four youths, all in Roman dress, the top three airborne, the lowest standing on a ledge. Each supports a shield. On the left-hand side the topmost figure has a shield showing a monkey crouching and eating; he carries in his other hand a cornucopia; next down, the shield shows a dog, while he carries a bouquet; next, the shield shows an antlered deer and he carries a horn held to his ear; last, with the shield showing an eagle, while he carries a bunch of peacock feathers. On the right side each figure carries the same object as his opposite number, but the shields in descending order show the dog impaled with the monkey, the monkey impaled with the dog, the eagle impaled with the deer and last the deer impaled with the eagle.

In the foreground a group of three figures; left, a laurelled musician in classical dress singing and accompanying himself on a six-stringed *viola da gamba*; the instrument has a little human head instead of a scroll. Kneeling alongside, a boy in short wide trousers or robe, shirt and loose jerkin with close-cropped hair; his mouth is placed to the ear of the head of the *viola*; with his left hand he points to his own ear and with his other to the man seated at a table, full-face to the spectator. This person wears an academic cap, a fur-lined gown and fur cape with a small ruff showing at the neck. Before him on the table are left, an oval picture (probably intended for a miniature) showing the head and shoulders of a woman, centre, a censer exhaling puffs of perfume, right a dish of fruit. Dotted lines run from these objects to the man's face— that from the dish to his nose, from the censer to his mouth, from the picture to his ear. Running across the engraving from the mouth of the musician is a 'balloon' representing the sound of the song; it ends in a dotted line carried to an eye placed under the ear of the seated man; along it is the inscription, *ad/motum labiorū!* (according to the movement of the lips). At the bottom, in the margin on a long scroll, four roundels containing heads; extreme l., shorn head with badly formed mouth and cavity in the nose; next, shorn head with a nose without nostrils and bar over the bridge of the nose; next, shorn head with lids lowered and eyes in the ears; extreme right, head with straggly hair, no ears and one ear set in the right eye. Signed lower left margin: *W. Marshall Sculpsit.*

Opposite are the explanatory verses:

A Reflection of the sence and minde of the Frontispiece.

> Nature reliev'd by Arts new might,
> *Reasons* obnubilated sight
> Cleares up, and things which lay conceal'd,
> Are to her doubtful eyes reveal'd.
> To make the *Deafe* and *Dumbe* amends,
> Illustrious Nature heere descends
> To dance the *Senses Masque*; a Ball,
> Which we their *Anagram* may call:
> On each Hand the Scene keeping *Tact*,
> Without whome life can nought transact;
> The other Senses with this close:

The *Right*, the *Foure transpos'd*, oppose,
The *impresse* of whose shields relate,
Which for the other doth officiate.
Terpander who with *Lyrique* Aire,
Could to the *Deafe* their losse repaire,
Directs them by his Musick's sound
To a late consecrated ground;
Where the *Common-Sense* a Gaest,
They find at an exchanging Feast
Of objects where each Sence may tast
The Pleasures of that *Sence* lyes wast:
When lo! the *Genius* of that place,
Spake thus with a Majestique grace:
Sceptiques henceforth shall this repute,
The *Academy of the Mute*.
An Architectures highest grace
Let there herein be no *Deafe place*! . . .

The continuation of the title on the printed title-page sets out the purpose and content of the book:

EXHIBITING THE Philosophical verity of that subtile Art, which may inable one with an *Observant Eie*, to *Heare* what any man speaks by the moving of his lips. UPON THE SAME Ground, with the advantage of an Historicall Exemplification, apparently proving, That a Man borne Deafe and Dumbe, may be taught to *Heare* the sound of *words* with his *Eie*, and thence to speake with his Tongue.

As we saw in the *Chirologia*, Bulwer had earlier shown his great interest in means of communication other than by the ear and voice. 'I who was the first that made it my Darling study to interpret the natural richnesse of our discoursing gestures.'[1] The *Chirologia* came into the hands of William Gostwick, a very intelligent young man who was born deaf and dumb; he had understood the alphabets of gestures included in it and could already express himself by signs. But this was not enough. Bulwer addresses him,[2]

having well observed . . . that you earnestly desired to unfold your lips to an *orall elocution*; seeming as if you accounted your

[1] *Philocophus*, Sig. A₃v.
[2] Ibid., Sig. A₄ʳv.

213

dumbnesse to be your greatest *unhappinesse*; in tender pity of your
case, . . . When coasting along the borders of *gesture*, and
voluntary motion, I discovered a community among the *Senses*, . . .
a *Terra incognita* of *Ocular Audition*; . . . .

The doctor's interest and pity were the genesis of the *Philocophus* in
which he found his true vocation.

There was in fact a rising interest in the deaf and dumb from the
latter part of the sixteenth century onward. Cardanus and Campanella
had made studies and various deductions from them. The most striking
example of a solution to the problem of the deaf was the case of 'the
younger brother of the Constable of Castile'. This youth was taught to
lip-read and to speak by a Spanish Benedictine, John Paul Bonet.
Teacher and pupil were both present at the Spanish court when Prince
Charles was in Madrid in 1620–1. Sir Kenelm Digby, who was in the
prince's entourage, wrote an enthusiastic account of the demonstration
of speaking by the young nobleman in his book, *Two Treatises*,[1] first
published in 1644. Bulwer incorporated this account almost *verbatim*
in his work and used it as a text on which to make his philosophical and
practical observations.

The engraved title-page is a pictorial allegory of the philosophy
which underlines the possibilities of teaching the deaf and dumb to
understand and speak by lip-reading.

The first four lines of the 'Reflection' are illustrated at the top of the
engraving; they refer to Bacon's inauguration of a new era in the
development of thought which has given fresh powers to Nature and
rolled back the clouds from the darkened skies where for so long they
obscured the workings of reason. Nature is seen descending to dance a
masque with two sets of the personified senses; they are the medium
through which she will act 'To make the Deafe and Dumbe amends'.
The five senses were first identified and described by Aristotle.[2] Some
of the animals peculiarly associated with a single sense were described
by Pliny;[3] the spider, sensitive to any touch on his web, for the sense of
touch, and the monkey for the sense of taste, were added in the twelfth
century—the monkey's predilection for apples and his discrimination
between good and bad fruit were well known.[4] Two illustrated cycles

---

[1] Sir Kenelm Digby, *Two Treatises* . . ., 1644, 'A Treatise of Bodies', ch. xxviii, pp.
254–6.

[2] Aristotle, *De Anima*, II, 8–11.

[3] Pliny, *Hist. Nat.*, X, 69.

[4] H. W. Janson, *Apes and Ape Lore* . . ., 1952, ch. VIII, pp. 239ff.

are extant from the fourteenth century but it was not until the six-teenth century that 'the Senses' became a popular subject as five pretty women each with her 'sensory champion'. The spider appears in an engraving by George Pencz,[1] the monkey, the dog, the deer and the eagle, in engravings by Adrian Collaert, one of them after Adam van Oert[2] and four separate subjects after Martin de Vos.[3] Such works were often accompanied by well-turned verses perhaps with a moral lightly pointed. But Marshall's representation is not meant to entertain but to convey certain scientific truths.

> On each Hand the Scene keeping Tact,
> Without whome life can nought transact;

The verse encapsulates the ideas developed by Tommaso Campanella,[4] from whom Bulwer quotes. He held that all the senses were senses of touch or contact. This idea was based on the classical theory concerning the forces of the physical world in which movement is affected by contact of one object with another; as an example, a sound comes into contact with the air, so moves it and reaches the ear. So Nature holds the hands of the all-important masquers personifying Touch.

'Al *sensation* is performed by contact';[5] it follows, therefore, that '*one sense* may be exercised by the Organs of another, by changing the offices of the *Senses*'.[6] This is the 'anagram' or 'transposition to make something new' which is going to make it possible for the deaf and dumb to hear and speak. On the left of the arch are the personified senses each carrying the object which exemplifies his particular sense and a shield showing his own symbol: the monkey for taste, the dog for smell, the deer for hearing and the eagle for sight; on the right, the masquers show the transpositions: at the top the first masquer's shield displays the monkey and the dog, signifying that smell may substitute for taste. The next down reads a similar lesson, if smell fails taste may take its place; and so on—if hearing fails sight will come to its assistance, likewise if sight fails hearing will help the blind 'to see'.

Now for the means by which these substitutions are made. Aristotle adumbrated the theory of the body as the cohering medium for the faculty of touch, through which the plurality of sensation is

[1] Bartsch, VIII, nos 354, 109.
[2] Hollstein, IV, Adrian Collaert, 465.
[3] Ibid., 437–40.
[4] Tommaso Campanella, *De sensu rerum* . . ., 1620. lib. II. c. XII.
[5] *Philocophus*, p. 65.
[6] Ibid.

communicated.[1] Campanella saw the different senses as the organs of one given power of feeling.[2] This was the 'Common-Sense', personified perhaps for the first and last time, as the magisterial gentleman at the table. There is 'no absolute necessity that *Sensation* must be made by an organical part made for that purpose',[3] so the 'exchanging Feast' shows the sight of the portrait going to his organ of hearing, the smell from the censer to his mouth, and the taste of the fruit to his nose. He points to the boy who is the beneficiary of this interchange; he has got 'a paire of *Eare-Spectacles* before his eyes, whereby the dependencie that *speech* had upon the *eare* was taken away'.[4]

Terpander is the Greek musician who is said to have added a chord to the lyre. As the agent

> . . . who with Lyrique Aire,
> Could to the Deafe their losse repaire, . . .

he has the most important role in helping the boy. His song is directed to an eye placed in the right ear of 'Common-Sense'. The inscription completed reads, 'audiat ad motum labiorum!' (let him hear by the movement of the lips). There does not seem to be a record of an occasion in antiquity when Terpander made the deaf hear.

The boy with his mouth placed over the ear of the head of the *viola* is perhaps practising '*Orall* and *Dentall Audition*, of which wee have discovered sufficient ground to raise a new Art upon, directing how to convey intelligible and articulate sounds another way to the braine then by the eare or eye';[5] he refers again to this manner of helping his sufferers in his 'Table of such hints and notions' and precedes it with a suggestion '*That words may be tasted by Deafe and Dumbe men*'.

Though only a guess it seems possible that the representation shows the empirical discovery of the use of vibrations in enabling deaf people to understand the nature of sound. Bulwer does not go into any more detail and indeed at this period there was not sufficient scientific basis for the understanding and describing of vibrations.

In the four heads along the margin Bulwer attempts a pseudo-physiological demonstration of his thesis. The first has no sense of taste but savour will reach him through the nose; the second lacks nostrils

[1] Aristotle, op. cit., III, 13.
[2] Campanella, op. cit., lib. I. c. VI.
[3] *Philocophus*, p. 65.
[4] Ibid., p. 114 (the first of two pages both numbered *114*).
[5] Ibid., Sig. A$_5$.

and the bar shows that if for some reason odours cannot reach the brain from the nose, then the mouth must be smell's understudy; the third cannot see, so hearing will be the more acute; the fourth cannot hear but sight will come to the rescue.

The spacious modern hall has no part cut off from another in order that sounds may circulate. It is intended to hold 'The Academy of the Mute' which Bulwer proposed to found. In it there would be 'no Deafe Place!' The idea was badly received and institutions for training the deaf and dumb came into existence only very much later.

20

THOMAS HOBBES

Leviathan

1651

(Abraham Bosse, Johnson, Anon., no. 78)

The title-page is divided horizontally. At the top is a landscape of hills enclosing a valley. Beyond the furthest ridge of hills tower the head and upper half of the body of a man with flowing moustache, small beard and hair to his shoulders. He wears a closed imperial crown decorated with fleurons springing from the circling band. He is Leviathan; across the top of the engraving runs the quotation from the Vulgate, *Non est potestas Super Terram quae Comparetur ei Iob. 41.24* (There is no power on earth which can be compared to him). His body is made up of innumerable men, the greater part wearing the contemporary outdoor dress of gentlemen, a cloak and tall hat, though a few bare-headed men in overalls are incorporated in the right arm where also are two men kneeling; just above them is a priest in skullcap and Geneva bands; a bare-headed youth carrying side-arms stands at the waist. In his right hand the figure holds aloft a sword, in his left he grasps a crozier with a richly foliated crook of Baroque type; at the top of the pole of the crozier are two sets of carved and beaded mouldings enclosing carved niches which frame full-length male figures, presumably saints. His span is so huge that the tip of his sword and the end of the crozier reach beyond the edge of the engraving. On the hills below him are various edifices; extreme l., a chapel with central spire; to the right of it a village with a church with spire; above it on a spur a forti-fied building with four towers crowned with pignons; on the horizon, l., cypress trees behind a wall, and r., the tall spire of another church; below r., a river emerging from a gorge; on its banks in star-shaped defences a fortress with four bastions; flags flying from it and a soldier standing below the moat; small boats moored nearby and small houses on the other bank; extreme r., a village with church with central spire and small buildings round it. Nearer to the spectator, on a central buff with plateau top, lies a considerable city with a big star fortress with four bastions on the left; a flag flying from it; two men on the ramparts, and on an open space beyond the moat, others, two of them carrying pikes, possibly at drill practice. From the rear bastion stretches the machicolated city wall which continues interspersed with turrets, two of which rise on either side of a large roofed gateway surmounted by a statue; it encircles the main part of the city ending in a bastion. At right angles to the city wall and parallel to the fortress runs another wall, flat-topped, with two bastions pointing towards the city. In the foreground is a large church with simple west façade flanked by small square turrets; the body of the church has a row of round-headed windows above a second row of square windows; twin towers with two rows of round-headed windows and crowned with spires rise from short transepts. There are several streets of two-storey houses with one or two bigger houses among them; the rest of the city is cut off by the moulding which runs along the top of the lower part of the title-page. This is divided into three sections; on either side, a set of five compartments and in the centre an aperture over which is suspended by cords from the moulding, a heavy richly fringed and embroidered curtain carrying the title: LEVIATHAN/Or/THE MATTER, FORME,/and POWER of A COMMON:/wealth ECCLESIASTICALL/and CIVIL./ By THOMAS HOBBES/of MALMESBVRY. Below in an oval cartouche with foliated mouldings, the imprint, London/Printed for Andrew Crooke/1651. In the left-hand top compartment a castle is seen on top of a hill; it has machicolated walls and towers, the front wall being pierced by a gateway leading to the gabled structure within; two cypress trees appear above the hill on the left. In the frame below is a coronet with fleurons; below again is a cannon of contemporary design. Next down is a trophy made up of muskets, a drum and sticks, a cannon, flags, including one showing St Andrew's cross, swords and fasces. At the bottom two scenes of war; in the foreground cavalry meeting cavalry, the men wearing plumed helmets and surcoats; they are discharging firearms, a horse lies fallen; further off two forces of confronting pikemen, their standards flying; the leader of each force appears to be discharging a musket. On the right-hand side of the title, a church in the top compartment, similar in design to the one in the city, but smaller with a single row of windows round the side walls and the apse; the pediment of the façade surmounted by a cross; above the apse a statue of the Redeemer; flat-topped towers rise from the ends of the transepts. Next down a bishop's mitre with a cross on the front; next down again a thunderbolt. In the fourth frame a trident and three forks rise from behind a pair of bull's horns; the trident is lettered *Syl./ logis./me*, the fork in the centre, *Spiritual* and *Temporal*; the fork with one straight and one curved prong, *Directe* and *Indirecte*, the one on the right, *Real* and *Intentional*; the horns are lettered *Di/lem/ma*. At the bottom a disputation is represented, taking place in a modern hall lighted by round-topped windows; the president, centre, the two pairs of disputants, l. and r.; one protagonist, l., holds a book and his opponent is gesticulating with his hand; seated on benches facing the president, two rows of doctors wearing bonnets and gowns.

Leviathan, as is well known, was written during Hobbes' residence in Paris from 1640 to the end of 1651. The book itself was printed in London: Clarendon[1] writes in the Introduction to his *Survey of . . . Leviathan* that

> he [Hobbes] frequently came to me, and told me his Book (which he would call *Leviathan*) was then printing in England, and that he receiv'd every week a Sheet to correct, of which he shewed me one or two Sheets, and thought it would be finished within little more than a month; and shewed me the Epistle to Mr Godolphin which he meant to set before it, and read it to me, and concluded, that he knew when I read his Book I would not like it.

The title-page is invariably described as anonymous in the English literature, bibliographical and otherwise, of Hobbes and his *Leviathan*. Yet in France it has been ascribed since the middle of the seventeenth century to one of the most famous Parisian engravers of the day, Abraham Bosse (1602–76) and it has figured regularly in the literature of this artist as an unsigned work. The ascription dates back to Bosse's Parisian contemporary, the Abbé Michel de Marolles (1600–81), a famous connoisseur and collector of engravings, who included the frontispiece in his volumes of engravings by Bosse. The collection, now

---

[1] Clarendon, *Brief View and Survey of the Dangerous and Pernicious Errors to Church and State in Mr Hobbes book entitled Leviathan*, Oxford, 1676, p. 7. For the bibliography of *Leviathan*, see H. Macdonald and M. Hargreaves, *Thomas Hobbes: a Bibliography*, 1952, pp. 27–37.

in the Cabinet des Estampes of the Louvre, was purchased by Colbert for Louis XIV in 1667, so that the attribution to Bosse must be earlier than this date and falls well within Bosse's own lifetime. The attribution was formally made by another celebrated French connoisseur and collector of somewhat later date, P. J. Mariette (1694–1774) in his *Table manuscrite des oeuvres d'Abraham Bosse*. The attribution to a French engraver is supported by certain details of costume, such as the tall bonnets worn by the disputing ecclesiastics in the scene at the bottom right and by a version made in pen on vellum for presentation to Charles II.[1] This pen drawing is dated 1651, and is in a French style. It can be attributed with some confidence to Bosse. The drawing differs in various ways from the engraving; the body of Leviathan is made up of heads, not whole figures of men; the face of Leviathan is rounder; the church in the first compartment on the right has a curved top to its façade on which a statue of the Redeemer is clearly shown. These details suggest that it represents a finished version of the penultimate stage in the evolution of the design.

The anonymous French writer who wrote an article[2] on the title-page in 1852 correctly deduced from Bosse's authorship that Hobbes must have devised the title-page in Paris and closely supervised its execution. In themselves the English inscriptions are sufficient proof that the invention of the imagery with its carefully tabulated parallels is Hobbes' own work. This was not the first title-page that Hobbes had devised in France for execution by a French engraver. That of his *De Cive*, published at Paris in 1642, bears the signature *Math.f.* for Jean Matheus who was both an engraver and a publisher.[3] Here too the imagery is devised with close aptness to fit Hobbes' philosophical concepts and was certainly his invention.

Our title-page is dominated by the great half-length figure of Leviathan or the Commonwealth rising above the landscape which he holds under his sovereign sway with the sword of secular rule and the crozier of

---

[1] BL, MS. Egerton 1910, 'in a marvillous fair hand', Clarendon on op. cit., p. 8.

[2] In *Magasin pittoresque*, xx, May 1852, pp. 153–5, the writer collects the earliest references to Bosse's authorship. The attribution to Bosse is accepted by Duplessis, 'Abraham Bosse: catalogue de son oeuvre', in *Revue universelle des arts,* no. 297, pp. 362–363; Blum, *L'Oeuvre gravé.*

[3] The signature has not previously been identified. For Matheus see C. Leblanc, *Manuel de l'amateur des estampes*, ii, 1856, p. 623. For the bibliography of *De Cive*, see Macdonald and Hargreaves, op. cit., pp. 16–23.

ecclesiastical rule. He is formed, in the words of Hobbes' *Introduction,* as an 'Artificiall Man; though of greater stature and strength than the Naturall, for whose protection and defence it was intended'. Leviathan is shown with a body composed of men, that is with an artificial body, 'for by Art', says Hobbes in his *Introduction,* 'is created that great LEVIATHAN called a COMMONWEALTH, or STATE (in latine CIVITAS)'. The figure is therefore a strikingly literal image of Hobbes' conception of the Commonwealth as an 'Artificiall Covenant' into which men enter in order to 'erect such a Common Power, as may be able to defend them from the invasion of Forraigners, and the injuries of one another, and thereby to secure them in such sort, as that by their owne industrie, and by the fruites of the Earth, they may nourish themselves and live contentedly'.[1]

The only way by which men can do this is 'to conferre all their power and strength upon one Man, or upon one Assembly of men, that may reduce all their Wills, by plurality of voices, unto one Will: which is as much as to say, to appoint one Man, or Assembly of men, to beare their Person.' Hobbes therefore envisages two forms of commonwealth monarchical and republican. Hobbes' covenant as he explains is more than a consent or concord of wills, it is[2]

> a reall Unitie of them all, in one and the same Person, made by Covenant of every man with every man, in such manner, as if every man should say to every man, *I Authorise and give up my Right of Governing my selfe, to this Man, or to this Assembly of men, on this condition, that thou give up thy Right to him, and Authorize all his Actions in like manner.*

The verse from Job is taken from the description of Leviathan and wittily appropriated to Hobbes' conception of sovereign power. Hobbes used the image of Leviathan for his title because in Job God cites the great fish which He has created as a work of greater power and grandeur than any which a mortal man can achieve. Similarly a Commonwealth is the great Leviathan created by the art of the sovereign power. We have seen that Hobbes expressly makes the comparison in his introduction, and in his chapter on the generation of the commonwealth, he says,[3]

---

[1] *Leviathan,* edn of 1651, Introduction, pp. 1–2, p. 87.

[2] *Leviathan,* ed. cit., 2.17, p. 87.

[3] *Leviathan,* ed. cit., 1.10, p. 41 and loc. cit.

the Multitude so united in one Person, is called a COMMON-WEALTH, in latine CIVITAS. This is the Generation of that great LEVIATHAN, or rather (to speake more reverently) of that *Mortall God*, to which wee owe under the *Immortall God*, our peace and defence.

Leviathan is shown crowned because the Person of the Commonwealth 'is called SOVERAIGNE, and said to have *SOVERAIGNE POWER;* and every one besides, his SUBIECT'.[1] As is well known, Hobbes believed that the sovereign power has sole, indivisible and absolute authority over subjects, who have no right of rebellion against it. Accordingly he has emphasised the supremacy of Leviathan by giving him an imperial crown, the symbol of supreme earthly dignity. It is important to bear in mind that Hobbes uses the term sovereign to mean both monarchical and republican forms of ruling power. In the words which continue the verse from Job, 'Leviathan . . . is made so as not to be afraid. He seeth every high thing below him: and is a king of all the children of pride.'[2] These are the passages that Hobbes has sought to illustrate in visual form on the title-page. In the engraving Leviathan's even, fearless gaze also proclaims him monarch; his size, compared with the mountains, spires and fortresses beneath, implies a supreme power, an impression enhanced by the omission of a top border so that the tip of his sword is not so much cut off as lost in the skies. The sword is the emblem of the sovereign's temporal power which in the last resort he must use 'for the preserving of Peace and Security, by prevention of Discord at home, and Hostility from abroad'.[3] He holds the crozier as head of the Church, because 'the Church, if it be one person, is the same thing with a Common-wealth of Christians; . . . it consisteth in Christian men, united in one Christian Soveraign.'[4]

The men who make up the body of Leviathan are portrayed in the act of making the covenant, of literally uniting themselves in the person of the sovereign; those on either arm are moving forward, those in the centre have arrived and are gazing up towards the head. This pictorially complex conception, expressing Hobbes' final ideas on men and society may be compared with the earlier and simpler representation in *De Cive*[5] in which one of the scenes shows men organised under a just rule

---

[1] *Leviathan*, ed. cit., 2.17, p. 88.
[2] Ibid., 2.28, p. 167.
[3] Ibid., 2.18, pp. 90f.
[4] Ibid., 3.33, pp. 205f.
[5] *Elementorum Philosophiae. Sectio tertia De Cive*, Paris, 1642.

peacefully reaping their crops, and another, in contrast, the American Indians fighting each other savagely, every man for himself.

Leviathan wields his power over a walled city and its surrounding countryside—the *civitas*, the Latin name for city which embraces the classical conception of the city-state. Though Hobbes was writing about nation-states he uses the term *civitas* because it was the unit of political power in ancient Greece and his political thought, though profoundly original, was based on the works of the classical philosophers. The word 'city' is used in the same sense in *Philosophical Rudiments*.[1]

The spire indicates that the church of the city, placed for greater conspicuousness in the immediate foreground, belongs to northern Europe. Its classical façade and large windows show it to be a modern construction. It resembles the large church in the representation of the city of Erfurth in Merian the Elder's publication[2] of 1650; the citadel, though earlier in design, is also similarly placed in relation to the church as the one in our engraving. It seems likely that a view of a modern citadel was selected (to which the wall to the right with the star bastions belonged as part of its defence system), and combined with the view of a city perhaps suggested by Erfurth. The whole is fitted to Hobbes' theme since the citadel lies under the sword of Leviathan and the church under the crozier.

On either side of the title, tabulated directly under the sword and the crozier, are further scenes and symbols showing the sovereign's exercise of temporal rule on the left and ecclesiastical rule on the right. They are meant to be read both downwards and across; this is indicated by the designer, who has made each compartment of a different size to that below and above but a pair to its opposite number. For Hobbes the absolute supremacy of the sovereign power gave it in temporal rule, the right to judge of the means necessary for peace and war, the right to censor doctrines, the rights to establish laws of property, the right to appoint the judicature, to declare war and peace, to choose counsellors and magistrates, to reward with riches and honour and to grant titles of honour. The images on the left are concerned above all with war and peace. At the top, the castle, impregnably placed, is presumably a royal seat, the symbol of military might. From such a castle, well-garrisoned and secure, the sovereign may use the 'Power and Strength conferred on him' to keep 'Peace at home' and ensure 'mutuall ayd against their

---

[1] *Philosophical Rudiments . . .*, 1651, pp. 119, 333.

[2] Matthias Merian, *Topographia Germaniae Faksimile – Ausgabe*, 1964. M.Z., *Topographia Superioris Saxoniae . . .* Matthaeus Merian, 1650, between pp. 74 and 75.

enemies abroad'.[1] The coronet is one of the 'Titles of *Honour*' and belongs to a 'Duke, Count, Marquis, . . . [or] Baron'. These are 'Honourable; as signifying the value set upon them by the Soveraigne Power of the Common-wealth:' in other words, to whom they owe what rights they now possess in the state, though 'in old time [they were] titles of Office and Command'.[2] Third down is the cannon; 'making of Engines, and other Instruments of War; because they con-ferre to Defence, and Victory, are Power';[3] for over two hundred years the cannon had been the most effective weapon in existence. It was the sole armament of ships of war on which Britain's power depended, and since the time of Elizabeth cannon could only be manufactured under royal licence. The classical trophy of weapons, flags, etc., shows the instruments of war whose use belongs to the sovereign power; the *fasces* may be a backward glance at the insignia of consular power in republican Rome, but more probably was included by Bosse as a con-ventional motif in a trophy. The scene of battle exemplifies the manner in which temporal states settle their differences and by implication the sole right of the sovereign to make war. The conflicting armies are using modern weapons and tactics.

Hobbes believed unreservedly in the Erastian doctrine of the relation of church and state, that '*The Civill Soveraigne if a Christian, is head of the Church in his own Dominions.*'[4] For him this entails the sovereign's exercise of authority by divine right over and within the Church.

Seeing then in every Christian Common-wealth, the Civill Soveraign is the Supreme Pastor, to whose charge the whole flock of his Subjects is committed, and consequently that it is by his authority, that all other Pastors are made, and have power to teach, and performe all other Pastorall offices; it followeth also, that it is from the Civill Soveraign, that all other Pastors derive their right of Teaching, Preaching, and other functions pertaining to that Office; and that they are but his Ministers; in the same manner as the Magistrates . . . Judges . . . and Commanders of Armies.

Hobbes also held that Christian kings had the authority not only to preach but even to baptise, to administer the sacrament of the

[1] Hobbes, op. cit., 2.17, pp. 87f.
[2] Ibid., 1.10, p. 46.
[3] Ibid., 1.10, p. 42.
[4] Ibid., 3.42, pp. 299, 295.

Lord's Supper and to consecrate temples and pastors to God's use.
Accordingly, they may[1]

> commit the care of Religion to one Supreme Pastor, or to an
> Assembly of Pastors; and give them what power over the Church,
> or over one another, they think most convenient; and what titles
> of honour, as of Bishops, Archbishops, Priests, or Presbyters, they
> will. . . . It is the Civill Soveraign, that is to appoint Judges, and
> Interpreters of the Canonicall Scriptures; for it is he that maketh
> them Laws. It is he also that giveth strength to Excommunications
> . . . In summe, he hath the Supreme Power in all causes, as well
> Ecclesiasticall, as Civill. . . . And these rights are incident to all
> Soveraigns, whether Monarchs, or Assemblies.

These doctrines are illustrated in the right-hand compartments, and
matched, as already said, with their temporal expressions on the left.
Again there is an emphasis on the sovereign's ultimate power to settle
all disputes. At the top of the right side is the church—'*Christs House*'[2]—
which matches the castle. But a church is also defined as '*A company of
men professing Christian Religion, united in the person of one Soveraign*'.[3]
The bishop's mitre matches the secular coronet since the Lords Spiritual
like the Lords Temporal owe their dignities and honours to the
sovereign: 'by the Law of Nature . . . the Civill Soveraign in every
Common-wealth, is the *Head*, the *Source*, the *Root*, and the *Sun*, from
which all Jurisdiction is derived. And therefore the Jurisdiction of
Bishops, is derived from the Civill Soveraign.'[4] The thunderbolt
opposite the cannon signifies ecclesiastical punishment, that is excom-
munication; it was taken over by Christian symbolism from the
thunderbolt of Zeus. Hobbes himself refers explicitly to this derivation
of both metaphor and image:[5]

> The name of *Fulmen Excommunicationis* (that is, the *Thunderbolt of
> Excommunication*) proceeded from an imagination of the Bishop
> of Rome, which first used it, that he was King of Kings, as the
> Heathen made Jupiter King of the Gods; and assigned him in their
> Poems, and Pictures, a Thunderbolt, wherewith to subdue, and
> and punish the Giants, that should dare to deny his power.

[1] Ibid., 3.42, p. 300.
[2] Ibid., 3.39, p. 247. Sig. [I i 4].
[3] Ibid., 3.39, p. 248. Sig [I i 4].
[4] Ibid., 3.42, p. 312.
[5] Ibid., 3.42, p. 279.

Hobbes argues at length that the right to excommunicate belongs in fact not to the Pope, but solely to the civil sovereign. The next compartment down shows the weapons of logic used in the discussion of ecclesiastical questions; they are placed parallel to the weapons of war. The motif illustrates Hobbes' doctrine, inspired by the religious dissensions of the past century and a half and in particular by bitter experience of the Civil War in his native England, that 'It belongeth . . . to him that hath the Soveraign Power to be Judge, or constitute all Judges of Opinions and Doctrines, as a thing necessary to Peace; thereby to prevent Discord and Civill War.'[1] He does not intend, he says, this doctrine as a restriction on private opinion, but as imposing on subjects the absolute duty of putting obedience to the sovereign in religion as well as in temporal affairs before their own private beliefs. He illustrates his view by the example of scripture. Man is intended to study the Bible with the aid of his senses, experience and natural reason, but 'when any thing . . . is too hard for our examination, wee are bidden to captivate our understanding to the Words; and not to labour in sifting out a Philosophicall truth by Logick, of such mysteries as are not comprehensible. . . .'

The inclusion of the instruments of logic under the crozier of Leviathan symbolises then the sovereign's absolute right to demand submission to the official doctrines of the state religion from its subjects, while allowing the right to private opinion.

> But by the Captivity of our Understanding, is not meant a
> Submission of the Intellectual faculty, to the Opinion of any other
> man; but of the Will to Obedience, where obedience is due. . . .
> We then Captivate our Understanding and Reason, when we
> forbear contradiction; when we so speak, as (by lawfull Authority)
> we are commanded; and when we live accordingly.[2]

'Forked' was used as an adjective to describe a kind of argument in the sixteenth century but here real forks, akin to pitchforks, have been represented and labelled with pairs of terms from logic and philosophy in general. The syllogism is represented by the trident because it must contain three terms; the horns of a dilemma, here wittily given pictorial expression, are the equally disagreeable alternatives open to an adversary in an argument. The fork in the centre marked '*Spiritual*' and '*Temporal*' may be an allusion to that part of Book III of *Leviathan* in which

[1] Ibid., 2.18, p. 91.
[2] Ibid., 3.32, pp. 195, 196.

Hobbes argues the case for the supremacy of the monarch in the spiritual as well as the temporal sphere against the papal theologian Cardinal Bellarmine,[1] whose opinions, set out in his great polemic *De Summo Pontifice*,[2] he confutes with the whole armoury of logic. The fork immediately behind could refer to forms of adequate proof which may be direct or indirect, indirectness being indicated by the curved prong; or again Hobbes may be referring to the power claimed by the Pope who if he has it not 'directly' may possess it indirectly 'by a Right given him by God, . . . in his Assumption to the Papacy'.[3] '*Real*' and '*Intentional*' are terms belonging to scholastic philosophy. This fork,' therefore, may be meant to recall the theological controversies of the Middle Ages and seventeenth-century neo-scholasticism.

At the bottom the disputation shows the ecclesiastical way of settling a dispute in contrast to the battle opposite—the disputes of the schools in fact. These were a normal feature of theological education. In addition, during the sixteenth century disputations were frequently held in France between churchmen of the papal and reforming parties to try to reach agreement on questions of doctrine and church government. An ecclesiastical dispute was conducted much like a court of law with each side arguing its case and bringing citations to support it from acknowledged authorities—hence the book held by the one protagonist from which he reads. But all the members of the assembly on the title-page are doctors wearing the tall biretta of the Roman church; it is therefore a disputation held by a Roman Catholic body, most probably the theological school of the Sorbonne meeting in one of the spacious rooms of the newly rebuilt College. The designer may have had in mind two disputations held in Paris in 1643 and 1649 to consider the opinions of the Jansenists. The scene is a further illustration of the right of the sovereign to be the determining authority in all ecclesiastical disputes.

A comparison with the portrait by J. B. Jaspers given to the Royal Society by John Aubrey and with the engraving after it by Hollar[4] shows unmistakably that the face of Leviathan is that of Hobbes himself.[5] This fact is borne out by the description of him by Aubrey:[6]

[1] Ibid., 3.42, pp. 300ff.

[2] *Tractatus de Potestate Summi Pontificis*, 1610.

[3] Hobbes, op. cit., 3.42, p. 314.

[4] G. Parthey, *Wenzel Hollar . . .*, 1853, no. 1417.

[5] Mr John Gere, Keeper of Prints and Drawings, British Museum, has kindly confirmed my opinion.

[6] Aubrey's *Brief Lives*, ed. O. Lawson Dick, 1950, p. [154].

Face not very great; ample forehead: whiskers [moustache] . . .
which naturally turned up. . . . Belowe he was shaved close, except
a little tip under his lip. Not but that nature could have afforded
a venerable Beard, but being naturally of a cheerfull and pleasant
humour, he affected not at all austerity and gravity to looke severe.
He desired not the reputation of his wisdome to be taken from the
cutt of his beard, but from his reason. He had a good eie, . . .
which was full of Life and Spirit, . . . when he was serious and
positive, he open'd his eies round [i.e. his eye-lids].

The title-page portrait is of course of a younger man since Jaspers, who
was in England during the Commonwealth, must have made the
painting after 1660 when Hobbes was over seventy-two; it was probably done from the life since the engraving and the drawing in ink on
vellum (see above p. 222) differ slightly, the latter being rounder and
livelier.

The ingeniously complex figure of *Leviathan* is therefore given yet
another significance—it becomes a version of the traditional author-
portrait in which the author and the concepts he expounds in his book
are united into a single image. With this last illustration of the intimate
link between author and engraved title-page our book may fittingly
end.

INDEX